Our Republican Constitution

ADAM TOMKINS

John Millar Professor of Public Law
University of Glasgow

·H A R T·
PUBLISHING

OXFORD AND PORTLAND, OREGON
2005

Hart Publishing
Oxford and Portland, Oregon

Published in North America (US and Canada) by
Hart Publishing c/o
International Specialized Book Services
5804 NE Hassalo Street
Portland, Oregon
97213-3644
USA

Hart Publishing is a specialist legal publisher based in Oxford, England.
To order further copies of this book or to request a list of other
publications please write to:

Hart Publishing, Salter's Boatyard, Folly Bridge,
Abingdon Road, Oxford OX1 4LB
Telephone: +44 (0)1865 245533 or Fax: +44 (0)1865 794882
e-mail: mail@hartpub.co.uk
WEBSITE: http//www.hartpub.co.uk

British Library Cataloguing in Publication Data
Data Available
ISBN 1–84113–522–4 (paperback)

Typeset by Hope Services (Abingdon) Ltd.
Printed and bound in Great Britain by
MPG Books, Bodmin, Cornwall

For Lauren, of course

Preface

This book presents a republican reading of the British constitution. It offers an interpretation of contemporary constitutional practice, of aspects of constitutional history and of the state of constitutional reform that is, in each respect, radically critical of orthodoxy.

The book opens with an exposition of what I perceive to be the currently dominant view of the British constitution as it is discussed, analysed and taught by lawyers. I call this view 'legal constitutionalism'. Chapter one sets out the various tenets of legal constitutionalism and offers a detailed and critical analysis. For all its popularity among public lawyers (both academic and judicial), the model of legal constitutionalism is, it seems to me, dangerously misguided. It is the purpose of chapter one to demonstrate why this is so.

It is one thing to criticise orthodoxy; it is another to seek to replace it. Chapters two, three and four set out an understanding of constitutionalism that I argue can and ought to be adopted in Britain instead of the model of legal constitutionalism. The alternative advocated in this book returns to an older, political, approach to the constitution, an approach which I contend should be seen as resting on republican foundations. It is not a novel argument to suggest that the British constitution is primarily political rather than legal in character—the model of the political constitution is one that I seek not to invent but to revive. What is new in this book is the attempt to ground the political constitution on values and practices of republicanism.

This, the core argument of the book, proceeds in three stages. First I explain what is meant (and, just as importantly perhaps, what is not meant) by republicanism. Chapter two surveys previous constitutional writings to have considered this issue and constructs a conception of republicanism that borrows extensively from recent and ground-breaking scholarship in political philosophy and in the history of political thought. The second stage of the argument moves from the domain of ideas to that of constitutional practice. I argue that British constitutional practice has, at key moments in its history and especially in the seventeenth century, been profoundly influenced by republican ideas. Indeed, the argument in chapter three suggests that the constitution is, at least in part, founded upon republican ideals. The final stage of the argument moves back to the present and addresses the (some would maintain, rather sizeable) gap between contemporary constitutional reality and the republican ideal presented in chapter two. The book closes with a series of suggestions as to reform with a view to establishing an agenda for change that would help to close the gap.

The republican approach to constitutionalism presented in this book is not an import, constructed out of ideas borrowed and transplanted from elsewhere, but is one that derives from an analysis of the values inherent within the British constitutional order. At first glance this may strike us as a rather bizarre claim to make. After all, is Britain not one of the world's longest-lasting and most stable monarchies? Is our state not the United *Kingdom*, rather than the United *Republic*, of Great Britain and Northern Ireland? Furthermore, is it not the case that, in the last thirty years, the single most potent *threat* to the United Kingdom government has come from a certain species of republicanism, in the form of the terrorism of the IRA, the Irish Republican Army? Given this, how could it be said that republicanism is an approach to politics that is in harmony, rather than in conflict, with British constitutional traditions?

As with all political 'isms', republicanism is a term that can be used in a variety of ways. Just as liberalism is a term broad enough to accommodate a bewildering range of positions, from the neo-Conservative libertarianism of a Ross Perot or a Pat Buchanan to the social welfarism of a Gordon Brown, and just as socialism covers a wide spectrum from the romantic democratic trade unionism of Tony Benn to the totalitarianism of Stalin, so too with republicanism. That the IRA and George W Bush (for example) both use the word republican as a label to describe themselves does not mean that they share the same policies, any more than Pat Buchanan shares those of Gordon Brown or Tony Benn those of Stalin. Political labels can be extremely misleading. Mrs Thatcher was one of the late twentieth century's most important Conservative politicians, but her brand of market liberalism was far from conservative of the economic structure that was in place when she arrived at Downing Street. Similarly with republicanism: the republican constitutionalism advocated in this book has nothing to do with Northern Irish republicanism. Neither is it an endorsement of anything associated with the current leadership and direction of the Republican party in the United States. Indeed, as we shall come to see, the republicanism defended here is in many instances the direct opposite of much of what the Republicans stand for on the right wing of contemporary American politics.

The argument here will be that, notwithstanding the monarchic nature of the British state, values and practices of republicanism can nonetheless be found within it. This is not an entirely new claim. Montesquieu wrote as long ago as 1748 of 'a nation where the republic hides under the form of monarchy'.[1] A century later Walter Bagehot echoed the remark and applied

---

[1] Montesquieu, *The Spirit of the Laws* [1748] (ed and trans A Cohler, B Miller and H Stone, Cambridge, Cambridge University Press, 1989), at 70.

it specifically to Britain where, he stated, 'a republic has insinuated itself beneath the folds of a monarchy'.[2] The meaning of these famous but somewhat cryptic remarks will be uncovered and explored as this book proceeds.

This book grew out of the inaugural lecture I delivered on 17 March 2004 as John Millar Professor of Public Law in the University of Glasgow. I am grateful to the Dean of my faculty, Noreen Burrows, for chairing the lecture and to the School of Law for hosting the reception that followed it. The arguments presented here are the product of research I was able to undertake only with the support of a large number of colleagues and institutions. I am especially grateful to the Research School of Social Sciences and the Humanities Research Centre at the Australian National University for awarding me a research fellowship for three months in 2000 and to the Faculty of Law at the University of New South Wales for awarding me a visiting research fellowship for two months in 2003. Both the time away from home and the exposure to so much outstanding Australian scholarship were invaluable. My ideas on republican constitutionalism were shaped in numerous ways through the feedback my presentation of them provoked from audiences in several universities in Britain, Australia, New Zealand and the United States. I am very grateful to all those who gave me opportunities to present my work at faculty seminars at Kent Law School, the University of Aberdeen, Newcastle Law School, the University of Manchester, the University of Oxford, the Australian National University, Griffith University, the Queensland University of Technology, the University of New South Wales, the University of Auckland, Texas Law School and Cardozo Law School.

Finally, I would like to record my thanks to the friends and colleagues who have given generously of their time and energy to help me with this book. I have benefited from numerous conversations with Joshua Getzler, Mark Godfrey and Victor Tadros. Nick Barber, Lionel Bently, Brian Bix and Emilios Christodoulidis each read several chapters in draft and offered helpful advice. Scott Veitch read the entire book, some of it more than once. He saved me from numerous errors and sustained me throughout the writing process with encouragement, sound advice and some fine whisky. Above all, my wife Lauren Apfel, whose insights, expertise and tireless editorial efforts have once again been invaluable, was a constant source of both support and inspiration. It is to her, of course, that this book is dedicated.

---

[2] W Bagehot, *The English Constitution* [1867] (ed P Smith, Cambridge, Cambridge University Press, 2001), at 44. For discussion, see A Tomkins, 'The Republican Monarchy Revisited' (2002) 19 *Constitutional Commentary* 737.

Table of Contents

1

On the Political Constitution

———»·•·«———

'There are only two things that ever stop the government from doing
anything: money or politics.'[1]

I THE IDEAL OF POLITICAL ACCOUNTABILITY

Political Accountability and the British Constitution

THE BRITISH CONSTITUTION is a remarkable creation. It is
no exaggeration to say that there is nothing quite like it anywhere else
in the world. Both in its famously 'unwritten' form and in aspects of
its content it is extraordinary. At its core lies a simple—and beautiful—rule.
It is a rule that has formed the foundation of the constitution since the seventeenth
century. It is that the government of the day may continue in office
for only as long as it continues to enjoy the majority support of the House of
Commons. The moment such support is withdrawn is the very moment that
the government is required to resign. By this one rule is democracy in Britain
secured;[2] by this one rule are 'we the British people' able, through our elected
representatives in Parliament, to 'throw the scoundrels out'.[3] The rule is
known as the convention of ministerial responsibility or as the doctrine of
responsible government. For now, the most important thing to note about
the rule is that it stipulates that the government is constitutionally responsible
to Parliament.

The extreme step of forcibly removing the government from office is not,
of course, an everyday occurrence. This is not to say that it never happens.

---

[1] Words spoken by the character Josh Lyman, Deputy White House Chief of Staff, in *The
West Wing*, written by Aaron Sorkin. (The episode is 'Noel', from season two.)

[2] Although this was not its original function, as we shall see. The rule that the government is
accountable to the House of Commons dates from the 1640s, a time well before the emergence
of British democracy.

[3] Compare JHH Weiler, 'To be a European Citizen: Eros and Civilization', in his *The
Constitution of Europe* (Cambridge, Cambridge University Press, 1999), at 329.

The Labour government led by prime minister James Callaghan fell in 1979 because it lost a vote of confidence in the House of Commons. Callaghan's successor as prime minister, Margaret Thatcher, reluctantly resigned from office eleven years later when it was explained to her by her Cabinet colleagues that they felt she had lost the support of the majority of backbench Conservative MPs.[4] It is not only prime ministers who are responsible to Parliament: all government ministers are constitutionally responsible to Parliament.

Votes of no confidence and prime ministerial resignations are relatively rare but, in addition to providing the occasional drama of high political theatre, there is a second aspect to our rule. It is less spectacular, perhaps, but it is no less important. The government is required to secure the support of a majority in Parliament not only when ministerial careers are on the line, but every single day. It is a routine obligation on the part of the government that it must ensure that its policies, decisions and actions enjoy parliamentary backing. Parliament is the institution through which the government must legislate;[5] Parliament is the institution that controls the government's purse strings; and Parliament is the institution that will continuously inquire into the 'expenditure, administration and policy' of every government department.[6] It follows that in order for it to realise its legislative ambitions, the government will have to persuade a majority in Parliament that its policies are the right ones; that in order for the government to enjoy financial freedom, it will have to persuade a majority in Parliament that its spending plans are the right ones; and that in order for government departments to achieve success they will have to ensure that their expenditure, administration and policy are sustainable.

The beauty of our rule lies in its recognition of what may be called the 'reality of government'. Government is not (or at least is not always) an especially attractive occupation: it can be cynical, even dirty. One way of expressing the 'reality of government' is to say that those in political office are liable to try to do whatever they can politically get away with.[7] What is special about the British constitution is that it recognises this reality and acts on it. It does this by building it into the very heart of what the constitution tries to do. The purpose of all constitutions is to find ways of insisting that the government is

---

[4] See G Marshall, 'The End of Prime Ministerial Government?' [1991] *Public Law* 1 and R Brazier, 'The Downfall of Margaret Thatcher' (1991) 54 *Modern Law Review* 471.

[5] There are exceptions: these are considered in ch 4, below.

[6] These words are taken from the Standing Order of the House of Commons that governs the powers of Departmental Select Committees (Standing Order No 152). On select committees, see G Drewry (ed), *The New Select Committees* (Oxford, Clarendon Press, 1989, 2nd ed).

[7] See n 1, above.

held to account for its actions. What is unusual about the British constitution is the way it sets about accomplishing this task.

Most modern constitutions in the western world are not founded on an ideal of making government responsible to a political institution such as a Parliament. Most Western constitutions may *recognise* what I am calling the reality of government but they do not *act* on it in the way that the British constitution does. Rather than building constitutional structures of political accountability around this realisation, the bulk of Western constitutional practice has in modern times tended to focus instead on legal controls. Ideals of the 'rule of law' or of respect for 'fundamental' or 'human' rights form the backbone of today's constitutionalism in both continental Europe and North America. Ideals such as these are generally enforceable in courts of law rather than in political institutions such as Parliament. Accordingly it is to the judges, rather than to parliamentarians, that these constitutions look to provide the lead role in securing checks on government.

Instead of incorporating the fact that governments are liable to try whatever they think they can politically get away with into the fabric of constitutional accountability, such constitutions turn their backs on politics. It is as if they regard politics as part of the problem—as something that requires to be checked—rather than as part of the solution. What is beautiful about the British constitution is that it does not do this. It uses politics as the vehicle through which the purpose of the constitution (that is, to check the government) may be accomplished. This is beautiful for at least two reasons: first, because it is democratic; and secondly, because it can actually work. Politics really can stop governments from abusing their authority.

Turning instead to the courts to provide ways of holding the government to account endangers both democracy and effectiveness. No matter how democracy is defined, judges can never hope to match the democratic legitimacy of elected politicians. Whether you conceive of democracy in terms of the representativeness of the personnel or in terms of the openness and accessibility of the institution, Parliaments will always enjoy greater democratic legitimacy than courts. As for effectiveness, we shall come to examine this in more detail later in this chapter, and when we do we shall see both how and why it is that courts—or at least British courts—are unable to secure the same results in terms of government accountability as Parliament can.

Before we come to consider this issue, it is important to add some further remarks on just how unusual the British prioritisation of political over judicial accountability is. It is easy to take one's routines for granted, but central constitutional traditions such as prime minister's question time are no mere habits. The weekly half-hour that the prime minister must endure at the despatch box in the House of Commons is one of the most important reminders of the constitution's core rule: that the prime minister and his government are accountable to Parliament and require its ongoing support if they are to continue in office. The prime minister may appear to be the most powerful politician in the country, but his power is not his to keep. He is but its temporary custodian. His power is held on trust. At election time it is the electorate itself that may, indirectly,[8] remove it from him. But general elections normally occur only once every four or five years, and between elections it is Parliament, not the people themselves, to whom the prime minister must report if he is to be permitted to continue in office.

Traditions such as prime minister's question time and the doctrine of ministerial responsibility are so familiar to us in Britain and form such a central component of our political experience and expectations that we are in danger of assuming that they are shared everywhere. However, such an assumption would be sorely misplaced. There is simply no direct equivalent to the British system of political accountability in the United States, for example, in the traditions of many of our continental European neighbours or in the constitutional order of the European Union.

The US has in recent years suffered more than most from the absence of an effective mechanism of political accountability. Think, for example, of the protracted and hugely expensive procedures involved in the unsuccessful attempt to impeach President Clinton in the late 1990s. Bruce Ackerman, one of America's most astute constitutional commentators, has observed that:

> Bill Clinton would not have lasted a month as a prime minister in a parliamentary system. His backbenchers would have revolted, or his coalition partners would have ushered him out the door in a desperate effort to move into the next election with a new face at the head of the old government. In contrast, Americans had to waste a year on the politics of Clinton's personality.... [G]iven the American separation of powers, Bill Clinton's failings did not provide a constitutionally adequate basis for Congress to override the judgment rendered by the voters in 1996. But compared with the way a parliamentary system would have handled the affair, [the US Constitution] did a spectacularly bad job in dealing with this minor scandal.[9]

Under the terms of the US Constitution it is Congress, not a court of law, that is empowered to impeach the President. But short of this extreme step

---

[8] 'Indirectly' because under the British system the prime minister and his government ministers are not elected to office. They must all be members of one of the two Houses of Parliament (Commons and Lords). Those who are peers in the Lords are appointed rather than elected. Those who are MPs in the Commons are elected as MPs but not as ministers. The only part of the electorate that may directly remove the prime minister from office is that part of it which happens to reside in the prime minister's constituency.

[9] B Ackerman, 'The New Separation of Powers' (2000) 113 *Harvard Law Review* 633, at 659.

congressional powers to subject the executive branch to account are severely limited. Professor Ackerman's argument in the article just quoted from is that what he calls a 'constrained' form of parliamentarianism would make for a more suitable and more effective (as well as a more democratic) system of constitutional accountability than American presidentialism is capable of. We shall have cause to return to the United States at several points later in this book, but for now let us turn our attention briefly away from America and towards Europe.

It has been suggested that the English word 'accountability' does not even have an exact translation in some other European languages, such as French and German.[10] But it is not just the word that is difficult to translate: British practices of political accountability have few parallels elsewhere in Europe.[11] In France, for example, the current constitution (the Constitution of the Fifth Republic, dating from 1958) was expressly designed to limit the extent to which the National Assembly could subject the government to account. The Constitution provides that the prime minister is to be appointed by the President of the Republic, not by the National Assembly,[12] and stipulates that the government is accountable to the National Assembly only in strictly limited ways. Thus, while a government must resign if its general programme is defeated in a parliamentary vote, it is under no obligation to present such a programme to the National Assembly in the first place.[13] Further, the availability of censure motions is strictly curtailed, such that they may be passed only by an absolute majority of all members of the National Assembly.[14]

British policy-makers and constitutional practitioners have been painfully slow to realise just how special our expectations of political accountability are. Particularly in the context of developing a constitution for the European Union, Britain could have done much more to export its notions of political accountability, so that they could have been built into the political framework of the EU. Other leading European nations have been far keener to export their constitutional ways—whether it be German concepts of proportionality, French ideas of institutional design or Scandinavian traditions of transparency and open government—than Britain has. This is a great pity,

---

[10] See R Mulgan, '"Accountability": An Ever-Expanding Concept?' (2000) 78 *Public Administration* 555 and C Harlow, *Accountability in the European Union* (Oxford, Oxford University Press, 2002), at 14–15.

[11] 'Few', but not 'none'. Ireland, the Netherlands and Denmark are all examples of European countries that do share something of the British notion of political accountability.

[12] Constitution of 1958, Art 8.

[13] *Ibid*, Art 49. See J Bell, *French Constitutional Law* (Oxford, Clarendon Press, 1992), at 17.

[14] As John Bell has noted (*ibid*), when British prime minister James Callaghan lost a vote of no confidence in 1979 he lost it by 311 votes to 310. The absolute majority at that time would have been 315.

as it would have been significantly to the benefit of the EU's citizens had its constitution more enthusiastically embraced British ideas and practices of political accountability.[15]

Political Accountability under Challenge

The British reluctance to export its most cherished constitutional ideas on the European stage is, regrettably, a somewhat typical symptom of a broader malaise. We just do not seem to like our constitution very much any more.[16] In Charles Dickens' *Our Mutual Friend*, written in 1864-65, the character Mr Podsnap proclaims that:

> We Englishmen are Very Proud of our Constitution, Sir. It Was Bestowed Upon Us By Providence. No Other Country is so Favoured as This Country.[17]

Mr Podsnap is, of course, a preposterous figure—pompous, shallow and insular. But it is as if we have now made a sort of association in our minds that all those who seek to praise the British constitution do so in the manner of a Mr Podsnap, or that admiring it is somehow to condone the imperial values of the Victorian age. That greatest of British Victorian constitutionalists, Walter Bagehot, had no doubt that the British constitution was 'a model and an exemplar for liberals everywhere'.[18] As Vernon Bogdanor has suggested, 'most educated Englishmen of his day would almost certainly have agreed'.[19] Even into the 1950s, it was commonplace on both the political left and right for the British constitution to be described as 'nearly as perfect as any human institution could be'.[20] At the beginning of the twenty-first century, views such as these have become more than unfashionable. They have become anathema. No doubt it is appropriate for both the ignorant bluster of Podsnappery and the smug self-satisfaction of the 1950s to have been consigned to the dustbin. But it is not only such hyperbolic views of the British constitution that have fallen by the wayside: even moderate support for it is now relatively difficult to find.

---

[15] I have argued this point more fully elsewhere: see A Tomkins, 'Responsibility and Resignation in the European Commission' (1999) 62 *Modern Law Review* 744 and 'The Draft Constitution of the European Union' [2003] *Public Law* 571.

[16] For a stimulating account, see C Harlow, 'Export, Import. The Ebb and Flow of English Public Law' [2000] *Public Law* 240.

[17] C Dickens, *Our Mutual Friend*, ch 11.

[18] V Bogdanor, 'Introduction', in V Bogdanor (ed), *The British Constitution in the Twentieth Century* (Oxford, Oxford University Press, 2003), at 1.

[19] *Ibid.*

[20] See V Bogdanor, 'Conclusion', in *ibid*, at 689.

Indeed, in the past thirty years the British constitution has taken a real beating, coming under sustained and unprecedented criticism. Argument has spanned the political spectrum, from the left-leaning liberal reformism of Charter 88[21] to the right-wing critiques of frustrated politicians and journalists alike.[22] Remarkably, among the most persistent advocates for constitutional change have been the judges. For a quarter of a century their pet project was to cajole Britain's political parties into accepting the merits of incorporating the European Convention on Human Rights into domestic law so that Britain could have a Bill of Rights,[23] a policy that was finally implemented when the Human Rights Act 1998 came into force in October 2000, and one which has vastly increased the constitutional power of the judiciary.[24]

Away from the London-based 'juristocracy'[25] the British constitution also came under sustained attack from the Scots, who felt particularly disenfranchised during the Thatcher era when the government allowed the problems of the Scottish economy to be neglected while simultaneously imposing one of its most controversial policies (the poll tax) on Scotland before it was made to apply south of the border. The British constitution, it was felt, had allowed a distant and authoritarian executive to centralise power in Whitehall. The solution, it was urged, was for both legislative and executive power to be devolved to new institutions in Edinburgh. Scotland needed not only an executive but also a Parliament of its own.[26] When the Blair government came into office in 1997 it did so promising a package of devolution measures

---

[21] See, eg, A Barnett, C Ellis and P Hirst (eds), *Debating the Constitution: New Perspectives on Constitutional Reform* (Cambridge, Polity Press, 1993) and A Barnett, *This Time: Our Constitutional Revolution* (London, Vintage, 1997).

[22] See, eg, L Hailsham, *The Dilemma of Democracy: Diagnosis and Prescription* (London, Collins, 1978) and F Mount, *The British Constitution Now: Recovery or Decline?* (London, Heinemann, 1992).

[23] See, among many, many examples, L Scarman, *English Law—The New Dimension* (London, Stevens, 1974); L Browne-Wilkinson, 'The Infiltration of a Bill of Rights' [1992] *Public Law* 397; T Bingham, 'The European Convention on Human Rights: Time to Incorporate' (1993) 109 *Law Quarterly Review* 390.

[24] As Lord Hope put it in one of the first Human Rights Act cases to reach the House of Lords: 'the incorporation of the European Convention on Human Rights into our domestic law will subject the entire legal system to a fundamental process of review and, where necessary, reform by the judiciary'. See *R v Director of Public Prosecutions, ex parte Kebilene* [2000] 2 AC 326, at 374–75.

[25] I have borrowed this word from Keith Ewing: see KD Ewing, 'The Bill of Rights Debate: Democracy or Juristocracy in Britain?', in KD Ewing, CA Gearty and BA Hepple (eds), *Human Rights and Labour Law: Essays for Paul O'Higgins* (London, Mansell, 1994), ch 7. See also now R Hirschl, *Towards Juristocracy: The Origins and Consequences of the New Constitutionalism* (Cambridge, Harvard University Press, 2004).

[26] See, eg, the influential paper formulated by a body known as the Scottish Constitutional Convention, *Scotland's Parliament, Scotland's Right* (Edinburgh, Scottish Constitutional Convention, 1995).

not only for Scotland, but also for Wales and, on condition that the paramilitary ceasefires held, also for Northern Ireland.[27]

In addition to these various pressures for constitutional change, for a written constitution, for a Bill of Rights and for devolution, the British constitutional order has also had to cope in the last thirty years with the vast impact upon it that has been made by the United Kingdom's membership since 1973 of the European Union. Not only has membership of the EU posed unique challenges to the law of parliamentary supremacy,[28] it has also resulted in the courts being able to extend the range and variety of judicial remedies available in public law cases. Injunctive relief has become more widely available, while damages and compensatory remedies are similarly being used more broadly in public law.[29]

Perhaps the greatest European impact on British constitutional law, however, has come through the simple exposure of European ideas to domestic practitioners who would formerly have been unaware of them. This is obviously true for parliamentarians and for government ministers, who must now spend significant portions of their time attending various Council of Europe or European Union meetings. But it is also true for Britain's judiciary. Until the 1990s few if any senior judges in Britain could boast of substantial direct or professional experience of European law. But when (in 1992) Lord Slynn was appointed to the judicial committee of the House of Lords, he came not from the English Court of Appeal or from the Scottish Court of Session, but from the European Court of Justice in Luxembourg, where he had served as an Advocate-General since 1981.[30] Britain's senior judiciary now has far greater experience of both EU law and the case law and internal workings of the European Court of Human Rights in Strasbourg than ever before.

At the same time, conversations between judges on various high and supreme courts across the Commonwealth have grown in regularity and importance. As the Supreme Court of Canada and the Court of Appeal

---

[27] See now the Scotland Act 1998, the Government of Wales Act 1998 and the Northern Ireland Act 1998. For early assessments, see A Tomkins (ed), *Devolution and the British Constitution* (London, Key Haven, 1998) and N Burrows, *Devolution* (London, Sweet and Maxwell, 2000). For a more recent overview, see A Trench (ed), *Has Devolution made a Difference?* (Exeter, Imprint Academic, 2004).

[28] See *R v Secretary of State for Transport, ex parte Factortame (No 2)* [1991] 1 AC 603. For discussion, see A Tomkins, *Public Law* (Oxford, Oxford University Press, 2003), ch 4.

[29] The move to damages has been further encouraged by the Human Rights Act 1998, s 8: see, eg, *Anufrijeva v Southwark LBC* [2004] 2 WLR 603. It should be noted that there are several differences between English law and Scots law in the context of judicial remedies: see, eg, *McDonald v Secretary of State for Scotland*, 1994 SLT 692 and *Davidson v The Scottish Ministers*, 2002 SLT 420.

[30] For a clear example of how Lord Slynn's European exposure helped to shape his views on domestic public law, see his judgment in *R v Chief Constable of Sussex, ex parte International Trader's Ferry* [1999] 2 AC 418.

of New Zealand started to grapple with those countries' new Bills of Rights,[31] and as the Australian High Court started to read implied rights into the text and structure of the Australian Constitution,[32] the judges serving on these courts could attend Commonwealth conferences, exchange war-stories, engage in mutual encouragement, and further expose the British judiciary to the delights and challenges of enforcing a Bill of Rights and to the greater constitutional role for the courts that necessarily comes with it.[33]

When, in 1989, the Soviet bloc collapsed and the newly independent countries of eastern Europe desired a fresh constitutional start, they did not turn to Britain as an 'exemplar for liberals everywhere'.[34] Rather, they turned principally to the United States and to Germany. What they wanted were written constitutions with clear separations of power and judicially enforceable bills of rights.[35] This brings us full circle. We have identified here six different ways in which the British constitution was criticised, was placed under pressure or became unfashionable in the last decades of the twentieth century: the internal reform argument of the Charter 88 liberals, who wanted much the same for Britain as the post-Communist states of eastern Europe wanted for themselves; the juristocratic argument for a Bill of Rights; the regional pressures within the United Kingdom for devolution of power; the vast impact of European Union law; the juridical influence of other leading nations in the Commonwealth; and the fact that the world's liberal exemplars had, by the 1990s, become the US and the German constitutions rather than the British.[36]

Aside perhaps from the argument for devolution, underlying all of these sources of pressure lurks a common idea. It is an idea that is both simple and powerful. It is that Britain's traditional, political manner of dealing with the problem of constitutional accountability is no longer (even it if ever was) the best method, and that a better approach would be to turn instead to the courts. Such a move would bring the British constitution into line with the legal model of constitutionalism that is common in both North America and continental Europe. A move from the political constitution to the legal is the necessary result of a Bill of Rights.[37] It is also the likely result of a written

---

[31] See the Canadian Charter of Rights and Freedoms (1982) and the New Zealand Bill of Rights Act (1990).

[32] See A Stone, 'The Australian Free Speech Experiment', in T Campbell, K Ewing and A Tomkins (eds), *Sceptical Essays on Human Rights* (Oxford, Oxford University Press, 2001), ch 21.

[33] See C McCrudden, 'A Common Law of Human Rights? Transnational Judicial Conversations on Constitutional Rights' (2000) 20 *Oxford Journal of Legal Studies* 499, at 510–11.

[34] See above n 18.

[35] See B Ackerman, 'The Rise of World Constitutionalism' (1997) 83 *Virginia Law Review* 771.

[36] For an excellent and detailed account of these various pressures, see D Oliver, *Constitutional Reform in the UK* (Oxford, Oxford University Press, 2003).

[37] See, eg, the comments of Lord Hope: above n 24.

constitution. And it is certainly the direction in which both European law and Commonwealth constitutional law have been pushing.

The argument here is not that all of this is a terrible mistake and that we should return as quickly as possible to the values of Podsnappery, or to the late-imperial complacency of the 1950s. It is no part of the case put forward in this book that the British constitution was (or is) in no need of reform. On the contrary, the position adopted here is that there are aspects of our constitutional order that remain in urgent, indeed desperate, need of reform.[38] But I do want to suggest that the move away from a political constitution and towards a legal one is a mistake. It is a mistake because it risks losing sight of what was referred to above as 'the reality of government': that is, the idea that the government of the day is liable to try to do whatever it thinks it can politically get away with. Politics is able both democratically and effectively to stop government, to check the exercise of executive power, to hold it to account. The courts, no matter what their powers and no matter what their composition, will always find it more difficult. Chapters two and three of this book are concerned with a detailed defence of the political constitution, which seeks to ground it in both political theory and in Britain's political history. But before we can come to these issues, we must first outline what is wrong with the juridical alternative. Why is legal constitutionalism so undesirable? Why is it so undemocratic? And why is it so ineffective?

II THE MODEL OF LEGAL CONSTITUTIONALISM

The Six Tenets of Legal Constitutionalism

In order to answer these questions, we must first outline, as clearly as possible, exactly what is meant by legal constitutionalism. The first thing to be noted is that it is an approach to constitutionalism that has many authors, not all of whom necessarily agree with all the others on all points. John Gray has put it well: a construct such as legal constitutionalism is recognisable, he says,

> by virtue of its exhibiting a family of commitments and presuppositions, not all of them shared by every one of its theorists, but having resemblances enough in common to represent a distinctive and in some respects novel contribution ...[39]

---

[38] See ch 4, below.

[39] J Gray, 'After the New Liberalism', in his *Enlightenment's Wake* (London, Routledge, 1995), at 120.

It is, in other words, 'an outlook, or a framework of categories, more than it [is] a doctrine, or a substantive philosophical position'.[40] Among the leading proponents of legal constitutionalism are the academics TRS Allan, Jeffrey Jowell and Dawn Oliver, along with the Court of Appeal judge, Sir John Laws.[41] From a close reading of these authors' work, legal constitutionalism can be seen to be composed of the following main tenets.

1. Law is an activity that is not only distinctive from but also superior to politics.
2. The principal arena in which the activity of law takes place is the courtroom.
3. Individuals should, as far as possible, remain free of interference by the government.
4. Where government interference is unavoidable, it should be limited and justified by reason.
5. Both the extent of and the justification for government interference are questions of law for the judges to determine.
6. The law should control government through the enforcement of specific rules and general principles of legality (such as human rights).

Each of these six tenets will now be considered in turn. In what follows we will outline what each tenet requires and will offer, where appropriate, critical analysis.

Tenet one: law is an activity that is not only distinctive from but also superior to politics.

The claim of distinctiveness is not especially new. Since the early nineteenth century most British public lawyers have seen their business as being a different enterprise from that of the politicians. Taking their cue from the positivism of Bentham and Austin, public lawyers from Dicey to Wade would have found obvious and uncontentious the proposition that law and politics are not the same things as one another.[42] The claim has, however, come under sustained attack. The American legal realists wrote as early as the

---

[40] *Ibid.*

[41] In addition to these four, aspects of Paul Craig's vigorous defence of the common law model as the foundation of judicial review may also be read as supporting many of the tenets of legal constitutionalism. Likewise, Sir Stephen Sedley's approach to public law shares some similarities with legal constitutionalism. See, eg, P Craig, 'Competing Models of Judicial Review' [1999] *Public Law* 428 and 'Constitutional Foundations, the Rule of Law and Supremacy' [2003] *Public Law* 92 and S Sedley, 'Human Rights: a Twenty-First Century Agenda' [1995] *Public Law* 386.

[42] See M Loughlin, *Public Law and Political Theory* (Oxford, Clarendon Press, 1992), chs 1 and 5 and at 139–65 and 184–90. The work of Dicey and Wade is considered briefly at the beginning of ch 2, below.

1880s that 'a proper understanding of judicial decision-making would show that . . . judges' decisions were often based (consciously or unconsciously) on personal or political biases and constructed from hunches'[43] and that public policy played a significant role in judicial decision-making. American legal realism reached its height from the 1920s to the 1940s, but its insights did not appear to penetrate British public law scholarship until the 1970s (perhaps because, until then, and in marked contrast to the US Supreme Court, British judges tended to play such a small role in public law disputes).[44] Only at this point did British constitutional commentators such as John Griffith start to point out that judicial law-making is just as much a political enterprise as is parliamentary law-making.[45]

The claim of superiority is a rather newer one. While there are figures from the past who have clearly believed common law judicial law-making to be a superior form of reasoning,[46] the claim of law's superiority over politics has come to the fore of legal constitutionalism only recently. Modern legal constitutionalists believe that politics should be enclosed within what Martin Loughlin has described as 'the straitjacket of law':[47]

> Once viewed as a noble craft, politics is now conceived as an activity in which the passions hold sway. The political sphere, being one of power conflicts, is danger-ous and potentially destructive. Constraints are therefore required to ensure that passions are channelled towards right conduct . . . Politics must be tamed and placed within bounds so that its energies can be harnessed positively, that is, in accordance with the dictates of reason and justice.[48]

Politics is dangerous because it is ruled by the passions, which can run wild. In order to safeguard liberty (see tenet three, considered below) politics needs to be tamed, or kept in check, by the law. In the words of Sir John Laws,

> a democratic constitution is in the end undemocratic if it gives all power to its elected government . . . the survival and flourishing of a democracy in which basic rights . . . are not only respected but enshrined requires that those who exercise democratic, political power must have limits set to what they may do: limits which they are not allowed to overstep.[49]

[43] B Bix, *Jurisprudence: Theory and Context* (London, Sweet and Maxwell, 2003, 3rd ed), at 178.

[44] See R Stevens, *The English Judges: Their Role in the Changing Constitution* (Oxford, Hart Publishing, 2002), chs 2–3.

[45] See JAG Griffith, *The Politics of the Judiciary* (London, Fontana, 1997, 5th ed). The first edi-tion of this ground-breaking book was published in 1977. See further on Griffith ch 2, below.

[46] Sir Edward Coke CJ is an important seventeenth-century example: see ch 3, below.

[47] M Loughlin, *Sword and Scales: An Examination of the Relationship between Law and Politics* (Oxford, Hart Publishing, 2000), at 5.

[48] *Ibid*, at 223.

[49] Sir J Laws, 'Law and Democracy' [1995] *Public Law* 72, at 73 and 81. Laws stressed that in this essay he was using 'the term "government" indifferently as between Legislature and Executive' (at 90).

The common law is able to set (and enforce) such limits because, unlike politics, it speaks dispassionately in the cool language of reason and logic: in the words of one of Britain's leading academic legal constitutionalists, common law serves 'as a bulwark between governors and governed, excluding the exercise of arbitrary power'.[50] The assumption that underpins this remark (and, indeed, that underpins the entire model of legal constitutionalism) is that it is only the political branches that are capable of acting arbitrarily; the courts of law, apparently, never can. As Judith Shklar expressed it in her pioneering study,

> politics is regarded not only as something apart from law, but as inferior to law. Law aims at justice, while politics looks only to expediency. The former is neutral and objective, the latter the uncontrolled child of competing interests and ideologies.[51]

This 'politics bad, law good' approach to legal constitutionalism is sometimes carried to bizarrely exaggerated lengths. TRS Allan, for example, has suggested that in Britain 'the rule of law [has] serve[d] as a form of constitution' and that 'if important liberties are given protection, and standards of justice and fairness upheld, it is ultimately because—and largely to the extent that— they find expression in the common law'.[52] Acts of Parliament, then, are instruments only of repression and not of liberation. All our freedom we owe to the courts and to the common law they develop; without them there would be no standards of justice, and no fairness.

There are two major problems with Allan's position. The first is that it is simply wrong, empirically. In Britain we do not owe our freedom only to the courts. Parliament has frequently legislated, often in face of overt judicial hostility, to extend liberty, whether it be in conferring on women the right to vote,[53] in enacting prohibitions against discrimination,[54] or in providing for essential welfare services, such as health care and social security.[55] Far from there being in Britain no standards of justice other than those conferred by

---

[50] TRS Allan, *Constitutional Justice: A Liberal Theory of the Rule of Law* (Oxford, Oxford University Press, 2001), at 3. This book is one of the most important statements of legal constitutionalism. For critical discussion, see the review articles by T Poole, 'Dogmatic Liberalism? TRS Allan and the Common Law Constitution' (2002) 65 *Modern Law Review* 463 and J Goldsworthy, 'Homogenising Constitutions' (2003) 23 *Oxford Journal of Legal Studies* 483.

[51] J Shklar, *Legalism* (Cambridge, Harvard University Press, 1964), at 111.

[52] TRS Allan, *Law, Liberty and Justice: The Legal Foundations of British Constitutionalism* (Oxford, Clarendon Press, 1993), at 4.

[53] Representation of the People Acts 1918 and 1928. For comparison with the position preferred by the courts, see KD Ewing and CA Gearty, *The Struggle for Civil Liberties: Political Freedom and the Rule of Law in Britain, 1914–1945* (Oxford, Oxford University Press, 2000), at 17–21.

[54] See, eg, Sex Discrimination Act 1975, Race Relations Act 1976, Disability Discrimination Act 1995.

[55] See, eg, National Assistance Act 1948, National Health Service Act 1977.

the courts, the entirety of British social justice—of the welfare state—is a creation of progressive governments enacting law in Parliament. The second problem with Allan's position is that it does not allow for the situations in which the judges have failed to protect liberty. His faith in the common law would perhaps be less objectionable if the judicial record showed that British courts really were the guardians of freedom. But of course the record shows no such thing: on the contrary, it reveals a judiciary that is, all too often, 'more executive minded than the executive', as Lord Atkin famously expressed it in his dissent in *Liversidge v Anderson*.[56] As well as *Liversidge*, the litany of well-known judicial failures to protect liberty includes *R v Halliday, ex parte Zadig*,[57] *Thomas v Sawkins*,[58] *Duncan v Jones*,[59] *Council of Civil Service Unions v Minister for the Civil Service*,[60] *Attorney-General v Guardian Newspapers*,[61] and *A and others v Secretary of State for the Home Department*;[62] all of this without even mentioning Northern Ireland.[63]

Tenet two: the principal arena in which the activity of law takes place is the court-room.

The constitutional control and regulation of public power is, in the modern world, a complex and multi-faceted activity. From what has been written here thus far, it is obvious that it involves institutions such as Parliament and the courts. But in addition to these, many other institutions are also implicated. Ombudsmen such as the Parliamentary Commissioner for Administration,[64] the Commissioners for Local Administration[65] and the Scottish Public Services Ombudsman[66] investigate complaints of maladministration. Auditors such as the Comptroller and Auditor General, the National Audit

[56] [1942] AC 206, at 244.

[57] [1917] AC 260 (upholding the legality of internment during the First World War). See D Foxton, '*R v Halliday, ex parte Zadig* in Retrospect' (2003) 119 *Law Quarterly Review* 455.

[58] [1935] 2 KB 249 (holding that the police possess a common law power to enter and remain on private property in order to prevent anticipated breach of the peace). See KD Ewing and CA Gearty, above n 53, at 289–95.

[59] [1936] 1 KB 218 (holding that the police possess a common law power to obstruct a public meeting where deemed necessary in order to prevent anticipated breach of the peace). See KD Ewing and CA Gearty, *ibid*, at 261–70.

[60] [1985] 1 AC 374 (upholding decision of Mrs Thatcher unilaterally and without consultation to withdraw trade union rights from government employees at GCHQ).

[61] [1987] 1 WLR 1248 (holding that the publication by the *Guardian* newspaper of allegations contained in former MI5 officer Peter Wright's book, *Spycatcher*, was in breach of confidence).

[62] [2003] 2 WLR 564 (upholding the legality of the provisions in the Anti-Terrorism, Crime and Security Act 2001 permitting indefinite detention without trial of suspected international terrorists; also upholding legality of the UK government's derogation from Art 5 ECHR).

[63] On which see C Gearty, 'The Cost of Human Rights: English Judges and the Northern Irish Troubles' (1994) 47 *Current Legal Problems* 19.

[64] See Parliamentary Commissioner Act 1967 and <www.ombudsman.org.uk>.

[65] See Local Government Act 1974, Part III and <www.lgo.org.uk>.

[66] See Scottish Public Services Ombudsman Act 2002 and <www.scottishombudsman.org.uk>.

Office[67] and the Audit Commission[68] inquire into the economy, effectiveness and efficiency of public spending. Regulators abound in the modern state, from the offices that oversee the privatised utilities (gas, telecommunications, electricity, water and the railway) to the Health and Safety Executive, the Civil Aviation Authority and the Office of Fair Trading. Public inquiries provide for a further series of ways in which government may be subjected to scrutiny, sometimes of the most penetrating and politically damaging nature.[69] Finally, there are dozens of different species of tribunal that between them make several hundred thousand decisions each year.[70]

Notwithstanding this complex matrix of institutions, however, legal constitutionalists focus almost exclusively on public law as it is developed and enforced in the courts.[71] Perhaps this is nothing more than the application of the common law mindset to the realm of public law.[72] Very many British academic lawyers focus their research sharply (that is, narrowly) on case law. In this sense there is nothing particularly unusual about such a focus being a feature of legal constitutionalism—many lawyers would find it unexceptional. It is important nonetheless to appreciate that legal constitutionalism is a constitutionalism that places the common law courts absolutely centre-stage. Routine as this may be for the classic common law domains of private law (contract, tort and the like), in constitutional terms it is a striking move.[73]

Tenet three: individuals should, as far as possible, remain free of interference by the government.

Tenets three and four reveal the underlying political theory of legal constitutionalism. The political theory on which legal constitutionalism rests is

[67] See National Audit Act 1983 and <www.nao.org.uk>.

[68] See Audit Commission Act 1998 and <www.audit-commission.gov.uk>.

[69] The Hutton inquiry into death of Dr David Kelly (and the lead-up to the Iraq war of 2003) (HC (2003–04) 247, January 2004) and the Fraser inquiry into the management and costs of the Holyrood Parliament building project (see SP Paper 205, September 2004) are two of the most notable recent examples: see, respectively, <www.the-hutton-inquiry.org.uk> and <www.holyroodinquiry.org>.

[70] For an overview, see the annual reports of the Council on Tribunals, available at <www.council-on-tribunals.gov.uk>.

[71] A good example is the work of Jeffrey Jowell: see for example his 'Administrative Law', in V Bogdanor (ed), *The British Constitution in the Twentieth Century* (Oxford, Oxford University Press, 2003), ch 10.

[72] On the relationship between the common law mindset and legal constitutionalism see T Poole, 'Back to the Future? Unearthing the Theory of Common Law Constitutionalism' (2003) 23 *Oxford Journal of Legal Studies* 435.

[73] See TRS Allan, *Law, Liberty and Justice*, above n 52, at 4–16. Placing the common law centre-stage is not unique to modern writers: it was an abiding feature of Dicey's work, more than a century ago. See further on Dicey, below, ch 2.

liberalism. Tenet three makes this explicit: the essence of liberalism is that individuals should be able to enjoy their liberty. They should remain free from interference. Some liberal thinkers refer to this in terms of individual autonomy, others in terms of human dignity.[74] By adopting liberalism as their foundational argument, legal constitutionalists exhibit an ambivalent attitude towards government. Government is something which, on the one hand, may enable individuals to enjoy their freedom—so legal constitutionalists recognise that government is necessary, as the anarchic chaos that would ensue without it would not provide the conditions under which liberty could be safely enjoyed. On the other hand, legal constitutionalists also view government with suspicion, as an institution with the potential of doing great damage to individuals by virtue of its being able to act arbitrarily, interfering with individuals' lives and diminishing or curtailing the extent of their freedom.

Sir John Laws has spelled this out as clearly as any other legal constitutionalist: the 'true starting-point in the quest for the good constitution consists', he has suggested, in the concept of 'the autonomy of every individual, in his sovereignty . . . In the good constitution the principle of minimal interference is compulsory, because its refusal would cripple or destroy the autonomy of every individual.'[75] TRS Allan has written in similar terms: 'Majority rule deserves no special political or constitutional reverence except in so far as it is truly consistent with the values of equal human dignity and individual autonomy . . .'[76] The primary values, for writers such as Laws and Allan, are human dignity and individual autonomy. Government, politics and majority rule should be able to prosper only if and in so far as they do not trespass on these fundamentals. No matter how democratic their legitimacy, the political branches must stay within the confines of that which is required by this conception of individual freedom.

---

[74] For a useful overview, see J Gray, *Liberalism* (Buckingham, Open University Press, 1986). On dignity, see D Feldman, 'Human Dignity as a Legal Value' [1999] *Public Law* 682 (Part I) and [2000] *Public Law* 61 (Part II). Dawn Oliver has suggested that, along with 'respect, status and security', both autonomy and dignity are 'key values' in public law: see D Oliver, 'Underlying Values of Public and Private Law', in M Taggart (ed), *The Province of Administrative Law* (Oxford, Hart Publishing, 1997), at 225.

[75] Sir J Laws, 'The Constitution: Morals and Rights' [1996] *Public Law* 622, at 623 and 627. This is one of a series of lectures and articles in which Laws has set out his position. For a critical appraisal, see JAG Griffith, 'The Brave New World of Sir John Laws' (2000) 63 *Modern Law Review* 159.

[76] TRS Allan, *Constitutional Justice*, above n 50, at 25.

Tenet four: where government interference is unavoidable, it should be limited and justified by reason.

Tenet four entails three separate but closely related claims. It insists that government should intervene only when strictly necessary (that is, only when it is unavoidable); that government intervention should be limited; and that it should be justified by reason. As with tenet three, here again we can see an ambivalence towards government. There is a recognition that government interference with individual liberty may sometimes be necessary in the public interest. But this is coupled with an insistence that such interference is both limited and justified by reason. This approach to government is one that is clearly expressed in the European Convention on Human Rights. Consider for example Article 8 of the Convention, which provides that:

(1) Everyone has the right to respect for his private and family life, his home and his correspondence.

(2) There shall be no interference by a public authority with the exercise of this right except such as is in accordance with law and is necessary in a democratic society in the interests of national security, public safety or the economic well being of the country, for the prevention of disorder or crime, for the protection of health or morals, or for the protection of the rights and freedoms of others.

The structure of this Article is repeated elsewhere in the Convention. Article 9 (freedom of thought, conscience and religion), Article 10 (freedom of expression) and Article 11 (freedom of peaceful assembly and association) are all structured identically to Article 8. In each of these Articles the first paragraph confers the right and the second provides for the criteria that must be satisfied in order for state interference with the right to be justified. In every case there are three such criteria: first the interference must be 'in accordance with the law',[77] secondly the interference must be 'necessary in a democratic society' and thirdly the interference must be in order to promote or protect a certain specified objective (national security, prevention of crime, etc).[78] Since the coming into force of the Human Rights Act 1998 these provisions of the Convention have of course become part of domestic law enforceable by courts throughout the United Kingdom. But even

---

[77] Arts 9–11 use the phrase 'prescribed by law' rather than 'in accordance with the law', but there is no material difference between the two formulations.

[78] Arts 8–11 each contain slightly varying lists of objectives. Art 10 has the longest list of the four; Art 9 the shortest.

beforehand the reasoning of tenet four had begun to influence the development of British public law.[79]

Tenet five: both the extent of and the justification for government interference are questions of law for the judges to determine.

This is perhaps the most controversial claim made by advocates of legal constitutionalism. It is closely connected to (and builds on) the superiority claim in tenet one—that is, the notion that the adjudicative environment of common law reasoning constitutes a superior forum for decision-making to the deliberative democracy of legislative assemblies. It is important to appreciate that not all those who would subscribe to tenets three and four necessarily subscribe also to tenet five. Tenets three and four contain, as we have seen, the foundational claims of liberalism and are, as such, accepted by all liberals. But not all liberals go on also to accept the claims made in tenet five: Jeremy Waldron, for example, is one legal philosopher whose work is rooted in liberalism but who maintains a deep scepticism about the appropriateness of seeing questions of constitutional justice as being only (or even mainly) for the courts to determine.[80] Waldron, recognising that radical disagreement—even about such apparently fundamental values as justice and human rights—is a feature of modern society, would prefer to locate decision-making about such issues in a democratic institution such as Parliament, rather than in the courts.

Legal constitutionalists, by contrast, have few such doubts. Dawn Oliver, unusual among legal constitutionalists in being a student of Parliament as well as of the common law, has come to regard Parliament with such disdain that she now describes the public law court, rather than Parliament, as being the 'forum for political debate and settlement of disputes with a political dimension' and as being the 'Grand Inquest of the Nation' in response, as she puts it, to 'the increasingly obvious inability and unwillingness of the House of Commons to do so'.[81]

It is important to recognise that on tenet five legal constitutionalists do vary a little in their approaches (a reflection, perhaps, of its controversial

---

[79] See, for example, *R v Secretary of State for the Home Department, ex parte Pierson* [1998] AC 539 (esp L Steyn at 575) and *R v Secretary of State for the Home Department, ex parte Simms* [2000] 2 AC 115 (esp L Hoffmann at 131). Scottish courts have been rather more sceptical: see for example the doubt expressed as to Lord Steyn's approach in *Pierson* in *Davidson v The Scottish Ministers*, 2002 SLT 420, at 425–6.

[80] See J Waldron, *Law and Disagreement* (Oxford, Clarendon Press, 1999) and *The Dignity of Legislation* (Cambridge, Cambridge University Press, 1999).

[81] D Oliver, 'The Underlying Values of Public and Private Law', above n 74, at 241. The issue of how to return the 'Grand Inquest of the Nation' role to the House of Commons (where it properly belongs) is considered in ch 4, below.

nature). Jeffrey Jowell's view, for example, is considerably more moderate on this aspect of legal constitutionalism than is Trevor Allan's. The difference between Jowell and Allan is that whereas for the latter it would seem that questions of the extent of and justification for government interference are always questions of law for the courts, for Jowell there will be some circumstances where these will remain political questions not suitable for resolution by judges. In Jowell's view there are both 'constitutional' and 'institutional' limitations on the competence of the courts. Constitutional limitations relate to those matters which, in a democracy, do not fall within the province of the courts. Evaluations of the public good and assessments of social and economic advantages are presented as examples: thus, 'we should not expect judges ... to decide whether the country should join a common currency, or to set the level of taxation' as these are matters of 'policy' and are, as such 'the preserve of other branches of government'.[82] Institutional limitations relate to those matters that are 'not ideally justiciable' due to the 'inherent limitations of the process of adjudication'.[83] Thus,

> courts are limited in their capacity to decide matters which admit of no generalised or objective determination ... In addition, the adjudicative process is not ideally suited to deciding polycentric questions—those which cannot be settled in isolation from others which are not before the court—such as whether scarce resources should be allocated to one project or proposal in preference to others ...[84]

Jowell's suggestions as to the limitations of the judicial role in the model of legal constitutionalism are a rarity. As he has himself expressed it, the model as it is presented in most of the literature 'presents a provocative challenge to traditional British constitutional doctrine by seemingly conferring an open-ended law-making power on unelected judges'.[85]

Unfortunately, not all legal constitutionalists have stated their claims in terms as moderate as those of Jowell. Consider, for example, the following statement, made by TRS Allan:

> common law adjudication is superior to the legislative process as a means of resolving questions of justice, even where the latter is accompanied by wide consultation to ascertain public opinion and preceded by vigorous political debate. In highly sensitive matters, where moral and ethical opinions are most personal and deeply divided, legislation may be hard to formulate in generally acceptable terms; and a negotiated compromise is likely to produce radically inconsistent results ... The common law method of reasoning by analogy, where the appropriateness of

---

[82] J Jowell, 'Of Vires and Vacuums: The Constitutional Context of Judicial Review' [1999] *Public Law* 448, at 451.

[83] *Ibid.*

[84] *Ibid.*

[85] *Ibid*, at 449.

the suggested analogy is always a matter for closely reasoned argument, may often provide a more sensitive and generally satisfactory mode of decision-making, better able than statute to accommodate all the complex and critical features of specific cases.[86]

The breadth of this statement is staggering. The common law court-room is preferred over Parliament to resolve even 'highly sensitive' questions where personal opinion is 'deeply divided'. Adjudicative techniques of decision-making are preferred over the open and deliberative processes of parliamentary government even where the matter to be addressed is 'complex'. Neither public consultation nor political debate—no matter how vigorous—can compensate for the deficiencies of the political process. Allan's position may be summarised in the following way: for him, it seems, there is no constitutional problem that is incapable of being solved by the courts, and no constitutional problem is solved until it is solved by the courts. This is legal constitutionalism at its most extreme.

To give an example from practice of what is advocated in tenet five—that is, of what is advocated both by hardliners such as Allan as well as by more moderate legal constitutionalists such as Jowell—let us consider again the structure of ECHR Article 8, outlined in relation to tenet four. We saw that under the terms of Article 8 there are three criteria to be satisfied before state interference with privacy may be justified. The first is that the interference must be in accordance with the law; the second is that the interference must be 'necessary in a democratic society'; and the third is that the interference must have the aim of protecting or promoting a certain, specified, objective. Legal constitutionalists posit that the application of each of these three criteria is properly a judicial role for the courts to determine. This is as true for the more moderate proponents such as Jowell as it is for the more extreme such as Allan.[87]

Now, there is an argument that the first criterion may indeed be a matter that lends itself to resolution in a court-room. Deciding what is 'in accordance with the law' seems on the face of it to be an appropriate activity for a judge. The second and third criteria, however, pose quite different sorts of questions. The European Court of Human Rights has ruled that the phrase 'necessary in a democratic society' requires the court to determine whether the state has shown its action to be justified by what the court calls a 'pressing social need'. It is to be noted that this is not a straightforward necessity test—

---

[86] TRS Allan, 'Common Law Constitutionalism and Freedom of Speech', in J Beatson and Y Cripps (eds), *Freedom of Expression and Freedom of Information* (Oxford, Oxford University Press, 2000), at 22.

[87] See, eg, J Jowell, 'Beyond the Rule of Law: Towards Constitutional Judicial Review' [2000] *Public Law* 671.

the test here is not simply that the state's actions must be necessary, but must be necessary *in a democratic society*. Consequently the state will be able to justify its actions only if they are proportionate and can be shown to be in accordance with what the Court has described as the spirit of 'pluralism, tolerance and broadmindedness'.[88]

Unlike the first criterion it is far from self-evident that these questions are appropriate for determination by judges. The following examples (all of them real) illustrate the problems. In 2000 the home secretary decided to exclude from the United Kingdom a (non-British) controversial political activist, whom many regard as racist and anti-Semitic, on the ground that his presence in the UK would not be 'conducive to the public good'. Why should it be the courts, rather than the home secretary, accountable as he is to the democratically elected House of Commons, who decide whether such a decision is in accordance with the spirit of 'tolerance and broadmindedness'?[89] How could a court weigh and assess the various factors that must go into making a decision such as this: the intelligence advice, the risks to public order, the sensitive issues of inter-community relations, even the delicate foreign affairs considerations, and so forth? In 2002 the Scottish Parliament passed legislation to criminalise the hunting of wild mammals with dogs. Why should a judge (rather than the electorate) have the last word on whether the policy choices made by the democratically elected Parliament are 'proportionate' or sufficiently 'pluralist'?[90] Hunting is a politically controversial matter that raises a great number of issues, from control of land to management of wild animals and from cruelty to tradition. Are these not precisely the sorts of issues that should be debated in a Parliament rather than litigated in a court-room?

The third criterion raises similar problems. Who should determine what is necessary in the interests of national security, or for the prevention of disorder, or for the protection of public health? Are these issues that lend themselves to resolution through the adjudicative techniques of the courts or through the political processes of parliamentary government?

Tenet six: the law should control government through the enforcement of specific rules and general principles of legality (such as human rights).

What is striking about this, final, tenet of legal constitutionalism is its reliance on both 'specific rules' and 'general principles'. It is the inclusion of the

[88] These phrases are widely used in the Court's case law: see, eg, *Smith and Grady v United Kingdom* (2000) 29 EHRR 493.

[89] See *R (Farrakhan) v Secretary of State for the Home Department* [2002] QB 1391.

[90] *Adams v The Scottish Ministers*, decision of the Inner House of the Court of Session, 28 May 2004. For commentary, see B Winetrobe, 'The Judge in the Scottish Parliament Chamber' [2005] *Public Law*, forthcoming.

general principles that makes legal constitutionalism distinctive. The proposition that the courts should have the power to declare government action unlawful where it flouts a specific rule that Parliament has laid down is uncontroversial. If Parliament passes legislation which provides that a public authority may (for example) withdraw a certain welfare benefit from a person only after giving that person an opportunity to make representations to the authority, and a public authority withdraws the benefit from someone without giving them such an opportunity, it is clear that the court should have the power to declare that the authority has acted unlawfully, on the ground that the authority has acted in a way that was not authorised by statute.

This situation, however, stands in stark contrast to the legal constitutionalist position with regard to general principles. Legal constitutionalists posit that the courts should be able to declare government decisions to be unlawful not only where they breach specific rules that Parliament has laid down, but also where they breach general principles of legality.[91] Such general principles do not have to be enshrined in legislation, but may be the creations of the courts. The source of such general principles may be the rule of law, which some legal constitutionalists define spectacularly broadly,[92] or may lie in other principles that are said to inhere within the common law constitution—principles such as equality or freedom of expression.[93]

Thus, the courts have ruled that the actions and decisions of public authorities must be 'reasonable', or at least, that they must not be so unreasonable that no reasonable public authority could have taken them. This is known as the '*Wednesbury*' formulation of unreasonableness.[94] The difficulty with this ruling is that it is impossible to predict what the courts will hold to be unreasonable and what they will not. Such an approach to public law seeks to control the problem of executive discretion simply by replacing it with untrammelled judicial discretion. For sure, a constitution should guard against capricious or arbitrary executive action. But so too should it guard against capricious or arbitrary judicial decision-making. The creation by the courts of general principles of legality is no way to control arbitrariness in public life, as the use and abuse of the *Wednesbury* doctrine in English law has shown.[95]

---

[91]   Further, they posit that the courts should be able to declare Acts of Parliament to be unlawful where they breach general principles of legality: see, eg, Sir J Laws at n 49 above.

[92]   Most notably TRS Allan, in his *Constitutional Justice*, above n 50. For a stimulating critique, see C Gearty, *Principles of Human Rights Adjudication* (Oxford, Oxford University Press, 2004), at 61–68.

[93]   This is the approach adopted by Jeffrey Jowell (who, incidentally, is critical of the breadth of Allan's definition of the rule of law): see J Jowell, 'Of Vires and Vacuums', above n 82, at 456.

[94]   *Associated Provincial Picture Houses v Wednesbury Corporation* [1948] 1 KB 223.

[95]   The story is a well-known one: for a brief account, see A Tomkins, above n 28, at 176–82.

In a similar vein, and more recently, the courts have ruled that an Act of Parliament cannot be interpreted as authorising a public authority to infringe what the court called a 'constitutional right' unless that Act says so expressly.[96] The 'constitutional right' at issue in the case in which this rule was invented was the right of unimpeded access to the court. Never before had such a right been recognised in English law, and nowhere in the court's judgment is it made clear what in the future will be added to the list of constitutional rights recognised by the common law. This was a development in public law that pre-dated the coming into force of the Human Rights Act 1998, but there is nothing in the Act, nor in the courts' subsequent interpretation of it, to suggest that the Convention rights the Act incorporates into domestic law have replaced common law constitutional rights.

Whether courts are enforcing Convention rights incorporated into domestic law by force of statute, or constitutional rights invented by the courts through the development of the common law, the danger remains the same: it is what we saw earlier that Jowell referred to as the conferring of 'an open-ended law-making power on unelected judges'.[97] Jowell's purported safeguard against this danger is to posit a radical separation between questions of policy and matters of principle, a separation that he avowedly borrows from the work of Ronald Dworkin.[98] Thus, constitutional questions, even when they are overtly political in character, may be adjudicated upon and ultimately decided by judges rather than by Parliament as long as they relate to principle rather than to policy. Civil and political rights and the limitations that may be placed upon them are, in this analysis, questions of principle rather than of policy and, as such, are matters for the courts to determine. Questions such as the allocation of limited public resources, on the other hand, are policy matters for Parliament.

Laws has adopted a broadly similar approach, in which he distinguishes between 'negative' rights such as those found in the European Convention on Human Rights, which are legal in character and are therefore questions for the courts, and 'positive' rights which are aspirational in character and which are best left to Parliament. Among the positive rights Laws identifies are education, health care, national security and a clean environment.[99] About positive rights, Laws says:

---

[96] *R v Secretary of State for the Home Department, ex parte Leech* [1994] QB 198.

[97] See above n 85.

[98] See R Dworkin, *Taking Rights Seriously* (London, Duckworth, 1977), ch 4. In his earlier work TRS Allan also took this Dworkinian line (see *Law, Liberty and Justice*, above n 52, at 7–8 and 53–59), but he appears to have dropped it in his more recent work, presumably on the ground that he now considers both matters of principle and questions of policy to fall within the domain of the courts: see above, at n 86.

[99] See J Laws, 'The Constitution: Morals and Rights' above n 75, at 628.

there will always be hard choices about which ... decent and honourable people will disagree. At the level of political decision-making such choices find expression in rival policies ... This is the area in which constitutional responsibility rests on the shoulders of our elected politicians. It is not the domain of the judges ... In relation to positive rights, Parliament is necessarily and rightly supreme.[100]

For once, Laws is right. Or at least, he is partly right. These are indeed matters that are properly regarded as being for government and Parliament to determine. But so too are the issues which the legal constitutionalists characterise as being matters of 'principle'. The difficulty with the legal principle/political policy distinction is that it is never justified (or indeed grounded in principle). It is merely asserted. The only explanation for treating (say) freedom of expression as a legal principle but the right to a clean environment as a political aspiration can be a political one—that is to say, it is nothing more than mere political preference.[101]

The distinction between positive and negative rights is illusory. Many of the so-called negative rights contained in the European Convention require states (that is, governments) to take extensive positive action, whether it be to ensure that the 'right to life' of the vulnerable is appropriately safeguarded or to ensure that adequate inquiries are made by coroners and others in circumstances of suspicious deaths in custody. The realisation of freedom of expression in the modern world is impossible without broadcasting, which requires considerable state regulation. The right to a fair trial requires the state to establish an elaborate system of criminal and civil justice. And so on. Laws' inclusion of national security in his list of positive rights further undermines the distinction he seeks to make between the two forms. As we saw above, national security is one of the prescribed objectives listed in Articles 8, 10 and 11 of the ECHR on which a state may rely in order to justify interference with the rights set out in those Articles. How can national security simultaneously be a limitation to a justiciable right and a political aspiration best left to Parliament? Education is another example of a right that is contained in the Convention (and incorporated into domestic law by virtue of the Human Rights Act)[102] yet which is listed by Laws as being positive. Where does this leave us? Is state intervention in education a matter for the courts to determine or an issue for Parliament?

The distinction (relied upon by Jowell) between legal principle and questions concerning the allocation of limited public resources is also illusory. Civil and political rights such as those contained in the ECHR are neither free

---

[100] See J Laws, 'The Constitution: Morals and Rights' above n 75, at 629.

[101] For an excellent discussion, see KD Ewing, 'Social Rights and Constitutional Law' [1999] *Public Law* 104, esp at 113–21.

[102] ECHR, First Protocol, Art 2 and Human Rights Act 1998, s 1(1)(b).

nor cheap. Court structures, prison services, broadcasting regulators and so on—all of which are required state services necessary for the delivery of civil and political rights—are expensive. The conclusion to be drawn is that Laws' analysis of what he calls positive rights applies to all rights, as it applies to Allan's 'rule of law' as well to Jowell's 'legal principles'. On all of these matters there will always and inevitably be hard choices to make about which we will disagree. In a democracy such choices find expression as rival policies, constitutional responsibility for which properly rests on the shoulders of our elected politicians.

What's Wrong with Legal Constitutionalism?

This completes our examination of the six tenets of legal constitutionalism. Several criticisms have been made in relation to particular tenets as we have considered them. Before we move on to formulate a response to the model we must first attempt to draw some threads together. It was suggested above that legal constitutionalism is undesirable for two main reasons: first because it is undemocratic and secondly because it is ineffective. Let us now say something more about each of these. Legal constitutionalism may be said to incorporate undemocratic aspects in three respects. The first relates to the (lack of) accountability of the prime decision-makers—that is to say, of the judges; the second concerns problems of access; and the third problems of representation.

We saw above that at the core of the British constitutional order lies a rule of accountability that requires all members of the government to subject themselves both individually and collectively to the rules of ministerial responsibility to Parliament. The MPs to whom ministers are responsible are themselves responsible, of course, directly to the electorate. There are no equivalents to these structures of accountability for the judges. The judiciary is not elected; neither is it responsible to any elected body. First instance judges are, in a sense, accountable by virtue of the possibility of appeal to a superior court. Even Court of Appeal (or, in Scotland, Court of Session) judges are similarly accountable in such cases that are further appealed to the House of Lords. But this is only a very limited notion of accountability, akin to saying that a junior minister is accountable to the secretary of state that is for the time being her immediate superior. All public sector professionals know that there is the world of difference between being answerable to one's immediate boss and being part of an institution that is accountable to some external form of public assessment through audit, whether it be the accountability of the NHS to the Audit Commission or of universities to the Quality

Assurance Agency.[103] Moreover, of course, even if the prospect of an appeal were to constitute a form of accountability, this cannot apply to the most senior judges. There is, by definition, no appeal from the highest court—the very court which is likely to make the most controversial constitutional decisions. The House of Lords remains wholly unaccountable even in this very limited sense of accountability through appeal.[104]

This lack of accountability is relatively unobjectionable while the courts are confined to the resolution of legal disputes. But questions such as whether a government minister has acted as is required in a democratic society in the interests of national security or public health are not purely legal, as we have seen. They necessarily and inevitably raise difficult political questions. This claim is no longer controversial, or even contested. Even the most ardent legal constitutionalists recognise (indeed, positively welcome) the fact that their model grants to judges not merely a licence but a 'duty' to decide 'wide questions of policy'.[105] Yet, in a democracy, those who are empowered for the time being to resolve political disputes are required to be politically accountable. Judges are not, which makes the transferring to the courts of responsibility for answering political questions objectionable.

The second democracy-related problem with legal constitutionalism concerns participation and access. Democracy requires not only that those in positions of political power be politically accountable. It also requires that those who are subject to the exercise of political power have ready access to political decision-makers. Courts are notoriously expensive to access and often have strict rules of standing that limit the availability of judicial redress to small classes of applicants. From the perspective of participatory democracy, then, legal constitutionalism suffers from a number of drawbacks. The final democracy-related problem with legal constitutionalism concerns the representativeness of the decision-makers (that is, of the judges). In a representative democracy, political power should be exercised by persons 'representing' the community over whom they exercise power. This notion of 'representing' has two dimensions: representation and representativeness. On the one hand the decision-maker should act as a representative (in the sense of 'delegate') of the people. That is, the people should nominate or elect the decision-maker. On the other hand the decision-makers should constitute a representation (in the sense of 'reflection') of the people. Yet, whom

---

[103]   See R Mulgan, above n 10.

[104]   That there are limited circumstances in which a reference may be made to the European Court of Justice or in which further action may be taken before the European Court of Human Rights is not to answer the problem but merely to shift it, as the issue then becomes the lack of accountability of the ECJ or ECtHR.

[105]   J Laws, 'The Limitations of Human Rights' [1998] *Public Law* 254, at 256.

do the appeal court judges represent? In the House of Lords there are currently twelve lords of appeal. All are over sixty years old and six are over seventy; all are white; eleven of the twelve are men; and they are no more representative of the British people in terms of class, educational background or wealth.

So much, for the time being, for democracy. We will return to some of these themes in more depth in chapter two. First we must turn our attention briefly to issues of ineffectiveness. There are two main dimensions to the claim that the model of legal constitutionalism suffers from problems of ineffectiveness. The first concerns the nature of the judicial forum and the second relates to the judicial record.[106] The forum in which judges operate is, of course, the court. A case will come before the court where there is a dispute between two parties who cannot agree or settle. Argument in court is structured around the two parties to the case, now known in English law as the 'claimant' and the 'defendant' (Scots law employs different terms). The role of the judge is to adjudicate between the arguments of the two parties and to give a judgment that will, ultimately, hold either that the claimant's case is made out or that it is not. It is to be noted that judges cannot choose the cases that come to court—litigation happens by accident, not by design, and is in this sense always haphazard, not systematic.[107] The contrast here with Parliament is stark: Parliament may legislate on any issue, for any reason and at any time. Judges also have limited room for manoeuvre in terms of the arguments on which their judgments are based. Judges are generally required to decide cases on the basis only of the submissions made to them by counsel.

A striking example of just how limiting this can be for the effectiveness of legal constitutionalism arose in the *Prolife* case, arguably the most important free speech case so far decided by the House of Lords in the Human Rights Act era.[108] Prolife, a registered political party that campaigns against abortion, fielded a sufficient number of candidates in Welsh constituencies in the 2001 general election to entitle it to a party election broadcast (PEB) to be broadcast in Wales. Prolife submitted a tape of its PEB to the broadcasters, who refused to screen it on the ground that to do so would breach their statutory obligations to ensure that their broadcasts contained nothing likely to be 'offensive to public feeling'.[109] There was no objection to the text of the broadcast: only its pictures were deemed offensive. These contained

---

[106] There is, in addition, a third dimension, which concerns the effectiveness of judicial remedies: for a brief discussion, see A Tomkins, above n 28, at 208–9.

[107] The House of Lords, like most supreme courts, does filter the cases which may come before it, but this facility is not generally available to lower courts.

[108] *R (Prolife Alliance) v British Broadcasting Corporation* [2004] 1 AC 185.

[109] Broadcasting Act 1990, s 6(1)(a).

'prolonged and graphic images' of an abortion.[110] Prolife edited its proposed broadcast, blurring its pictures, but still the broadcasters refused to screen it. Finally, Prolife produced a version of its broadcast with a blank screen bearing the word 'censored' accompanied by a sound track describing the images that Prolife had desired to show.

Prolife sought judicial review of the decision to refuse to screen its original broadcast. The Court of Appeal held in favour of Prolife that the broadcaster's censorship of its PEB was neither necessary nor proportionate in a democratic society. When the broadcasters appealed to the House of Lords, their appeal was allowed and the decision of the Court of Appeal was overturned.[111] Why? The answer lies in the framing of the question in argument before the House of Lords. The question was split into two: (a) do the rules prohibiting broadcasters from screening pictures 'offensive to public feeling' comply with the principle of freedom of political expression and (b) did the broadcasters correctly apply those rules in this particular case? For reasons which are not readily apparent Prolife's counsel conceded before the House of Lords that only question (b) and not question (a) was in issue.[112] Whereas the two questions had been presented as one overall question in the Court of Appeal (ie, 'was the restriction on freedom of expression proportionate?') the division of the question on appeal into two separate issues enabled the Lords to focus on the narrower point ('did the broadcasters properly apply the law?') and to leave to one side the bigger question of whether the law properly respected or improperly interfered with Prolife's freedom of expression. In this way a potentially enormous case concerned with a right that many legal constitutionalists consider to be the most important of all— the right to freedom of political expression—became transformed into a perfectly ordinary administrative law case about the proper construction and application of a particular set of statutory obligations, the House of Lords holding that in refusing to screen the PEB the broadcasters had not misapplied the law.

A further limitation with regard to the judicial forum arises from the nature of common law adjudication. Decision-making through the bi-polar adjudicative techniques of the court room allows precious little room for compromise or for negotiated settlement. Resources are limited to the (largely legal) expertise of counsel. While third-party interventions do occur

---

[110] Per L Nicholls, at para [3].

[111] By a 4–1 majority, L Scott dissenting.

[112] See L Nicholls at para [10]: '[B]efore your Lordships' House Prolife Alliance accepted . . . that the offensive material restriction is not in itself an infringement of Prolife Alliance's Convention right under Article 10. The appeal proceeded on that footing. The only issue before the House is the second, narrower question.'

in some cases,[113] the bulk of cases continue to involve only two parties. As such, neither the range nor the variety of argument in court is anything like as plural or as open as is the case with parliamentary forms of decision-making, as, to their credit, judges do sometimes acknowledge. Complex questions of social policy, such as public housing or other welfare schemes, are often seen by judges as being matters requiring parliamentary legislation rather than judicial law-making.[114]

The issue goes wider than this, however. Even away from questions of social policy the limitations inherent within judicial forms of decision-making may significantly reduce the effectiveness of legal constitutionalism. The point has been powerfully made by Thomas Poole. In a careful and detailed analysis of the decision of the House of Lords in *Simms*,[115] a case decided very much in accordance with the model of legal constitutionalism and welcomed by the model's proponents, Poole has stated that:

> We would expect an exemplary forum of public reason . . . to operate a system which encourages or at least accommodates direct, open, wide-ranging, non-rigid, consequentialist argument. This is not what the examination of the process in a case like *Simms* reveals. *Simms* represents a process of reasoning which, while certainly public, rational and receptive to liberal norms and values, is narrowly focused on the needs of the parties to the case, almost devoid of consequentialist analysis and adheres quite rigidly to a limited number of pre-set forms of argument.[116]

Simms was concerned with a big question: to what extent should convicted prisoners enjoy the same opportunities the rest of us have as regards making contact with, and expressing ourselves through, the media. How far should imprisonment upon conviction curtail this aspect of freedom of expression—and, relatedly, how far should journalists and the commercial organisations for whom they write be permitted to profit from publishing the stories of convicted prisoners? Yet, as with the *Prolife* case considered above, in the hands of the lawyers the question is reduced to a far narrower one: where a prisoner requests an oral interview with a journalist, is a prison governor entitled to withhold permission in the event that the journalist concerned refuses to sign an undertaking that he will not publish the interview? This is not a criticism of the individual lawyers involved in Simms' case,

---

[113] See S Hannett, 'Third Party Intervention: In the Public Interest?' [2003] *Public Law* 128.

[114] See for example the discussion of this issue by L Millett (dissenting) in *Ghaidan v Godin-Mendoza* [2004] 3 WLR 113, esp at paras [96]–[101]. See also *Re S (Care Order: Implementation of Care Plan)* [2002] 2 AC 291, esp the criticism of the Court of Appeal's attempts in that case at judicial legislation.

[115] *R v Secretary of State for the Home Department, ex parte Simms* [2000] 2 AC 115.

[116] T Poole, 'Dogmatic Liberalism? TRS Allan and the Common Law Constitution' (2002) 65 *Modern Law Review* 463, at 472.

nor even of the judges who decided it. It is a reflection of the inevitable consequence of using the court-room as the forum for making big policy decisions.

As well as the limitations inherent in the structure of judicial argument, legal constitutionalism also risks being ineffective as a check on government for the reason that the courts are simply not very good at doing what the legal constitutionalists desire them to do. They are neither as liberal nor as eager to intervene as they would be required to be for the model of legal constitutionalism to be effective as a check on illiberal government. We saw above how a catalogue of repressive common law decisions, from *ex parte Zadig* and *Duncan v Jones* to the *GCHQ* case and the *Spycatcher* litigation, suggested that the courts might not be the best institution on which to rely in the struggle to secure civil liberties. The record since the coming into force of the Human Rights Act is no more encouraging. Two House of Lords cases serve to illustrate the point: *Rehman*[117] and *Shayler*.[118]

Rehman was a Pakistani national who had been given leave to enter and remain in the United Kingdom for a limited period of time. When he applied for indefinite leave to remain his application was refused and the secretary of state decided that he should be deported on the ground that he was a danger to national security. The House of Lords unanimously refused to quash the home secretary's decision, stating that notwithstanding the fact that 'it cannot be proved . . . that [Rehman] has carried out any individual act which would justify the conclusion that he is a danger',[119] determining what is in the interests of national security is a matter exclusively for the government of the day, the courts being simply 'not entitled' to disagree with the government's verdict.[120]

In *Shayler* the House of Lords was presented with an opportunity to declare certain provisions of Britain's notorious Official Secrets legislation (including section 1 of the Official Secrets Act 1989) to be incompatible with Article 10 of the European Convention on Human Rights. Section 1 of the 1989 Act makes it a criminal offence for a member or former member of the security and intelligence services[121] to disclose any information relating to security or intelligence which came into that person's possession by virtue of his employment in the services. No damage to Britain's national security need actually (or even potentially) be caused by the disclosure and it is no defence to a charge under section 1 that the disclosure was in the public interest (on

---

[117] *Secretary of State for the Home Department v Rehman* [2003] 1 AC 153.
[118] *R v Shayler* [2003] 1 AC 247.
[119] Per L Hutton, at para [65].
[120] Per L Hoffmann, at para [53].
[121] Shayler had been a member of the Security Service (MI5) from 1991–96.

the ground that, for example, it revealed corruption in the services). The House of Lords ruled that, notwithstanding the breathtaking scope of this section, it did not breach the protection of freedom of expression afforded by Article 10.

In the days before the Human Rights Act, liberal public lawyers used to boast that, if only the courts were able to enforce a Bill of Rights, political liberty in Britain would be safely secured. Yet cases such as *Rehman* and *Shayler*, decided since the Act came into force, suggest that liberty is no better protected now than it was before. Together with *Simms* and *Prolife*, these cases all serve to illustrate the limitations inherent within the model of legal constitutionalism, even *with* a Bill of Rights and even *with* a judiciary that is more highly schooled in the ostensibly liberal values of legal constitutionalism than ever before.[122]

The message to be gleaned from cases such as these is that the model of legal constitutionalism promises more than it is able to deliver: that in practice it is able neither to safeguard liberty nor to act as an effective check on the government of the day. If this message is correct—that legal constitutionalism fails—this means that those of us who are committed to the protection of liberty and to the checking of excessive government must find an alternative. For we can be sure that just as government will not check itself, neither can liberty be its own safeguard—it needs institutional protection, not mere rhetoric. It is the mission of this book to suggest what the alternative to legal constitutionalism might be. And it is the argument of this book that our alternative is to be found in the ideal of political accountability and in the theory of republicanism that underpins it. It is to these issues that we can now turn.

---

[122] For further argument to similar effect, see KD Ewing, 'The Futility of the Human Rights Act' [2004] *Public Law*, forthcoming.

2

Republican Constitutionalism

———➤·◆·◄———

'There is not a more unintelligible word in the English
language than republicanism.'[1]

I REPUBLICANISM AND CONSTITUTIONAL LAW

The Shape of British Public Law Scholarship

IN THE PREVIOUS chapter we saw how the model of legal constitutionalism has in recent years become the dominant discourse of public
law scholarship in Britain. It is important to appreciate just how novel a
move this is. The modern, liberal model of legal constitutionalism outlined in
chapter one is a recent innovation in British public law, having adopted its
current form only in the mid 1990s. Until the 1990s there had been only two
main schools of thought in British public law scholarship, one rather conservative and the other more progressive but strongly functionalist rather than
normative in character.[2] These various schools of thought have been well
documented by Martin Loughlin, whose *Public Law and Political Theory*
remains a leading work on this topic.[3]

---

[1] John Adams, founding father and second President of the United States, letter to Mercy
Otis Warren, 8 August 1807.

[2] For a while in the 1980s it appeared as if a new school was being developed, known as
the 'Sheffield School', but twenty years on it is difficult to see what, if anything, is left of this as a
distinctive approach. A number of its preoccupations have been absorbed into the mainstream
(seeing the subject as one of public law rather than as separate fields of constitutional and administrative law, and seeing freedom of information as being of central rather than marginal importance, for example). Some scholars associated with the Sheffield School have been at the
forefront of developing regulation as an area of scholarship, but by no means all regulation
scholars came from the Sheffield School. Probably the leading work of the Sheffield School is
I Harden and N Lewis, *The Noble Lie: The British Constitution and the Rule of Law* (London,
Hutchinson, 1986).

[3] M Loughlin, *Public Law and Political Theory* (Oxford, Clarendon Press, 1992). For a summary,
see A Tomkins, 'In Defence of the Political Constitution' (2002) 22 *Oxford Journal of Legal Studies*
157, at 157–61.

The conservative school, which Loughlin called 'conservative normativism' was, for most of the twentieth century, the dominant school of
thought. This approach to public law was fashioned by the greatest constitutional lawyer of the late nineteenth century, AV Dicey, and by his followers in
the twentieth. It is associated in particular with ECS Wade, who edited the
later editions of Dicey's key text, *The Law of the Constitution*, and with Sir
William (HWR) Wade, whose treatise on *Administrative Law* was one of the
first (and remains one of the leading) textbooks in that field, the later editions
of which were co-written with his Cambridge colleague, Christopher
Forsyth, another figure closely associated with this school.[4]

Conservative normativists believe strongly in the legal supremacy of
statute and in a rather weak, largely formal, notion of the rule of law. That is,
they believe that the executive should govern through legal forms and instruments, through rules rather than discretion. As long as this formal constraint
is applied, conservative normativists believe that the content of government
policy should, on the whole, remain a matter for parliamentary government
and should not be generally subject to wide-ranging substantive review by the
judges. In the model of conservative normativism the constitutional role of
the judges is minimal, concerned only with the enforcement of rules, leaving
law-making to Parliament, unchecked by the courts and leaving questions of
substantive policy to the government of the day.[5]

For most of the twentieth century the only significant challenge to the hege-
mony of conservative normativism came from a line of scholars based at the
London School of Economics. Taking their lead from the inspirational political theorist HJ Laski, two public lawyers at the LSE in the 1930s developed a
functionalist critique of the Diceyan model. William Robson focused on
administrative justice[6] while Ivor Jennings wrote two monumental accounts of
the main institutions of the British state: *Cabinet Government* and *Parliament*.[7]
The main thrust of Robson's and of Jennings' work was to describe the institutions of the state as they actually operated rather than to engage in argument
about what they dismissed as the conceptual 'fictions' (sovereignty, the rule of
law and so forth) with which the Diceyans were concerned.[8] Rather than
debating what were the values on which the constitutional order was founded,

---

[4] HWR Wade and CF Forsyth, *Administrative Law* (Oxford, Oxford University Press, 2004,
9th ed).

[5] For discussion, see M Loughlin, above n 3, at 139–62 and 184–90. See also C Harlow and
R Rawlings, *Law and Administration* (London, Butterworths, 1997, 2nd edn), ch 2.

[6] WA Robson, *Justice and Administrative Law: A Study of the British Constitution* (London,
Macmillan, 1928).

[7] WI Jennings, *Cabinet Government* (Cambridge, Cambridge University Press, 1936) and
Parliament (Cambridge, Cambridge University Press, 1939).

[8] See A Tomkins, '"Talking in Fictions": Jennings on Parliament' (2004) 67 *Modern Law
Review* 772.

the LSE scholars focused instead on how the institutions of state functioned in practice. Their work was grounded not in abstract political theory but in the social scientific techniques of empirical data gathering.[9]

Their findings effectively destroyed the basis on which conservative normativism rested: namely the purported distinction between rules and discretion. For the Diceyans the great evil was administrative discretion, which they associated with arbitrary government and tyranny.[10] Government, they argued, should govern through rules rather than discretion. As the state grew, however, and as it developed a greater role in the provision of welfare, exclusive reliance on rules became impossible. Discretion had become an inevitable aspect of modern administrative life. The issue for the law was not how to quash it, but how best to regulate it. For the functionalists the answer was clear: administrative discretion had to be regulated, but not through the courts. If the judges, imbued in the Diceyan tradition, could not even distinguish between discretion and tyranny, what hope was there in the court room for effective, functional regulation? Rather than rely on the common law courts, the functionalists argued that specialist, expert administrative tribunals were required, that the modern administrative state required a sophisticated and dedicated system of administrative law.

This, of course, is where legal constitutionalism comes in. The legal constitutionalists recognise, with the functionalists, that a modern public law needs to accommodate (rather than merely resist) the problem of discretion but they insist, contrary to the functionalists, that the common law courts are able to learn and to adapt to this new role. In this sense the legal constitutionalists agree with the Diceyans that the common law court is central and with the functionalists that one of the key tasks for public law is to regulate the exercise of political discretion.[11] We saw in the previous chapter how, in the model of legal constitutionalism, this is to be done through the enforcement of general principles of law and negative rights.

The LSE functionalists were clearer on what the institutional structure of the new public law needed to be than they were on what its content should be. The personal politics of the scholars of the LSE school may have been progressive but in their work they were less concerned to confront the political conservatism of Dicey and his followers than they were to challenge their methodology and their focus on the common law.[12]

---

[9] For discussion, see M Loughlin, above n 3, at 165–76 and 190–206 and C Harlow and R Rawlings, above n 5, ch 3.

[10] The classic text is Lord Hewart, *The New Despotism* (London, Benn, 1929).

[11] For discussion, see M Loughlin, above n 3, at 206–29 and C Harlow and R Rawlings, above n 5, ch 4.

[12] There were occasional exceptions, such as Jennings' attack on the Public Order Act 1936 (see WI Jennings, 'Public Order' (1937) 8 *Political Quarterly* 7) but even when considering matters

The pioneering work of Robson and Jennings was developed later in the century by their student, JAG Griffith, who spent virtually his entire career at the LSE, from undergraduate to Professor of Public Law. Griffith's best-known work, as well as his most controversial, is his brilliant polemic on *The Politics of the Judiciary*,[13] but for our purposes his most significant work is his lecture, delivered in 1978, on 'The Political Constitution'.[14] This lecture is the most important statement on the political model of constitutionalism we encountered at the beginning of chapter one and, as such, it requires careful consideration. Griffith's lecture was a response to three books published in the 1970s, books which were to pave the way for the development of the model of legal constitutionalism. His targets were Lord Scarman's Hamlyn lectures of 1974,[15] Lord Hailsham's *Dilemma of Democracy*[16] and Ronald Dworkin's *Taking Rights Seriously*,[17] all of which, in admittedly slightly differ-ent ways and for varying reasons, advocated greater judicial powers to con-strain the forces of parliamentary government. All three argued that general legal principles such as those found in a Bill of Rights should be available to the judiciary so as to provide legal limits to what both Parliament and government may do.[18]

Griffith outlined two sets of objections to such arguments, which he labelled the 'political' and the 'philosophical'. The political objection was rooted in Griffith's understanding of (and support for) parliamentary democracy. In a famous passage, Griffith insisted that:

> law is not and cannot be a substitute for politics. This is a hard truth, perhaps an unpleasant truth. For centuries political philosophers have sought that society in which government is by laws and not by men. It is an unattainable ideal. Written constitutions do not achieve it. Nor do Bills of Rights or any other devices. They merely pass political decisions out of the hands of politicians and into the hands of judges or other persons. To require a supreme court to make certain kinds of polit-ical decisions does not make those decisions any less political. I firmly believe that political decisions should be taken by politicians. In a society like ours this means by people who are removable.[19]

---

as ostensibly political as parliamentary reform Jennings preferred to focus on how to make the Commons more efficient in its functions rather than on how to democratise the composition of the House of Lords: see, eg, his *Parliamentary Reform* (London, Gollancz, 1934).

[13] JAG Griffith, *The Politics of the Judiciary* (London, Fontana, 1997, 5th ed), first published in 1977.

[14] JAG Griffith, 'The Political Constitution' (1979) 42 *Modern Law Review* 1.

[15] L Scarman, *English Law—The New Dimension* (London, Stevens, 1974).

[16] L Hailsham, *The Dilemma of Democracy: Diagnosis and Prescription* (London, Collins, 1978).

[17] R Dworkin, *Taking Rights Seriously* (London, Duckworth, 1977).

[18] JAG Griffith, above n 14, at 7–12.

[19] *Ibid*, at 16.

Griffith accepted that 'the responsibility and accountability of our rulers should be real and not fictitious' and conceded that

> our existing institutions, especially the House of Commons, need strengthening. And we need to force governments out of secrecy and into the open . . . Governments are too easily able to act in an authoritarian manner. But the remedies are political. It is not by attempting to restrict the legal powers of government that we shall defeat authoritarianism. It is by insisting on open government.[20]

He concluded his political objection with these words:

> [the] proposals by Lord Hailsham, Lord Scarman and others are not only mistaken but positively dangerous. They seem to indicate a way by which potential tyranny can be defeated by the intervention of the law and the invention of institutional devices. There is no such way. Only political control, politically exercised, can supply the remedy.[21]

So much for Griffith's political objection. His philosophical objection was an argument against the notion of fundamental individual rights, a category which he simply did not accept. 'There are no over-riding human rights,' he wrote. 'Instead there are political claims.'[22] For Griffith, the acceptance or rejection of such a human right/political claim is a matter for politicians rather than for judges, the advantage of such a system, in his view, being 'not that politicians are more likely to come up with the right answer but that . . . they are so much more vulnerable than judges and can be dismissed . . .'[23]

Griffith's objections are powerful and are reminiscent of many of the criticisms of legal constitutionalism that were outlined in chapter one. But there is one major limitation to Griffith's position, a limitation that he inherited from his mentors Robson and Jennings. This is that the argument presented in 'The Political Constitution', for all its passionate rhetoric, was in constitutional terms wholly descriptive. While Griffith expressed forthright political opinions (for example, 'political decisions should be taken by politicians . . . who are removable', and 'we need to force governments out of secrecy and into the open') these were articulated solely at the level of politics and not as matters of constitutional analysis. When he insisted that the 'accountability of our rulers should be real and not fictitious' he was not expressing his view of what the constitution requires, but merely his own political preference.

When it came to discussing constitutional questions, Griffith only ever described—he never prescribed. His position was not that the arguments of Scarman, Hailsham and Dworkin were unconstitutional: only that they were

---

[20] *Ibid*. We return to the issue of open government below and also in ch 4.
[21] *Ibid*.
[22] *Ibid*, at 17.
[23] *Ibid*, at 18.

politically unwise and philosophically mistaken. This was made clear at the end of the lecture, where Griffith reflected on the nature of the constitution in the following terms:

> The constitution of the United Kingdom lives on, changing from day to day *for the constitution is no more and no less than what happens. Everything that happens is constitutional. And if nothing happened that would be constitutional also.*[24]

So, for Griffith, when the prime minister answers questions in the House of Commons he is not doing so because the constitution requires it, but merely because he finds it politically expedient. If the prime minister were to refuse to attend question time, that would not be unconstitutional. It would simply be different, and it would reflect the fact that the constitution had changed. On this view, government ministers are not constitutionally required to be accountable to Parliament. It just so happens that for the time being they are. If they were to refuse to allow the House of Commons to hold them to account that would not be unconstitutional: it would merely mean that the constitution had changed.

Thus, Griffith's defence of the political constitution was entirely descriptive. He may have believed that the political model of accountability was to be preferred over the legal. He may have considered it to be both more democratic and more effective. But he did not believe the political model of accountability to be constitutionally required; still less constitutionally entrenched. It was, for him, simply what for the time being happened. When, more than twenty years later, Griffith came to review the legal constitutionalism of Sir John Laws, his preference for the political constitution over the legal had diminished not one jot. But neither had his constitutional descriptivism: 'it is not . . . possible,' he wrote, 'to argue that there is something unconstitutional or unhistorical or logically perverse in asserting as does Sir John [Laws], that judges should further invade the province of executive decision-making by the extension of judicial review. What can be argued is whether particular invasions are politically unwise or undesirable.'[25]

Republicanism to the Rescue

The argument in this book takes issue with Griffith's descriptivism. My view, *contra* Griffith, is that the government is accountable to Parliament not only because, as matter of fact this is true, but also because the constitution insists

---

[24] *Ibid*, at 19, emphasis added.
[25] JAG Griffith, 'The Brave New World of Sir John Laws' (2000) 63 *Modern Law Review* 159, at 175. Laws' legal constitutionalism was considered in ch 1, above.

upon it. Ministerial responsibility is, I will argue, a prescriptive rule as well as a descriptive practice. Similarly, I will suggest, when judges intervene in the business of parliamentary government they are not simply rewriting the unwritten constitution—they are not simply altering what the constitution describes—they are doing something which is different from what the constitution previously prescribed. In other words they are doing something that would previously have been unconstitutional.

We have seen that, in the course of the last century or more of British public law scholarship, three main schools of thought have been developed. First there was the conservative normativism of Dicey and his followers. Then there was the functionalism of the great LSE scholars, Robson, Jennings and Griffith. And finally there was the legal constitutionalism of John Laws, Trevor Allan, Jeffrey Jowell and others.[26] It is to be noted that of these three schools of thought, only two are normative in character—the first and the third. The values on which the first school was founded were those of political conservatism: protection of private property, preference for the minimalist, laissez-faire state and a deep antipathy towards collectivism and trade unionism. And as we saw in the previous chapter tenets three and four of legal constitutionalism reveal the liberalism on which the third school is founded. The second school, the LSE functionalism, while developed by people who were largely progressive in their personal politics, was not founded on progressive values. It is functionalist, or descriptive, in nature, rather than normative.

The absence of a 'progressive normativist' school of British public law thought has had incredibly important consequences. The most obvious is that in moving away from the political model of constitutionalism, the legal constitutionalists have not had to show that the loss of the political model entails risking anything of value. As we have seen, the political model was never grounded in any particular set of values—it was presented merely as description. Accordingly, to move away from it could be presented as jeopardising nothing that is normatively valuable.

This book argues that a good deal of value *is* lost by moving away from the political model of constitutionalism. For Griffith, all that those of us who are not legal constitutionalists can do is politically to lament the foolishness of

---

[26] As a map of the terrain of British public law scholarship this trio of schools is not complete. In particular, it does not account for the tradition of radical and progressive civil liberties scholarship found in the work of Harry Street, DGT Williams, Keith Ewing, Conor Gearty, Helen Fenwick and others (see, eg, KD Ewing and C Gearty, *Freedom under Thatcher: Civil Liberties in Modern Britain* (Oxford, Oxford University Press, 1990)). Such scholarship is both progressive and normative. However, it cannot be said to amount to a 'progressive normativist' school of public law thought because it is concerned not with public law as a whole but only with a particular aspect of the law—and, at that, with an aspect of the law that is not uniquely 'public', civil liberties being a concern of private as well as of public lawyers.

turning to the new model, of relying on the courts rather than on politicians to find ways of holding government to account. I disagree. I think that there is more we can do. For sure, we can show that legal constitutionalism is unwise. We can show that it is undemocratic, that it is ineffective, and that it is politically undesirable. But we can also take the argument to a new level. We can also show that it is unconstitutional.

In order to do that, we need to ground the model of the political constitution normatively. We need to show that it is not a mere description of what happens (or perhaps of what used to happen) but that it is also a prescription of what ought to happen. Griffith, for all his passionate advocacy of the political constitution, never did this. For him, no matter how earnestly he considered the model to be wise, he never thought of it as being required, ordained or entrenched.

The legal constitutionalists have found it remarkably easy to brush the political constitution to one side. This is, no doubt, at least partly because it has become such a widespread view that Parliament and politics are ineffective as checks on the government of the day.[27] But it is also because the model of the political constitution was never grounded in theory. Its advocates never explained the norms or values on which the model was founded. To unearth and reveal those values is what this book seeks to achieve. The argument is that the values on which the political model of constitutionalism is based are the values of republicanism. And it is to this topic, republicanism, that we can now, at last, turn.

Republicanism in the Constitutional Law Literature

The first thing that has to be said about republicanism is that when constitutional lawyers write about it they usually make a complete hash of it. As a topic in the literature of constitutional law, republicanism makes only infrequent appearances. Even when it is discussed its consideration is generally poor. In Britain constitutional lawyers have barely written about republicanism at all. One of the few exceptions is a recent essay in the *Cambridge Law Journal* by Rodney Brazier[28] but this piece, like so much legal writing about

---

[27] The view may be widespread, but it is in my view nonetheless wrong: for a detailed defence of the practice of political accountability, see A Tomkins, *Public Law* (Oxford, Oxford University Press, 2003), ch 5.

[28] R Brazier, 'A British Republic' (2002) 61 *Cambridge Law Journal* 351. M Sunkin and S Payne (eds), *The Nature of the Crown: A Legal and Political Analysis* (Oxford, Clarendon Press, 1999) offers as good an analysis as exists in English legal scholarship of the legal problems associated with the concept of the Crown, but it includes no essay on republicanism. J Jacob, *The Republican Crown: Lawyers and the Making of the State in Twentieth-Century Britain* (Aldershot, Dartmouth, 1996)

republicanism, proceeds on the basis that there is nothing more to it than the rather narrow question of who should be the head of state. Now of course it is the case that one element of republicanism does concern the issue of whether the head of state is elected by its citizens or inherits office via an accident of birth. But as we shall see this is but one, rather small, aspect of republicanism. To reduce republicanism to this single issue, as Brazier's article does, is to miss the bulk of what republicanism has to offer and is to mistake what, as an overall approach to politics, republicanism is primarily about.[29]

The same is true of the vast bulk of legal commentary on republicanism in Australia. This is surprising, since Australia, unlike the United Kingdom, has in recent times engaged in serious reflection on its future status as a monarchy. A referendum was held in 1999 in which Australians were asked whether they wished to remain a monarchy or whether they preferred a particular (and, it has to be said, not terribly impressive) alternative. The alternative was rejected at the polls and so Australia remains, for the time being, a monarchy. It might have been thought that such a period of national self-reflection would have been accompanied by a healthy academic literature on the potential that a move to a republic may bring but, at least as far as legal commentary is concerned, this was not the case. As with Brazier's article, most of the Australian constitutional lawyers who wrote about the issue focused exclusively on the narrow question of the identity of the head of state. George Winterton (one of Australia's leading constitutional lawyers and himself a committed republican activist) suggested for example that 'the advent of a republic would not require the alteration of any part of the Australian constitutional system except the identity of the Head of State'.[30] Like Brazier's version of republicanism, this is a depressingly thin, diluted account of what the republican alternative has to offer.[31]

is a book whose title promises a republican much but which on closer examination turns out to be a work whose themes are more accurately captured by the subtitle than the title.

[29] P Craig, *Public Law and Democracy in the UK and the USA* (Oxford, Clarendon Press, 1990), ch 10 is a rare example of discussion by a public lawyer of republicanism that extends beyond consideration of the narrow head of state issue. Craig's chapter is a survey piece, which describes a variety of republican thinking, but he makes no attempt (either here or elsewhere in his work) to apply republicanism to his analysis of British public law.

[30] G Winterton, *Monarchy to Republic: Australian Republican Government* (Melbourne, Oxford University Press, rev ed, 1994), at 5. A similar narrowness of focus is displayed in G Williams, 'A Republican Tradition for Australia?' (1995) 23 *Federal Law Review* 133. For criticism of the Winterton/Williams position, see A Fraser, 'In Defence of Republicanism: A Reply to Williams' (1995) 23 *Federal Law Review* 362. As Fraser notes (at 365), 'fixated on the monarchy as such, on its literal embodiment in the Queen . . . the question of what the Crown stands for' has been ignored.

[31] A deeper notion of republicanism than that discussed by the constitutional lawyers has penetrated other areas of the Australian legal academy, notably in the work of John Braithwaite. See for example J Braithwaite and P Pettit, *Not Just Deserts: A Republican Theory of Criminal Justice* (Oxford, Clarendon Press, 1990) and J Braithwaite, 'On Speaking Softly and Carrying Big Sticks: Neglected Dimensions of a Republican Separation of Powers' (1997) 27 *University of Toronto Law Journal* 305.

The position is quite different—but not much better—if we turn to American constitutional lawyers. There was a significant rekindling of legal interest in republican constitutionalism in the US about fifteen years ago, when some of America's foremost constitutional lawyers wrote high-profile articles on the topic.[32] Two essays by Frank Michelman[33] and one by Cass Sunstein[34] were particularly widely discussed and two major symposia on republicanism were published, one in the *Yale Law Journal*[35] and the other in the *Florida Law Review*.[36] These various essays and articles were inspired by, and constituted a sort of delayed lawyers' reaction to, the emergence in the late 1960s and early 1970s of a new and vigorously republican re-interpretation in American history of the nature of the American revolution and founding.

For more than a century Americans had seen their political thought as being dominated by liberalism, their revolution as being a liberal revolution and their founding as being a liberal founding. The leading influence on the founding fathers, it was said, was John Locke, who dominated American thinking 'as no thinker anywhere dominates the political thought of a nation.'[37] Eighteenth-century Americans took to Locke 'because American society was already Lockean in its social marrow: individualistic, ambitious, proto-capitalist, in a word, "liberal"'.[38] This interpretation of the American revolution came under republican challenge with the publication of three books: Bernard Bailyn's *The Ideological Origins of the American Revolution*,[39] Gordon Wood's *The Creation of the American Republic, 1776–1787*[40] and JGA Pocock's *The Machiavellian Moment: Florentine Political Thought and the Atlantic Republican Tradition*.[41] Bailyn started the ball rolling by offering a 'brilliant, contra-Lockean reading of revolutionary rhetoric' before reverting

---

[32] For critical overviews, largely unsympathetic to the republican project, see R Fallon, 'What is Republicanism and is it Worth Reviving?' (1989) 102 *Harvard Law Review* 1695 and S Gey, 'The Unfortunate Revival of Civic Republicanism' (1993) 141 *University of Pennsylvania Law Review* 801.

[33] See F Michelman, 'Foreword: Traces of Self-Government' (1986) 100 *Harvard Law Review* 4 and 'Law's Republic' (1988) 97 *Yale Law Journal* 1493.

[34] See C Sunstein, 'Beyond the Republican Revival' (1988) 97 *Yale Law Journal* 1539.

[35] 'Symposium: The Civic Republican Tradition' (1988) 97 *Yale Law Journal* 1493. This symposium comprised the two essays by Michelman and Sunstein (above) along with several shorter commentaries.

[36] 'Symposium on Republicanism and Voting Rights' (1989) 41 *Florida Law Review* 409. The centre-piece of this symposium was another Michelman article: 'Conceptions of Democracy in American Constitutional Argument: Voting Rights' (1989) 41 *Florida Law Review* 443.

[37] D Rodgers, 'Republicanism: The Career of a Concept' (1992) 79 *Journal of American History* 11, at 13, citing L Hartz, *The Liberal Tradition in America: An Interpretation of American Political Thought since the Revolution* (New York, Harcourt Brace, 1955), at 140.

[38] D Rodgers, *ibid*.

[39] Cambridge, Harvard University Press, 1967.

[40] Chapel Hill, University of North Carolina Press, 1969. See now also his follow-up work, *The Radicalism of the American Revolution* (New York, Knopf, 1992).

[41] Princeton, Princeton University Press, 1975.

to a liberal frame from the moment of independence.[42] Following Bailyn, it was 'in Wood's *Creation* in 1969 that republicanism first emerged as a distinct organizing theme, to which, six years later, Pocock's *Machiavellian Moment* gave a global context and history.'[43]

Pocock's project was twofold. On the one hand he sought to describe the evolution and features of Florentine republicanism from 1490–1530, examining the work not only of Machiavelli but also of Guicciardini and others. On the other he sought to trace the uses that were made of Florence's republican heritage in the revolutionary climates of seventeenth-century England[44] and eighteenth-century America. Pocock demonstrated that, notwithstanding the ostensibly hostile English political climate, dominated as it was by concepts and practices of monarchy, republican and Machiavellian ideas had in a number of ways become domiciled in seventeenth-century England.[45] The remarkable success of the Anglicisation of such ideas could be shown, in Pocock's view, from the fact that when monarchical rule collapsed in the 1640s, the terminology was immediately available for the political thinkers of the day to make sense of England's newly kingless government.[46]

The Machiavellian Moment presented republicanism as a complex set of ideas and practices concerned with the common good, the combating of tyranny and political corruption, the institutional importance of mixed government and the central role that is to be played in the republican polity by the concept of civic virtue. Pocock's was a distinctly Aristotelian understanding of republicanism, where man is conceived of as an essentially 'political being whose realization of self occurs only through participation in public life, through active citizenship'.[47] The Lockean interpretation had seen America as being founded on the liberal values of individualism and the protection of private rights. The republican challenge of Bailyn, Wood and Pocock emphasised instead the centrality in the founders' thinking of promoting the public good, civic virtue and political participation. According to the republican interpretation of the American revolution, the founders' aim to protect and promote individual freedom was concerned not only with the safeguarding

---

[42] D Rodgers, above n 37, at 16.

[43] *Ibid.* Rodgers' essay is an extremely useful historiographical survey of American republicanism that updates and refines two earlier such pieces: R Shalhope, 'Toward a Republican Synthesis: The Emergence of an Understanding of Republicanism in American Historiography' (1972) 29 *William and Mary Quarterly* 49 and I Kramnick, 'Republican Revisionism Revisited' (1982) 87 *American Historical Review* 629.

[44] Scotland received the occasional mention but was not discussed in any detail.

[45] JGA Pocock, above n 41, ch 10.

[46] Many of the seventeenth-century sources Pocock relied on are considered in ch 3, below.

[47] See I Kramnick, above n 43, at 630.

of Lockean rights (life, liberty and property) but also with the realisation of a political freedom to participate in and to form one's own government.

Michelman and Sunstein set out to incorporate this republican interpretation of the American founding into an analysis of contemporary American constitutional law. However, both did so in peculiarly minimal and limited ways. In contrast to the historians, neither Michelman nor Sunstein presented republicanism as a challenge to liberalism, but rather as a variant of it. And in keeping with the vast bulk of American constitutional law scholarship, both Michelman and Sunstein focused uniquely on the role of the courts and, especially, of the US Supreme Court. Sunstein presented republicanism as a form of liberalism whose core values focused on deliberative politics, political equality, universalism, and participatory citizenship.[48] Applying such a republicanism to American constitutional practice would, in Sunstein's view, lead to only minimal reform, the over-turning of the controversial Supreme Court ruling on campaign finance in *Buckley v Valeo*[49] being about the sum of it. Michelman's account was similarly thin. His argument recognised that republicanism invests more heavily in practices of citizenship than is the case with most readings of liberalism, but he proceeded on the basis that the only institution with responsibility for deepening our sense of citizenship is the courts, as if citizenship can be realised through litigation alone. A more court-centric (and one-dimensional) account of republican constitutionalism would be difficult to find. When Michelman applied his vision of republicanism to American constitutional practice he, like Sunstein, could find only one case that ought to have been decided differently, Michelman's candidate being *Bowers v Hardwick*.[50]

What is welcome about Michelman's and Sunstein's accounts is their recognition that there is more to republicanism than simply worrying about one's head of state. Borrowing from work of historians such as Wood and Pocock, notions of civic virtue, self-government, the promotion of the public good, active citizenship, deliberation and participatory politics are all, rightly, acknowledged to be key themes in republican thinking. Quite why it is that British and Australian constitutional lawyers have not absorbed this lesson is something of a mystery. Despite the fact that Michelman and Sunstein moved beyond the head of state issue, however, and that they saw something of the broader republican perspective, their accounts remain frustratingly limited. Two principal criticisms can be made. The first is their

---

[48] C Sunstein, above n 34, esp at 1548–58.

[49] (1976) 424 US 1.

[50] (1986) 478 US 186 (upholding Georgia statute criminalising homosexual sodomy as applied to adult defendant's conduct in own home with adult consenting partner). See F Michelman, 'Law's Republic', above n 33.

insistent attempt to sew liberalism and republicanism together, as if the latter is nothing more than a sort of communitarian take on the former. Republicanism is not simply a variant of liberalism. For one thing it pre-dates liberalism by some hundreds of years and for another (as we shall see) there are matters on which republicans and liberals profoundly disagree.

The second major criticism is their focus on courts, which, as one commentator expressed it, hugely 'undervalues the republican norm of self-conscious popular engagement'.[51] Republicanism is concerned not with government-through-judiciary but with *self*-government through processes of informed, public-spirited deliberation. To substitute the one for the other is to move republican thought away from questions of popular participation and to 're-direct our attention to the activities of a narrower citizenry: members of the judiciary'.[52] Another American lawyer, commenting on Sunstein and Michelman, forcefully argued that republican constitutionalism can be successful only if constitutional commentators first 'abandon [their] obsession with courts'.[53] But it is not just the academic obsession with courts that needs to be displaced: it is the power of the judiciary itself. There is a great tension between the ideals of republicanism and that most cherished of American constitutional practices, judicial review.

Yet for all the discussion of the centrality of civic virtue and popular participation in government, this is barely recognised anywhere in the American legal literature on republicanism. A rare exception is provided by Elizabeth Mensch and Alan Freeman who, in a penetrating critique of Michelman's arguments, acknowledged that American federal structure, especially since *Marbury v Madison*, 'with its crucial incorporation of the liberal individual rights model, signifies a wholesale rejection of an authentic republican tradition.'[54] Morton Horwitz made a similar point when he suggested that 'the dissenting opinion of Chief Justice Gibson of Pennsylvania in *Eakin v Raub* opposing judicial review . . . can be viewed not as some aberrational democratic protest but as part of a more deeply rooted republican conception of government.'[55] But even this comment is offered as an aside and is not further developed. It is Mark Tushnet who has done most in recent years to

---

[51] K Abrams, 'Law's Republicanism' (1988) 97 *Yale Law Journal* 1591, at 1592.

[52] *Ibid*, at 1603.

[53] P Brest, 'Further Beyond the Republican Revival: Toward Radical Republicanism' (1988) 97 *Yale Law Journal* 1623.

[54] E Mensch and A Freeman, 'A Republican Agenda for Hobbesian America' (1989) 41 *Florida Law Review* 581, at 600.

[55] See M Horwitz, 'Republicanism and Liberalism in American Constitutional Thought' (1987) 29 *William and Mary Law Review* 57, at 68. *Eakin v Raub* is reported at 12 Serg & Rawle 330 (Pa, 1825).

argue that the US constitution needs to be 'taken away from the courts'[56] but, while Tushnet flirted with republicanism in some of his earlier work,[57] he no longer presents his arguments in overt republican garb. Given the way republicanism was treated by the likes of Sunstein and Michelman, perhaps it is little wonder.

II REPUBLICANISM IN PHILOSOPHY AND HISTORY

For all the promise of the American republican tradition, then, the American legal academy is not the place to turn to for instruction in republican constitutionalism. Guidance will have to come from elsewhere—not from within the law, but from other disciplines, from philosophy and from history. While, to date, lawyers have generally failed to appreciate the richness of what republicanism may offer, this is less true of scholars working in our neighbouring disciplines. Indeed, in political and constitutional history, in philosophy, and in the history of political thought, there has in recent years been a remarkable increase in the attention devoted to questions of republicanism. And it is to these disciplines that we must turn in order to discover something of what it is that republicanism may offer us as lawyers. We will start with philosophy, and in particular with the work of Philip Pettit. We will then move to history and to the history of political thought, where our main focus will be on the work of Quentin Skinner.

Republican Political Philosophy

The leading modern work in republican political theory is Philip Pettit's *Republicanism: A Theory of Freedom and Government*, a widely read and influential work of analytical political philosophy, first published in 1997.[58] Like Pocock and others, Pettit recognises that republicans have distinctive things to say about the mixed constitution, checks and balances, the separation of powers and civic virtue, but his principal claim is that running throughout the vocab-

---

[56] See M Tushnet, *Taking the Constitution away from the Courts* (Princeton, Princeton University Press, 1999).

[57] See, eg, M Tushnet, *Red, White, and Blue: A Critical Analysis of Constitutional Law* (Cambridge, Harvard University Press, 1988).

[58] P Pettit, *Republicanism: A Theory of Freedom and Government* (Oxford, Clarendon Press, 1997). A considerable critical literature exists on Pettit's *Republicanism*. Among the more valuable works are H Richardson, *Democratic Autonomy: Public Reasoning about the Ends of Policy* (Oxford, Oxford University Press, 2002) and D Weinstock and C Nadeau (eds), *Republicanism: History, Theory and Practice* (London, Frank Cass, 2004).

ulary of republicanism is a distinctive idea of freedom, which he calls 'freedom as non-domination'. His book comprises a detailed working out of the contemporary meaning of freedom as non-domination, along with an account of the institutional structures that would be required for the idea to be realised in democratic practice. The republican conception of freedom as non-domination, in Pettit's analysis, finds its origins in ancient Rome, especially in the writings of Cicero,[59] with its early modern development coming first in Machiavelli's *Discourses*[60] and subsequently in the thinking (as well as the actions) of seventeenth-century English parliamentarians.

Its essence is that we are not free if we are subject to another who dominates us. That is, we are not free if there is another who possesses the capacity arbitrarily to interfere with our interests or to restrain us.[61] Under the republican conception of freedom we are not free even if such a capacity to interfere is not actually exercised—that is, even if we are not actually restrained. It is the domination that renders us unfree, not the restraint. On Pettit's analysis, restraint does not of itself necessarily render us unfree:

> on the contrary, the restraint of a fair system of law—a non-arbitrary regime—does not make [us] unfree. Being unfree consists rather in being subject to arbitrary sway: being subject to the potentially capricious will ... of another.[62]

Pettit rather unsurprisingly offers the relationship between master and slave as the exemplification of domination.[63] While a liberal might hold that the slave retains at least a degree of freedom as long as her master does not actually interfere with her interests,[64] for a republican, by contrast, the very fact of the slave's bondage makes her unfree, even if her master happens to be the most benign and benevolent of men. For a republican, it is the slave's *status qua* slave that renders her unfree. Wherever the 'dominating party can practise interference ... at will and with impunity', wherever 'they do not have to seek anyone's leave and ... do not have to incur any scrutiny or penalty' there is domination and those subject to it are unfree.[65]

---

[59] See esp Cicero, *De Republica* (c 52BC) and *De Officiis* (44BC). For modern editions in English, see *The Republic and The Laws* (ed and trans N Rudd, Oxford, Oxford University Press, 1998) and *On Obligations* (ed and trans PG Walsh, Oxford, Oxford University Press, 2000).

[60] Machiavelli, *The Discourses* [c 1517] (ed B Crick and trans LJ Walker, London, Penguin, 1998).

[61] These various terms are defined in detail by Pettit, above n 58, esp ch 2.

[62] *Ibid*, at 5.

[63] P Pettit, above n 58, at 22.

[64] Liberal conceptions of freedom are discussed further below.

[65] P Pettit, above n 58, at 22. See also to similar effect the excellent discussion of slavery in Q Skinner, *Liberty before Liberalism* (Cambridge, Cambridge University Press, 1998), at 36–57 and 69–72. Skinner's work is considered in detail below.

While the master/slave relationship is the most obvious instance of domination, it is far from the only one. A different sort of example is that of the present British monarch, Elizabeth II, over her subjects. The queen is a woman of remarkable legal power, even today. As a matter of law, she may appoint whomsoever she wishes to be prime minister. Indeed, if she wished, she could appoint no-one to the office. She may legally dismiss the government at any time for any reason or for none, and she has the legal power to refuse her assent to any Bill passed by the Houses of Parliament. Now, we know that there are all sorts of unwritten conventions that suggest that the queen will not actually exercise these powers, or at least that she will not do so absent extraordinary circumstances, but none of these conventions is legally enforceable and many of them are alarmingly unclear.[66] The monarch is an excellent example of someone who has the potential to exercise considerable power 'with impunity', and whose actions 'do not have to incur any scrutiny or penalty'. In this sense, for as long as Britons remain subjects of the Crown we remain unfree.[67] We will not be free until we emancipate ourselves from its domination. Even if the monarch's powers are not actually exercised,[68] for as long as there remains the potential that they may be exercised, we are not free.[69]

The republican conception of freedom as non-domination may usefully be contrasted with modern liberal understandings of freedom. Liberal freedom was famously analysed by Isaiah Berlin, who argued that there were 'two concepts of liberty': a negative concept of liberty that is encapsulated in the right to be left alone and a positive concept of liberty that is encapsulated in the notion of self-mastery.[70] The negative concept of liberty, which Pettit calls freedom from interference, has been the western world's dominant idea of freedom since at least the time of John Stuart Mill, indeed arguably since the time of Bentham.[71]

Notwithstanding its popularity, however, 'building a useful interpretation of freedom on the basis of an overly simple notion of non-interference' is

---

[66] For a detailed discussion, see A Tomkins, *Public Law* (Oxford, Oxford University Press, 2003), at 62–72.

[67] This may strike some as exaggerated, even inflammatory, language, but it is not intended to be. As we shall see, the view expressed here was commonplace in seventeenth-century English politics.

[68] And it is a myth that they are not: see A Tomkins, above n 66.

[69] This argument is developed further in ch 4, which considers also the exercise of Crown prerogative powers by government ministers.

[70] Berlin's writings on liberty, including his essay on the 'Two Concepts of Liberty' [1958] are conveniently collected in I Berlin, *Liberty* (ed H Hardy, Oxford, Oxford University Press, 2002).

[71] See P Pettit, above n 58, at 41–50. We encountered this notion of freedom in our exploration of legal constitutionalism (see esp tenet 3), above, ch 1.

extremely difficult.[72] This is because in some instances we *want*, indeed we *need*, government to restrain us by placing us under duties that we would not otherwise have. For example, as Richardson has argued:

> We need government (1) to co-ordinate our actions (on the roadways or the internet); (2) to resolve certain collective-action problems (in controlling arms races or environmental degradation), and (3) to enable us to achieve certain ends together that we cannot feasibly achieve through private action (exploring outer space or catching and punishing violent criminals).[73]

In all of these arenas states and governments (and, indeed, also international organisations) place us under various forms of restraint, they interfere with or limit our room for personal manoeuvre. Yet in none of these instances would we want to say that such restraint necessarily inhibits our freedom. The point of our freedom is not that it should never be interfered with but that, when it is (necessarily, inevitably) interfered with, the interference comes from a source whose authority over us is legitimate rather than illegitimate. Legitimate authority, for a republican, is authority without domination. This means authority that is neither arbitrary nor capricious, but which is reasoned and is contestable at the instigation of those who are subject to it. We shall return to these requirements shortly.

Berlin's taxonomy of positive and negative liberty echoed the distinction between ancient and modern ideas of freedom drawn in 1819 by Benjamin Constant.[74] Constant depicted ancient freedom as being concerned with the Aristotelian 'liberty of belonging to a democratically self-governing community,'[75] a notion that 'hails the democratic participation of the people as one of the highest forms of good and that often waxes lyrical, in communitarian vein, about the desirability of the close, homogeneous society that popular participation is often taken to presuppose.'[76] Pettit, as we have already noticed, locates the origins of republican freedom in the ancient world. But its source for him lies in the ancient world of the Roman republic and not in that of the Greek *polis*. Throughout his work Pettit is at great pains to stress that, despite its ancient origins, the idea of freedom as non-domination is not a positive, Aristotelian notion of liberty.

In this respect there is a critical difference between Pettit's understanding of republicanism and Pocock's account, which we encountered in the previous

---

[72] See H Richardson, above n 58, at 24.

[73] *Ibid*, at 26.

[74] See B Constant, *Political Writings* (ed and trans B Fontana, Cambridge, Cambridge University Press, 1988). On the parallels between Constant and Berlin, see P Pettit, above n 58, at 18.

[75] P Pettit, *ibid*.

[76] *Ibid*, at 8.

section of this chapter. For Pocock (and for those American lawyers such as Michelman and Sunstein who borrowed from him), republican freedom *is* a form of positive liberty: it is the right of citizens actively to share in the experience of self-government. Taken directly from Aristotle, their view is that 'man is by nature a political animal' and that, as such, if politics are denied him he is stripped of an element of his humanness.[77] Pettit does not exclude rights of participation or notions of self-government from his account, but in contrast with the Aristotelian view he insists that these are instrumental to the realisation of freedom as non-domination rather than intrinsic to it. They may help to facilitate republican freedom, but they do not of themselves constitute it.[78] It is important to understand this as many critics of republicanism, especially liberal critics, have assumed that there is nothing more to republican freedom than the right to popular participation. One of Pettit's most valuable contributions is to have shown that this is not the case.

For Pettit then, republican freedom, much like liberal freedom, is negative. The difference between the two is that whereas liberals cherish freedom from interference, republicans desire freedom from domination. For a liberal we are free even if there is a power that may interfere with us, as long as that power does not in fact so interfere. For a republican, as we have seen, we are not free if there is a power that dominates us even where that power does not for the time being interfere. Republican freedom as non-domination is however a more exacting standard than liberal freedom as non-interference. In this sense, while it is not, in Berlin's terms, positive, neither is it straightforwardly negative. Non-domination requires not only an absence of arbitrary interference, but also some form of positive 'security' against arbitrary interference.[79] This is where, for Pettit, popular participation comes in: it is one of a number of means by which non-domination may be secured.

---

[77] See Aristotle, *Politics* [c 330 BC], at I.2 and III.7, (ed and trans CDC Reeve, Indianapolis, Hackett, 1998), at 4 and 76.

[78] P Pettit, above n 58, at 8. When we come to consider the arguments of Quentin Skinner we shall see that he makes the same distinction. Republican freedom, in his view, cannot be equated with the right of political participation; it does not consist solely in membership of a self-governing state (see Q Skinner, above n 65, at 74). For an excellent discussion of the difference between the Aristotelian conception of liberty as membership of and participation in a political community and the Roman conception that is of interest to Pettit and Skinner, see N Buttle, 'Republican Constitutionalism: A Roman Ideal' (2001) 9 *Journal of Political Philosophy* 331. It should be noted that some modern scholars of republicanism (*contra* Pettit and Skinner) have continued to associate republican freedom with the Aristotelian notion of membership of a political community: this is true not only of Pocock's account but is also a feature of Hannah Arendt's and Paul Rahe's work. See, eg, H Arendt, *The Human Condition* (Chicago, University of Chicago Press, 1958) and P Rahe, *Republics Ancient and Modern* (Chapel Hill, University of North Carolina Press, 1992).

[79] See P Pettit, *ibid*, at 51.

Pettit is concerned not only to identify the idea of freedom as non-domination but also to explore something of the constitutional and institutional design that is required in order to secure its effective implementation.[80] How can the constitutional arrangements of a large, modern nation-state such as Britain facilitate non-domination so as to provide for legitimate authority? We have seen how an enemy of non-domination is arbitrariness (indeed, Pettit defines domination as the capacity arbitrarily to interfere). For Pettit, then, republicanism requires that those with the capacity to interfere (let us say, for convenience, the government)[81] are required to track the interests of those liable to suffer the interference (let us say, for convenience, the people). On Pettit's analysis, 'the only way for a republican regime to guarantee' that government does not exercise its power in a way that is hostile to the interests of the people at large, or of some section of the community,

> is to introduce systematic possibilities for ordinary people to contest the doings of government. This points us towards the ideal of a democracy based, not on the alleged consent of the people, but rather on the contestability by the people of everything that government does . . .[82]

It is here that we can begin to see the closeness of the connection between republicanism and the political model of constitutional accountability. For what is the contestability that Pettit alludes to in this passage other than an ideal form of responsible government? In the British system, we (Pettit's 'ordinary people') contest government policies and decisions by insisting that the government of the day is fully and openly accountable to our elected representatives in Parliament. As contestability may be grounded in a republican theory of freedom so too, in turn, may political accountability be grounded in a normative account of constitutionalism. In this way, responsible government ceases to be merely a descriptive practice and becomes instead an essential component in a constitutional structure designed to secure our non-domination. This is exactly the value of thinking about British constitutionalism from a republican point of view. It is through republican political philosophy that we can obtain a normative foundation for our practices of responsible government and political accountability (and, as we shall see

---

[80] See esp P Pettit, *ibid*, ch 6.

[81] Taking the government as our example is not meant to imply that republican theory applies only to the ability of the state to dominate. Multi-national corporations, international organisations such as the WTO, as well as many other agencies may, in addition to governments, possess powers of domination that would, on a republican analysis, render those subject to it unfree. For a penetrating application of republican separation of powers theory to the private sector, see J Braithwaite, 'On Speaking Softly and Carrying Big Sticks: Neglected Dimensions of a Republican Separation of Powers' (1997) 47 *University of Toronto Law Journal* 305.

[82] P Pettit, above n 58, at 277.

when we come to examine our history, this is a normative foundation that already inheres within the British constitutional order).

In its ideal form of full and open accountability, such a contestatory democracy as Pettit outlines would be both *deliberative* (requiring that decisions are based on reasoned considerations of allegedly common concern—that is, that they serve a public good) and *inclusive* (requiring that government is representative of different sections of the population, that channels of contestation are well established in the community and that government is adequately guarded against the influence of big business and other powerful interest groups).[83] This is a vision of political accountability that may be realised only with genuinely open government and radical freedom of information.

The ideal portrayed here may be some distance from our contemporary experience of accountable government. But what emerges from Pettit's account is a standard to which we can aspire and, just as importantly, against which we may judge current practices so that, when they fall short, we may say not only (as Griffith would) that something undesirable or unwise has happened, but that something unconstitutional has happened. As will be argued more fully in chapter four, the republican ideal of the British constitution would hold that whenever the government is less than fully and openly responsible to Parliament, whenever the practice of accountability is less than deliberative and inclusive, the government is acting unconstitutionally and it is the constitutional right, indeed duty, of Parliament to say so and to put it right.

Republicanism in the History of Political Thought

Pettit's scholarship is, in various ways, complemented by that of Quentin Skinner.[84] Skinner is, rather ironically perhaps, the current 'Regius' professor of history at Cambridge. Like Pocock, he is a formidable political historian and historian of ideas. In his most recent work, Skinner can be seen as attempting a sort of historicisation of the idea of freedom as non-domination. Skinner prefers to call this idea not republican freedom, but 'neo-Roman' freedom, but for my purposes the distinction between the two labels makes no material difference, and I shall use the two more or less inter-

---

[83]   P Pettit, above n 58, at 277 and, in more detail, at 183–205.

[84]   Pettit's and Skinner's positions are not absolutely identical to one another, but the differences between them are minor and make no material difference to the argument presented here. For an overview, see P Pettit, 'Keeping Republican Freedom Simple: On a Difference with Quentin Skinner' (2002) 30 *Political Theory* 339.

changeably.[85] The focus of Skinner's work has been to explore the meaning of republican freedom in seventeenth-century England. He tackled this theme in his inaugural lecture, *Liberty before Liberalism*, delivered in Cambridge in 1997[86] and has returned to and developed it in several essays since.[87]

Skinner's argument is that in the first decades of the seventeenth century a sense emerged in English politics that an individual citizen could not be free unless the state of which he was a citizen was itself free.[88] Freedom for a state, on this view, meant much the same as freedom for an individual:

> Just as individual human bodies are free . . . if and only if they are able to act or forbear from acting at will, so the bodies of nations and states are likewise free if and only if they are similarly unconstrained from using their powers according to their own wills in pursuit of their desired ends. Free states, like free persons, are thus defined by their capacity for self-government. A free state is a community in which the actions of the body politic are determined by the will of the members as a whole.[89]

Such freedom requires that a state's laws be enacted with the consent of its citizens, who must be able to exercise equal rights of participation in the law-making process.[90] Given, however, that even in the early modern state there were too many citizens for them all to assemble together, what is required is a representative body—a Parliament—'chosen by the people to legislate on their behalf'.[91]

On the structure of the representative assembly the seventeenth-century proponents of this view of freedom disagreed. Some, such as Marchamont Nedham[92] and John Milton,[93] thought that the House of Commons alone

---

[85] Skinner prefers the term neo-Roman because not all of those who, in the seventeenth century, advocated freedom as non-domination were opposed to monarchy outright. The term republican can, however, be used to describe not only those who are wholly opposed to monarchy but also to those who seek to subject a limited monarchy to constitutional checks. Algernon Sidney's *Discourses concerning Government* [1683] (ed T West, Indianapolis, Liberty Fund, 1996), for example, has long been seen as an essentially republican work notwithstanding the accommodation within Sidney's scheme of a limited monarchy. See further on Sidney, below n 95.

[86] See above, n 65.

[87] See esp his essays 'John Milton and the Politics of Slavery' and 'Classical Liberty, Renaissance Translation and the English Civil War', both in Q Skinner, *Visions of Politics, Volume II: Renaissance Virtues* (Cambridge, Cambridge University Press, 2002), chs 11–12.

[88] See Q Skinner, *Liberty before Liberalism*, above n 65, at 23. Even the most radical seventeenth-century conceptions of the citizenry were always limited to men, of course.

[89] *Ibid*, at 25–26.

[90] *Ibid*, at 27–30.

[91] *Ibid*, at 32.

[92] Editorialist of the newspaper of Cromwell's Commonwealth, *Mercurius Politicus* and author of *The Excellency of a Free State* [1656], the most accessible text of which is at <www.constitution.org/cmt/nedham/free-state.htm>.

[93] Author of numerous republican tracts, including *Tenure of Kings and Magistrates* [1648] and *Ready and Easy Way to Establish a Free Commonwealth* [1660], among others. For a modern edition, see J Milton, *Areopagitica and other Political Writings* (ed J Alvis, Indianapolis, Liberty Fund, 1999).

was sufficiently representative. Others vehemently disagreed, most notably perhaps James Harrington, whose *Commonwealth of Oceana*, published in 1656, is one the century's most important and influential republican works. Harrington's view of Parliament is famous, employing the celebrated analogy of two girls and a cake that is given to them to share: ' "Divide," says one unto the other, "and I will choose; or let me divide, and you shall choose." '[94] So too for parliaments: they should be bicameral, with one house for deliberating the laws and the other for enacting them. In the later seventeenth and throughout the eighteenth century it was Harrington's view that was to prevail over that of Nedham and Milton in republican thinking,[95] the ideal of a mixed and balanced constitution becoming one of the very cornerstones of republicanism, a point to which we shall return shortly.

For these thinkers there were two ways in which a free state could be rendered unfree. First, and relatively uncontentiously, they took it for granted that 'a body politic, like a natural body, will be rendered unfree if it is forcibly or coercively deprived of its ability to act at will in pursuit of its chosen ends.'[96] Indeed, such use of force against a free people was viewed as 'nothing less than the defining mark of tyranny'.[97] But secondly and more innovatively, these writers were

> no less insistent . . . that a state or nation will be deprived of its liberty if it is merely subject or liable to having its actions determined by the will of anyone other than the representatives of the body politic as a whole.[98]

Even if a state was not as a matter of fact governed tyrannically, and even if its rulers chose to follow the dictates of the law, a nation was nevertheless 'counted as living in slavery if its capacity for action [was] in any way dependent on the will of anyone other than the body of its own citizens.'[99] Such dependency could occur in either of two ways: as a result of colonisation or conquest or, more importantly for present purposes, when the 'internal constitution of a state allow[ed] for the exercise of any discretionary or prerogative powers on the part of those governing it.'[100]

---

[94] J Harrington, *The Commonwealth of Oceana* [1656] (ed J G A Pocock, Cambridge, Cambridge University Press, 1992), at 22.

[95] See, eg, Henry Neville's *Plato Redivivus* [1680] and Algernon Sidney's *Discourses concerning Government* [1683]. For modern editions, see respectively, C Robbins (ed), *Two English Republican Tracts* (Cambridge, Cambridge University Press, 1969) and A Sidney, *Discourses Concerning Government* (ed T West, Indianapolis, Liberty Fund, 1996).

[96] Q Skinner, *Liberty before Liberalism*, above n 65, at 47.

[97] *Ibid.*

[98] *Ibid*, at 49.

[99] *Ibid.*

[100] *Ibid*, at 50–51.

In the view of the writers Skinner is concerned with, you will be rendered unfree not only if the state actually coerces you but also if you 'merely fall into a condition of political subjection or dependence, thereby leaving yourself open to the danger' of being coerced.[101] Skinner continues:

> That is to say that, if you live under any form of government that allows for the exercise of prerogative or discretionary powers outside the law, you will already be living as a slave. Your rulers may choose not to exercise these powers, or may exercise them only with the tenderest regard for your individual liberties . . . The very fact, however, that your rulers possess such arbitrary powers means that the continued enjoyment of your civil liberty remains at all times dependent on their goodwill.[102]

And this, in the neo-Roman or republican view, is equivalent to living in a state of slavery. It follows that, if you wish to maintain your liberty, you must live 'under a system in which the sole power of making laws' rests with 'the people or their accredited representatives'.[103] You must live, in other words, in a system of self-government.

This account of freedom, according to Skinner, is not to be found in English politics prior to the early seventeenth century. Skinner argues that it emerged as a result of the influence of the great Roman orator Cicero and of the Roman historians, Livy, Tacitus and Sallust, each of whose work was translated into English during this period (hence Skinner's preferred label of 'neo-Romanism').[104] In the seventeenth century the neo-Roman account of freedom was concerned not only with the freedom of the individual and of the nation, but also with the extent to which the discretionary powers of the monarch undermined the freedom of Parliament. If the king could summon and dissolve Parliament at will, and if the king could grant or withhold his assent to Parliament's legislation at will, then Parliament was not free. And if Parliament was not free then neither was the nation, for Parliament was the representative of the people.

Skinner's argument is relatively uncontroversial insofar as it identifies a canon of republican thinking in seventeenth-century English political life. It has long been accepted, by proponents and critics of republicanism alike, that the most significant seventeenth-century contributions to the development of European republicanism were made in England.[105] However, the

---

[101] *Ibid*, at 69.

[102] *Ibid*, at 70.

[103] *Ibid*, at 74.

[104] See Q Skinner, 'Classical Liberty, Renaissance Translation and the English Civil War', above n 87, esp at 312–18.

[105] See, eg, B Worden, 'English Republicanism', in JH Burns and M Goldie (eds), *The Cambridge History of Political Thought, 1450–1700* (Cambridge, Cambridge University Press, 1991), at 443. So too is it generally accepted that England's most significant contributions to the development of republicanism were made in the seventeenth century.

orthodox view has been that republicanism emerged in English politics only after the execution of King Charles I in 1649 and not before it. Historians have long stressed that republican language began to be used only in the weeks and months following the king's execution in a retrospective attempt to justify it and that in no sense was the regicide caused by any earlier rise of republican sentiment. In his influential survey of English republicanism, for example, the historian Blair Worden argued that there were three periods in the seventeenth century in which republicanism figured in English politics. The first of these started in 1649 and continued until the restoration of Charles II in 1660, the second was 'a response to the political crisis of 1675–83' and the third was 'produced by the fresh constitutional anxieties of the 1690s'.[106] The first period produced the republican tracts of Nedham and Milton, as well as Harrington's *Oceana*; the second was the age of Henry Neville and Algernon Sidney; and the third saw further contributions from writers such as Robert Molesworth, Walter Moyle, John Trenchard, Thomas Gordon, John Toland and others.[107]

The radicalism of Skinner's argument lies less in his use of the relatively familiar figures who were writing in the 1650s and 1680s and more in two factors which combine to move his portrayal of neo-Roman republicanism significantly away from the orthodoxy. The first factor is his insistence that neo-Romanism featured prominently in English politics before the Civil War as well as after it; the second is his linking of republican writing and thinking with the political events of the time. Skinner sees elements of neo-Romanism in parliamentary debates as early as 1610 and 1628 and argues that it comes of age in the critical years 1640–42—well before the regicide of 1649. While he stops short of asserting that neo-Roman republicanism caused either the Civil War or the regicide, he does maintain that 'from the parliamentary perspective, the Civil War began as a war of national liberation from servitude'.[108] We will consider these historical arguments in the next chapter, which examines in detail the ways in which republican thinking has influenced and penetrated British constitutional practice. Before we move on to these issues, however, we need first to draw some threads together.

---

[106] B Worden, *ibid*, at 444. To similar effect, see also J Scott, *England's Troubles: Seventeenth-Century English Political Instability in European Context* (Cambridge, Cambridge University Press, 2000), esp chs 13–14.

[107] The best overview of the work of these writers is C Robbins, *The Eighteenth-Century Commonwealthman* (Cambridge, Harvard University Press, 1959).

[108] Q Skinner, 'Classical Liberty, Renaissance Translation and the English Civil War', above n 87, at 343.

III THE THREE THEMES OF REPUBLICANISM

Through our examination of the philosophical and historical work of such authors as Pocock, Pettit and Skinner we have encountered what might appear to be a pretty bewildering array of sources, sources that range not only across a number of disciplines but come also from a variety of periods. We have seen that republicanism is an approach to government that has ancient, indeed classical, roots, some looking to Aristotle and the Greek *polis*, others looking to the Roman republic of Cicero, Livy, Tacitus and Sallust. We have seen that it was first developed in the modern era by Machiavelli, whose *Discourses* exerted enormous influence in seventeenth-century England.[109] And we have seen that an entire canon of republican writing emerged out of the constitutional turmoil into which England fell in the period between the early 1640s and the late 1680s; and that this body of writing was widely read by and hugely influential upon the founding fathers of the American republic a century later, albeit that by the 1780s and 90s the liberal influence of Locke acted as a filter through which the pre-Enlightenment republicanism of the sixteenth and seventeenth centuries was reworked.

What are we to make of such a range of sources? Distilling from this mass of historical and philosophical material a coherent account of what republicanism consists in is not straightforward. As John Adams warned two centuries ago, republicanism is an approach to constitutional government that derives from such a rich variety of sources that its meaning can become unintelligible.[110] But notwithstanding the difficulties involved, we can plausibly identify three major themes that run through the republican literature we have surveyed. These are anti-monarchism and popular sovereignty; freedom as non-domination and its consequences; and the institutional design of accountability. By understanding republicanism as the combination of these themes its meaning will, I hope, become not only intelligible but clearly and plainly so. Each of our three themes will now be examined in turn.

Anti-monarchism and Popular Sovereignty

The first theme is anti-monarchism and popular sovereignty. This is perhaps the most obvious thing to say about republicanism, that it is anti-monarchic. Power has to start somewhere. For monarchists it starts at the top, with the

---

[109] See generally F Raab, *The English Face of Machiavelli: A Changing Interpretation, 1500–1700* (London, Routledge, 1964).

[110] See above n 1.

monarch. In an absolute monarchy it stays there; in what has become known as a constitutional (or limited) monarchy, it is allowed to filter down through the political system. This is what happened in England. Power started with the Crown and over the course of the last eight centuries it has been allowed to filter down, first through courtiers and subsequently through ministers.[111] For republicans, power starts not at the top but at the bottom, with the people. Power starts with the people, who delegate it upwards, to the institutions of government. This is the basis on which, for example, the US Constitution rests: 'we the people' (of the preamble) delegate power to the States, which in turn delegate power to the federal government of the United States. And the powers not delegated to the United States are, under its Constitution, expressly reserved to the States respectively, or to the people.[112] This is the very essence of the republican ideal. Indeed it explains the very word. The polity belongs to the people—it is a public thing, or in Latin, a *res publica*.

This may sound somewhat basic, even abstract, but it has a sharp practical consequence. Not all power is accounted for on the face of the constitution. Some, inevitably, gets overlooked or forgotten. So what do we do with it when it comes to our attention? The answer in the American constitutional order ought to be clear: power not delegated to the institutions of government is expressly stated to remain with the several States or with the people.[113] The answer in a monarchic constitutional order is quite different. In a monarchy, power not expressly dealt with by the law of the constitution will remain with the Crown.

Thus, when in the late 1980s the Thatcher government arrogated to itself the previously unheard-of power to issue police forces with plastic bullets and CS gas and to do so in certain circumstances notwithstanding the objections of the local police authority, the courts held that the government had not acted unlawfully.[114] It was not clear that Parliament had ever legislated to confer such a power on the government: on this issue the courts were divided, the Divisional Court holding that it had not, the Court of Appeal that it had. In some constitutional orders government decisions taken in want of clear legal authority would be struck down as being in violation of the rule of

---

[111] See A Tomkins, *Public Law* (Oxford, Oxford University Press, 2003), ch 2, esp at 39–44.

[112] See US Constitution, Tenth Amendment.

[113] This is not to say, however, that the US Supreme Court has as a matter of practice always interpreted the Constitution in this light. On the contrary, case law since *McCulloch v Maryland* 17 US (4 Wheat) 316 (1819) has demonstrated the Court's apparent readiness to read the Tenth Amendment (and similar provisions such as the 'necessary and proper' clause in Art 1 §8) all too flexibly.

[114] See *R v Secretary of State for the Home Department, ex parte Northumbria Police Authority* [1989] QB 26.

law, but not in the monarchy of Britain. The fact that there was an absence of specific statutory authority justifying the government's actions was held by both the Divisional Court and the Court of Appeal not to matter, as there was an historic Crown prerogative of keeping the peace on which the government could rely. The Court of Appeal conceded that precedent suggested this prerogative to be available only in the context of keeping the peace in the face of external attack rather than internal disorder, but held that, again, this was immaterial. The court allowed the government to turn to the authority of Crown prerogative as a sort of hidden reservoir from which it could draw, at its convenience, in the event of it running out of statutory authority.

A similar case occurred in Australia in 2001.[115] In August 2001 a Norwegian ship, the *MV Tampa*, rescued 433 mainly Afghan people from a sinking Indonesian boat. The 'rescuees', as they became known, had fled from the Taliban regime in Afghanistan and had been heading for Australia. The captain of the *Tampa* initially attempted to return the rescuees to Indonesia, but this proved impossible, so he set course for Christmas Island. The Australian authorities refused him permission to land at Christmas Island and he stopped, still in international waters, twelve nautical miles from shore. After drifting there in the tropical heat for three days, the captain decided that the medical condition of a number of the rescuees was so grave that he had no choice but to defy the Australian order not to enter its waters. When the *Tampa* was two nautical miles from Christmas Island, it was boarded by 45 Australian SAS troops in order to secure the vessel and to provide a modicum of food and medical assistance. Meanwhile, the government sought to make arrangements to have the rescuees transferred to such other jurisdictions as would accept them. New Zealand agreed to take a proportion of them, and the remainder were taken to the bankrupt island of Nauru in the South Pacific. Accordingly, the rescuees were transferred to an Australian troopship and were taken to Nauru, where they arrived two weeks later.[116]

When the *Tampa* was within Australian territorial waters, a Melbourne solicitor, Eric Vadarlis, and the Victorian Council for Civil Liberties (VCCL) brought legal proceedings in the Federal Court challenging the legality of the Australian government's actions. Argument focused on two main issues: first, whether the boarding of the *Tampa* by the SAS amounted to a 'detention' within the meaning of habeas corpus law, and secondly whether the government possessed the executive authority to expel the rescuees from Australian territorial waters. It is the second of these that concerns us here. Australia possesses a modern and comprehensive statutory

---

[115] *Ruddock v Vadarlis* (The MV Tampa Case) (2001) 183 ALR 1.
[116] The full story is told in D Marr and M Wilkinson, *Dark Victory* (Sydney, Allen and Unwin, 2003), chs 1–12.

code of immigration law—its Migration Act 1958 (Cth). The government conceded that no provision of the Migration Act conferred on it the authority to expel persons such as the rescuees. Yet it nonetheless insisted that its actions were lawful, relying (as the British government had in the Northumbria police case) on ancient prerogative powers of the Crown and on abstract theories of powers immanent to the executive authority of a country.

At first instance North J held that the rescuees had been unlawfully detained and that the government enjoyed neither statutory nor prerogative power to expel them. He ordered that they be released onto the mainland of Australia. The government appealed, winning its appeal by a majority of two to one. Black CJ, dissenting, delivered a lengthy judgment in which he forensically dismantled the government's legal claims and held, as North J had at first instance, that the government had acted without authority. For the majority, by contrast, one judge confined his judgment to matters of procedure, holding that Vadarlis and the VCCL had no cause of action and the other held simply that it was his 'opinion' that the executive power of the Australian government 'would extend to a power to prevent the entry of non-citizens'.[117] This was the judge's opinion notwithstanding the fact that, as Black CJ had demonstrated in his dissent, there was no clear or direct authority that could be cited in its favour.

Judicial decisions such as these are straightforwardly incompatible with republican constitutionalism. The British and Australian governments were able to win these cases only because they could rely on the prerogative authority of the Crown to supply them with the powers to act in the ways that the respective nations' Parliaments had not sanctioned. A republican constitution would accommodate no such reservoir of hidden, uncodified power. Power not expressly dealt with in the constitution would remain with the people, not lurk in the ancient authority of sovereign kings.

Before we leave this theme one word of clarification is called for. To suggest that the first theme of republicanism is anti-monarchism and popular sovereignty is not to say that a constitution cannot simultaneously embrace elements of both republicanism and monarchism. It is not only in the constitutions of states that are formal republics that republican notions of constitutionalism may be found. Thus, the fact that the United Kingdom is a monarchy does not mean that its constitution cannot contain elements of republicanism, although it does suggest that the UK's constitution is unlikely to be purely republican, of course. There is no reason to suppose that the

---

[117] *Ruddock v Vadarlis*, at para [193], *per* French J.

constitution of a monarchy cannot include some sense of popular sovereignty, or some sense even of anti-monarchism.[118]

The British constitution clearly accommodates ideas of popular sovereignty. Such sovereignty, in the British system, is not direct but is filtered through the institution that represents the people (and which is directly elected by the people)—the House of Commons. As we saw in chapter one, it is to the House of Commons that the prime minister and his government are constitutionally responsible. It is through Parliament that the government must legislate. When there are legislative disagreements between the two Houses of Parliament, it is the will of the Commons that will prevail over that of the Lords.[119] More fundamentally, when there are constitutional disagreements between the Houses of Parliament and the Crown it is the will of Parliament that will prevail over that of the Crown.[120] All of these rules of the British constitution are reflective of, indeed based on, the republican principle of popular sovereignty.[121]

Freedom as Non-domination and its Consequences

The second theme of republicanism is its understanding of freedom and the consequences that follow from it. We explored the idea of freedom as non-domination in some detail earlier in this chapter and there is no need to repeat here the analysis of it that was presented above. We also saw something of the institutional and constitutional consequences that flow from taking the idea of freedom as non-domination seriously. We saw, in particular, how it leads to the requirement of accountable government.[122] This analysis can now be taken further. What follows is an outline sketch of a number of further constitutional consequences that derive from the republican account of freedom as non-domination. The first concerns open government, the second citizenship and the third equality.

(i) Government in the Public Interest: Open Government

One security against domination is to insist that political decisions are made in the public interest—or in support of a common good—rather than in the

---

[118] Conversely there is no reason to suppose that the constitution of a republic cannot include some elements of monarchism: consider, eg, the apparently ever more powerful position within the US constitution of the Presidency.

[119] Parliament Acts 1911–1949.

[120] Bill of Rights 1689, Act of Settlement 1701.

[121] This analysis is carried further in ch 3, below.

[122] See above, at 51.

interests of a particular group. Indeed, the privileging of particular personal or private interests over the public good is presented in republican writing as the very definition of political corruption, as being the tyranny that republicanism is designed to combat.[123] Discovering what is a common good, what is in the public interest, requires the constitution to facilitate an inclusive, deliberative and openly reasoned style of politics and to ensure that participation in decision-making processes (whether it is direct or through elected representatives) is as widespread as possible.[124] Unless decision-making is open and deliberative there can be none of the contestation that we saw above to be essential to secure non-domination. In order for citizens to be able to contest what it is that the state is doing or is seeking to do in their name, government is required to be open and information free.

This presents an interesting contrast with the model of legal constitutionalism outlined in chapter one. There we saw that freedom of speech is often taken to be the paradigmatic civil right. For a republican it will often be freedom of information that has pride of place: if there can be no liberalism without free speech there can be no republicanism without freedom of information. Citizens and their representatives cannot hope to be able to subject the government to effective scrutiny (or contestation) unless they first know what it is that the government is doing or is proposing to do and what the reasons are for the government desiring to act in a certain way.[125]

(ii)   Citizenship in the Public Interest: Civic Virtue

The realisation of freedom as non-domination also requires something of us as citizens. Citizenship, for republicans, is not only a matter of rights that we hold against the state but is, just as importantly, a question of obligation on our part as to how we engage in the political process. As Iseult Honohan has put it, 'the idea that citizens need to be concerned with the common good and to take some personal responsibility for realising it is one of the longest-standing themes' of republicanism.[126] To this end, republican citizenship demands of us a deep and active sense of public-spiritedness. It is not just the government that is required to act in the public interest rather than in its own: it is us. We are required, when engaging in the public sphere, that is to say

---

[123] This is a particularly prominent theme in Machiavelli's *Discourses*: see above n 60.

[124] These themes are explored, often at great length, throughout the literature in political philosophy. Among the most rewarding of very many examples, see S Benhabib (ed), *Democracy and Difference: Contesting the Boundaries of the Political* (Princeton, Princeton University Press, 1996), IM Young, *Inclusion and Democracy* (Oxford, Oxford University Press, 2000) and H Richardson, above n 58.

[125] See further on this theme ch 4, below.

[126] I Honohan, *Civic Republicanism* (London, Routledge, 2002), at 147.

when engaging in politics, to be prepared where necessary to put our personal interests to one side and to act for the public good. This ideal of public-spirited citizenship is what is meant by the phrase 'civic virtue', widely employed in the republican literature.[127]

The notions of civic virtue, public spiritedness and the common good are often misunderstood. A frequent objection, particularly of liberals, is that these are dangerous ideas, that the prioritising of the public good over individual interests can lead to political oppression and to the denial of human rights. Without doubt we need to be careful that notions of the public good are not abused in this way. Such abuse, however, would be contrary not only to liberal values but to republicanism as well. To hold that citizens should be prepared to act to put public interests before their private concerns is not to say that the former is something that is centrally determined or imposed by the state. On the contrary (and as we have already seen) discovering what is in the public interest—what is the public good—is a question for the citizenry (acting, in the modern state, through its elected representatives in accordance with the principles of inclusive and contestatory deliberation). It is the government that is required to track the interests of its citizens, not the other way around. Tracking the interests of the citizens is what is meant by republicans as acting in the public good.

The classic example illustrative of what is meant by the public good is clean air. We all have an interest, rather obviously, in breathing clean air. None of us acting alone can realise that interest. It is only by acting together—by acting politically—that it can be realised. Now, some of us will have private interests that militate against the public interest of clean air. Some of us will be industrialists whose factories pollute the air. Others of us will be employees working in such factories, whose livelihoods depend on our employment. But even industrialists and their employees have an interest, as citizens, in breathing clean air. In this way the public interest is not something that is 'out there', imposed upon us by some external force, but is as much our own interest as are our private concerns. As Honohan explains it, civic virtue is

> an established disposition to act in certain ways, not a matter of acting in accordance with law or duty . . . It involves developing or modifying perceptions of where our interests lie. It is not a matter of choosing to be wholly altruistic or wholly selfish, but of identifying with an expanding range of others through action and experience. . .[128]

---

[127] For further elaboration, see the excellent discussion in I Honohan, *ibid*, ch 5.
[128] *Ibid*, at 159–60.

(iii) Equality

A further consequence of taking freedom as non-domination seriously concerns equality. As Pettit has observed, poverty is one of the forms of insecurity most likely to render a person liable to domination.[129] In today's world, freedom is as seriously challenged by the economic differences that exist in the private sector as it is by the power of states and governments. Our world is scarred by staggering differences in material conditions, which, as the French political philosopher Jean-Fabien Spitz has put it,

> cannot be proven to function for mutual advantages, so that liberty's main enemy is not only the state but also the extraordinary concentrations of private wealth and power which constrain those who are not members of the wealthy inner circle.[130]

Republicans since at least the time of Harrington have been concerned with the threat to freedom that is posed by such material inequality. Both Harrington and his ally Henry Neville devoted, in their writing, considerable attention to the problem that, as they saw it, 'prosperity and peace could only be achieved when the political system had been adjusted to the distribution of wealth'.[131] Inequality undermines republican citizenship and freedom in at least two ways. First and most obviously it subjects the poor to the dominion of the wealthy. Secondly, those in a state of abject material dependence have neither the time to engage in public life nor the opportunity of participating in the public-spirited manner that republicanism expects. A slave's interest is that of his master, not that of promoting the public good.

The Institutional Design of Accountability

The previous sections have set out something of the values of republican constitutionalism: popular sovereignty, non-domination, open government, civic virtue and equality. The third theme of republicanism concerns the question of how such values may be realised in constitutional practice. It addresses the structures—the institutional design—that we need in order to secure republican government. The centrepiece of republican constitutional structure is accountability: those in positions of political power must be accountable to those over whom (and in whose name) such power is

---

[129] P Pettit, 'Discourse Theory and Republican Freedom', in D Weinstock and C Nadeau (eds), above n 58, at 94, n 2.

[130] J-F Spitz, 'The Twilight of the Republic?', in D Weinstock and C Nadeau, *ibid*, at 58.

[131] C Robbins, above n 107, at 35. Harrington proposed, for example, that no-one should be permitted to inherit land worth more than £2000: see B Worden, above n 105, at 453.

exercised. As we have repeatedly seen, in the British experience this ideal is manifested by making the government of the day accountable to the people's representatives in Parliament.

This is the respect in which the British constitution is most obviously republican. Too few of the republican values we have identified here play central roles in the contemporary British polity.[132] But the institutional design of political accountability—even if many commentators would argue that it is not currently working as well as it might—remains absolutely central to British constitutional practice, as it has been for centuries.

How the practice of political accountability came to the fore of British constitutionalism, and how its development was shaped by republican thinking and action, are the issues that are explored in the next chapter. In the final chapter we return to the substantive values of republican constitutionalism and consider how the British constitution may be reformed so as more fully to accommodate them.

---

[132] See further on this issue ch 4, below.

3

The Making of the Republican Constitution

'The Parliament of England, . . . judging kingship by long
experience a government unnecessary, burdensome
and dangerous, justly and magnanimously abolished it,
turning regal bondage into a free commonwealth.'[1]

THE ACCOUNTABILITY OF the government to Parliament has
not always been the constitution's core rule. On the contrary, the
emergence of the republican notion of responsible government took
place at a particular—and critical—moment in Anglo-British constitutional
history. It is the purpose of this chapter to relate the story of the emergence
of responsible government, that is, to relate the making of the republican
constitution. The story will be told in two parts. The first concerns what is
sometimes referred to as the collapse of the ancient constitution. I prefer to
call it the failure of the common law constitution. It discusses the period
between the death of Elizabeth I in 1603 and the recall of Parliament (after an
eleven-year absence) in 1640. This period is marked by a series of cases in
which the common law courts were invited—but failed—to hold the governments of James I and Charles I to constitutional account. The second part
of our story examines Parliament's reaction to the failure of the common law
constitution and its construction of a new constitutional order, a construction that commenced in the pre Civil War parliaments of 1640–41 and which
culminated in the passing of the Bill of Rights 1689 and the Act of Settlement
1701.

It is the constitutional order that Parliament constructed between 1640
and 1701 that continues to form the bedrock of the British constitution to
this day. This is not to say, of course, that there have been no further changes
to the constitutional order since the early eighteenth century. But it is to say
that such development as has occurred since that time has been based on the

---

[1] John Milton, *The Ready and Easy Way to Establish a Free Commonwealth* [1660]. For a modern
edition, see J Milton, *Areopagitica and other Political Writings* (ed J Alvis, Indianapolis, Liberty Fund,
1999), at 416.

foundations that were laid between 1640 and 1701.[2] As we shall see, those foundations take as their starting-point the republican idea that the government is accountable to Parliament. Before we come to discuss this in more detail, however, we first need a clearer picture of what the parliamentarian founders of the mid and late seventeenth century were responding to. The republican constitution that was built after 1640 did not emerge out of thin air, but was a deliberate and considered reaction to the failure of the constitutional order that pertained before 1640, a constitutional order that had placed the common law courts centre-stage.

Seventeenth-century English political history has in recent generations been the subject of more intensely fought historiographical wranglings than perhaps any other aspect of England's past. Both the old, 'Whiggish' view that the period from 1603 to 1640 marked the self-destructive Stuarts on a constant 'high road to Civil War' and the Marxist interpretation of the mid seventeenth century as England's revolution have come under sustained criticism by so-called revisionist historians who have sought on the one hand to highlight the ruptures and discontinuities of the period and on the other to insist that the causes of its troubles were primarily religious rather than political or constitutional.[3] The revisionist accounts, however, have now come themselves to be substantially revised, with a variety of historians giving fresh credence to arguments that reinstate the importance of political and constitutional factors,[4] that suggest significant continuities between the struggles of the 1620s, the 1640s and the 1680s,[5] and that portray the earlier part of the century (as well as the later) as a time of revolution.[6] The value of these historians' work (on which I have relied considerably) lies in its having shown that there is a coherent story of revolutionary constitution-making to be told within the political history of England's seventeenth century and that to want to tell it does not mean that one necessarily has to embrace the values of either Whiggish or Marxist history.

---

[2] This position is not especially controversial or contentious: it is the view, eg, taken by Clayton Roberts in his definitive history of the seventeenth-century development of ministerial responsibility: see C Roberts, *The Growth of Responsible Government in Stuart England* (Cambridge, Cambridge University Press, 1966), at 430–31.

[3] For a good summary of (and references to) the voluminous literature, see D Underdown, *A Freeborn People: Politics and the Nation in Seventeenth-Century England* (Oxford, Clarendon Press, 1996), ch 1. See also D Cressy, 'Revolutionary England, 1640–1642' (2003) 181 *Past and Present* 35, at 37–41.

[4] See, eg, Q Skinner, *Liberty before Liberalism* (Cambridge, Cambridge University Press, 1998) and A Cromartie, 'The Constitutionalist Revolution: The Transformation of Political Culture in Early Stuart England' (1999) 163 *Past and Present* 76.

[5] See, eg, J Scott, *England's Troubles: Seventeenth-Century English Political Instability in European Context* (Cambridge, Cambridge University Press, 2000).

[6] For a particularly robust defence of this theme (which places, as this chapter does, the years 1640–42 at the heart of the revolution), see D Cressy, above n 3.

I THE FAILURE OF THE COMMON LAW CONSTITUTION

Common lawyers do not generally view the early seventeenth century as having been a time of common law failure. On the contrary, the period is celebrated as a moment of almost revolutionary constitutional triumph—as being the moment at which the common law courts stood up to the power of the Crown's government and insisted upon their independence from its authority. This position—the common law orthodoxy—is perhaps most clearly articulated in a recent paper by Paul Craig.[7] In his own words, the essence of Professor Craig's argument is that in a series of cases 'the courts have been forced to draw the boundaries of constitutional competence as between the executive and Parliament, and that they have consistently backed Parliament.'[8] Craig's argument relies heavily on an analysis of two critical, and famous, seventeenth-century cases, both decisions of Sir Edward Coke: *Prohibitions del Roy* in 1607[9] and the *Case of Proclamations* in 1611.[10] These he describes, in line with conventional legal interpretation, as 'the two central seventeenth-century authorities.'[11]

The orthodox legal position that Craig sets out is open to challenge in a number of respects. First, it will be shown that the courts were not forced to draw the boundaries of constitutional competence as between the Crown and Parliament: indeed, when the courts attempted to do this they buckled, and Parliament ultimately had to do it for itself. Secondly, it will be shown that in disputes between the Crown and Parliament the courts have not 'consistently backed Parliament': on the contrary, they have, on the whole, supported the Crown. But even where the courts have not supported the Crown, this does not mean that they have necessarily supported Parliament—even those cases which the Crown could be said to have 'lost' do not constitute clear parliamentary victories. The argument will proceed as follows: first, the two Coke decisions, *Prohibitions del Roy* and the *Case of Proclamations*, will be re-evaluated. Following this, the argument will then trace a series of further constitutional cases and parliamentary episodes from the same period, cases which, it will be shown, demonstrate the failure of the common law constitution.

---

[7] P Craig, 'Prerogative, Precedent and Power', in C Forsyth and I Hare (eds) *The Golden Metwand and the Crooked Cord* (Oxford, Clarendon Press, 1998).

[8] *Ibid*, at 65.

[9] (1607) 12 Co Rep 63; 77 ER 1342.

[10] (1611) 12 Co Rep 74; 77 ER 1352.

[11] P Craig, above n 7, at 67.

Prohibitions, Proclamations and Sir Edward Coke

Coke's decision in *Prohibitions del Roy* is generally regarded to have laid down fundamental restrictions on the prerogatives of the king as they affect judicial power. And, as Craig puts it, 'what *Prohibitions del Roy* achieved for the divide between executive and judicial power, the *Case of Proclamations* did for the crucial division between executive and legislative competence.'[12] These cases,[13] then, are taken as being fundamental to contemporary Anglo-British constitutionalism, cementing ideas of what we would now call the separation of powers and the independence of the judiciary. Coke is celebrated by lawyers such as Craig for having stood up to the coercive power of the Crown, and to have used his position as Chief Justice to lead the judiciary in the defence of Englishmen's rights, creating in the common law courts a powerful buttress against the abuse of prerogative authority.

Let us now take a closer look at *Prohibitions*, at *Proclamations*, and at the man who decided them. The dispute in *Prohibitions del Roy* arose out of two related uncertainties: what was the scope of the authority of the ecclesiastical judges, and how should such judges interpret statutes? In 1605 King James I had been advised by the Archbishop of Canterbury, Bancroft, that as to either of these uncertainties, 'the king may decide . . . in his royal person' and that in such matters the judges were but delegates of the king. When the issue came before him, however, Coke stood Bancroft's advice on its head. Coke's words on this matter are frequently quoted:

> His Majesty was not learned in the laws of his realm of England, and causes which concern the life, or inheritance, or goods, or fortunes of his subjects, are not to be decided by natural reason but by the artificial reason and judgment of law, which law is an act which requires long study and experience, before that a man can attain to the cognizance of it.

Coke's statement in *Prohibitions* is generally taken to be a striking constitutional defence of the autonomy of the courts from the power of the Crown, Coke insisting that the interpretation of statutes was a task which only the judges, and not the king himself, could authoritatively perform.

Is this interpretation correct? At the time of his statement in *Prohibitions*, Coke was Chief Justice of the Court of Common Pleas. During the reign of James I the church was in the process of launching a determined attempt to shake off the control of the common law courts, of which the Court of

---

[12] P Craig, above n 7, at 67.

[13] Despite the fact that it has generally been treated by lawyers as having been a case, *Prohibitions del Roy* was in fact more like a meeting (or a series of meetings) between the king and his political, legal and ecclesiastical advisers: see J Hart, *The Rule of Law, 1603–1660: Crowns, Courts and Judges* (Harlow, Longman, 2003), at 45–47.

Common Pleas was one. What seems to have motivated Coke, as a common lawyer, was a concern to consolidate the power and position of the common law courts over the church. Coke's attitude was that of a 'jealous lawyer', keen to consolidate his own power and influence over matters ecclesiastical.[14] Certainly, this was Maitland's view: in his lectures on constitutional history Maitland argued that in *Prohibitions* Coke was much less interested in limiting the powers of the Crown than he was in seeking to justify the controversial intrusion of the common law into ecclesiastical fields.[15] Defence of the common law, even when it appears as an attack on prerogative power, is not of course the same thing as defence of Parliament, and as we shall see it was the defence of the common law (and not of Parliament) which truly animated Coke throughout his time as a judge.

The *Case of Proclamations* concerned the legality of two proclamations made by James I. The first sought to prohibit new buildings in and about London, and the second sought to prohibit the making of starch from wheat. Coke held that the king cannot by his proclamation change any part of the common law. Nor could the king create any new offence by way of proclamation, for that would be to change the law. Coke summed up his position in the following well-known words: the king, he declared, 'hath no prerogative, but that which the law of the land allows him.'[16] Craig states that the significance of this decision is three-fold: first, 'it clearly established that the prerogative was bounded and not unlimited'; secondly, it established that it was for the courts (and not for the Crown itself) to determine where the boundaries to prerogative power lay and thirdly, 'the principal beneficiary of the court's judgment was, of course, Parliament'.[17] However, as with *Prohibitions del Roy*, we ought to treat such analysis with caution. This is for two reasons: first, any protection which Parliament gained from Coke's decision in *Proclamations* was purely incidental and secondly, Coke's decision was not based on grand constitutional theory, on seeking to subject the power of the Crown to the rule of law, but on something far more mundane: it was based simply on economics.[18]

Let us briefly examine each of these points in turn. On the parliamentary benefit point, the key is to understand what happened following Coke's judgment. What occurred was that despite the fact that the king had the

---

[14] This interpretation is offered in the lengthy entry on Coke in the *Dictionary of National Biography*. For a more recent authority to similar effect, see A Cromartie, above n 4, at 89–90.

[15] See F Maitland, *The Constitutional History of England* (Cambridge, Cambridge University Press, 1908), at 265–68.

[16] See 12 Co Rep, at 76.

[17] P Craig, above n 7, at 68.

[18] D Wagner has described the judicial safeguarding of economic liberalism as the 'ruling principle' of the common law at the time of Coke: see his 'Coke and the Rise of Economic Liberalism' (1935) 6 *Economic History Review* 30, at 44.

opinion of Coke and the judges against him, he nonetheless continued issuing proclamations. As Maitland observes,

> it is difficult for us to realise the state of things—that of the government constantly doing what the judges consider unlawful. The key is the Court of Star-chamber—the very council which has issued these proclamations enforced them as a legal tribunal, and as yet no-one dared resist its judicial power.[19]

The Court of Star-chamber, which was a prerogative court not a common law court, was abolished by Act of Parliament in 1641 but until that time the last word on proclamations did not rest with the common law judges, as the Court of Star-chamber would, and did, enforce proclamations. Maitland tells us that 'the proclamations of Charles I were far more numerous than those of his father. Prices were fixed by proclamation; houses were demolished, shops were shut in order that the new cathedral of St Paul might appear to better advantage; all persons who had houses in the country were directed to leave London' and all under the authority of proclamation.[20] Thus, the *Case of Proclamations* begins not to look so much the great parliamentary triumph that it is often made out to be.

Twentieth-century historians' assessments of Coke's role, and of his politics, have tended to be rather less generous than have those of the lawyers.[21] Christopher Hill rather rudely states that Coke was 'a lawyer, not an intellectual. The confusion and self-contradiction in his writings are so great that one is apt to dismiss them as of no significance'.[22] This view is echoed by Glenn Burgess, who describes Coke as 'an eccentric, and sometimes a confused, thinker.'[23] It is not only Coke's writing and thought which is criticised in this manner: even his basic legal skills are called into question. Hill says of Coke's relation with his beloved Magna Carta that it was just one of the many statutes which Coke interpreted 'so lovingly and so inaccurately'.[24] Kenyon similarly remarks on Coke's 'fluency in the invention of legal precedents.'[25]

---

[19]   F Maitland, above n 15, at 258.

[20]   *Ibid*, at 302.

[21]   One twentieth-century historian whose views of Coke should be cautiously treated is JGA Pocock. Coke plays a major role in Pocock's account of seventeenth-century English constitutionalism. Pocock's critics—particularly in this instance Glenn Burgess—have suggested that it is perhaps Pocock's 'major weakness' that he treats Coke 'as the norm rather than as the exception'. See JGA Pocock, *The Ancient Constitution and the Feudal Law* (Cambridge, Cambridge University Press, 1957, republished 1987), and G Burgess, *The Politics of the Ancient Constitution: An Introduction to English Political Thought 1603–1642* (Pennsylvania, Pennsylvania State University Press, 1993), at 58.

[22]   C Hill, *Intellectual Origins of the English Revolution Revisited* (Oxford, Clarendon Press, 1997, first published 1965), at 202. His chapter on Coke he aptly entitles 'Myth-Maker'.

[23]   G Burgess, above n 21, at 21.

[24]   C Hill, above n 22, at 229.

[25]   J Kenyon, *The Stuart Constitution 1603–1688: Documents and Commentary* (Cambridge, Cambridge University Press, 1986, 2nd ed), at 87.

Yet despite the contradictions and changes of mind, Coke does seem to have been animated by a number of causes and crusades at various points during his chequered career. Outward support for Parliament, however, was not one of them—at least not while Coke was active as a common law judge.[26] Rather, he seems more than anything else to have been motivated by the project of seeking to advance the cause of economic liberalism. This crusade overshadowed even his personal ambition and self-advancement—a view strongly expressed by Wagner, and endorsed by Hill. In his article, 'Coke and the Rise of Economic Liberalism,' Wagner argued that Coke had a strong 'bias in favour of economic liberalism' and that 'it is clear that in [Coke's] opinion the ruling principle at common law was freedom of enterprise.'[27] In this he was perhaps typical of the common lawyers: as Margaret Judson has argued, property rights were the 'principal concern of the common law.'[28] *Dr Bonham's Case* is a good example of this. The case is well-known by constitutional lawyers for Coke's statement that 'when an Act of Parliament is against common right and reason, or repugnant, or impossible to be performed, the common law will control it and adjudge such an act to be void'.[29] *Dr Bonham's Case* concerned the (statutory) power of the college of physicians to fine and imprison unlicensed physicians practising within seven miles of London. Of this decision, Hill suggests that

> lawyers and political theorists have perhaps made too heavy weather of this case. We need not read into it issues affecting fundamental law or the sovereignty of statute. Coke was faced with a monopoly which denied the right of men to sell their skills on the open market, and which made the monopolists at once prosecutors, judges, and beneficiaries from the fine.[30]

Even as a parliamentarian in the 1620s Coke continued to champion the cause of commerce and freedom of trade: his opposition in the Commons in

---

[26]   Coke was Chief Justice of the Common Pleas from 1606–13, and was Chief Justice of the King's Bench from 1613–16, at which point he was removed from office. In his later career Coke sat as a member of the House of Commons in the Parliaments of 1621–28, and played a leading role, as is discussed below, in the development and framing of the Petition of Right in 1628, but it is important to note that this was a role he played as a parliamentarian and not as a judge. It is also worth noting that even after his dismissal in 1616 as Chief Justice of the King's Bench, he continued to work closely with James I: he was consulted by the king on private matters, in 1617 he was recalled to the Council, and from then until 1621 he sat in the Star-chamber. Only after 1621 did James finally lose patience with Coke.

[27]   D Wagner, above n 18, at 44.

[28]   See M Judson, *The Crisis of the Constitution: An Essay in Constitutional and Political Thought in England, 1603–1645* (New Brunswick, Rutgers University Press, 1949), at 35.

[29]   (1610) 8 Co Rep 107a, at 118a; 77 ER 638, at 652.

[30]   C Hill, above n 22, at 210–11. See further on *Dr Bonham's Case*, S Thorne, 'Dr Bonham's Case' (1938) 54 *Law Quarterly Review* 543; T Plucknett, 'Bonham's Case and Judicial Review' (1926) 40 *Harvard Law Review* 30; and R MacKay, 'Coke—Parliamentary Sovereignty or the Supremacy of the Law' (1924) 22 *Michigan Law Review* 215.

1625 to the voting of subsidies for the new king, Charles, was based not on constitutional objections, but on economic grounds: 'pointing to the depression of trade and the inability of the people to bear a greater load,' Coke argued that the government's 'ordinary expense and charge should, and with an economical and honest administration could, be borne by the income from lands and revenues.'[31]

This brief reappraisal suggests that we should be cautious about celebrating Coke as a champion of the interests of Parliament over those of the Crown—at least as far as his career as a judge is concerned.[32] Neither *Prohibitions* nor *Proclamations* offer particularly strong support for the thesis that in disputes between the Crown and Parliament the common law courts will back Parliament. Even to the extent to which the Crown can meaningfully be said to have lost these cases (and we have seen that proclamations far from stopped after Coke's intervention), Parliament gained precious little. If we had to pick a victor it would not be Parliament, but the common lawyers and the economic freedom they so cherished.

Prohibitions and *Proclamations* were by no means the only occasions whereby the judges could express support for Parliament's concerns or for the Crown's executive interests. On the contrary, between 1603 and the outbreak of Civil War in 1642 there were at least four further episodes—all involving litigation of the highest constitutional significance—which show more clearly where the courts stood in the political and legal affairs of the time. Each of these episodes will now be considered in turn. They are *Bate's Case* on impositions, from 1606; *Darnel's Case,* or the *Case of the Five Knights* on the forced loan and discretionary imprisonment, from 1627—an extremely important case that led to the Petition of Right 1628, Parliament's first major statement of constitutional law in the seventeenth century; *Eliot's Case* in 1629 which concerned parliamentary privilege and the imprisonment of members of Parliament; and finally *R v Hampden*, the *Ship-money Case* of 1637.

Impositions and *Bate's Case*

The Crown had for centuries possessed a prerogative right to levy import duties, known as impositions, in order to regulate trade and to protect native producers and manufacturers. The merchant community strongly resented them. In 1606 John Bate, a merchant trading in the Levant, refused to pay a

---

[31] *Dictionary of National Biography.*

[32] As Alan Cromartie has suggested, 'Coke had a most suspicious attitude towards the institution—Parliament—that offered the best prospect of curbing any government excesses'. See above n 4, at 103.

levy of 5s per cwt on imported currants. The levy had been imposed in 1601 by James I by letters patent and was to be paid in addition to the statutory poundage of 2s 6d. Bate refused to pay James' levy on the ground that it amounted to indirect taxation without the consent of Parliament, in breach, so he argued, of statute.[33]

When Bate was sued in the common law Court of Exchequer, the judges upheld the king's right to levy impositions on the ground that it fell within his extraordinary or absolute prerogative—which operated outside the law—rather than his ordinary or legal prerogative. In his judgment Chief Baron Fleming stated that while the latter is exercised 'in ordinary courts ... and cannot be changed without Parliament', the absolute power of the king, on the other hand is not 'guided by ... the common law, and is most properly named policy and government; and as the constitution of this body varieth with the time, so varieth this absolute law according to the wisdom of the king.'[34] This absolute wisdom of the king, according to Fleming, was beyond any form of judicial review: 'all things done within these rules,' he declared, 'are lawful' and further, 'the wisdom and providence of the king is not to be disputed by the subject.'[35] Baron Clarke gave judgment in similarly sweeping style, arguing that just as England was 'not a kingdom without subjects and government', so too was James 'not a king without revenues ... The revenue of the Crown is the very essential part of the Crown, and he who rendeth that from the king pulleth also his Crown from his head.'[36]

Reaction in the Commons was uncompromising, if somewhat delayed. There was no sitting of Parliament from the middle of 1607 until early 1610.[37] In the 1610 session the Commons staged a great debate on impositions, which lasted from 23 June until 3 July. Prothero[38] reproduces two speeches delivered in the course of that debate, one of which was given by Hakewill. The 1610 debate marks an important stage in the progress of constitutional ideas in the early seventeenth century, and demonstrates how far—even at this point—the Commons had moved from the position defended by the common law courts. The following statements from Hakewill's speech give a flavour of the parliamentary disquiet. For Hakewill, the idea that 'the king

---

[33] *Bate's Case* is reported at (1606) 2 St Tr 371. For an excellent analysis, see P Croft, 'Fresh Light on *Bate's Case*' (1987) 30 *Historical Journal* 523. Much useful background information may be found in C Hall, 'Impositions and the Courts, 1554–1606' (1953) 69 *Law Quarterly Review* 200.

[34] 2 St Tr 389.

[35] *Ibid*, at 392.

[36] *Ibid*, at 382–83.

[37] James I's first English Parliament was called in 1604 and was not dissolved until 1611, but its five sessions were separated by lengthy breaks.

[38] GW Prothero, *Select Statutes and other Constitutional Documents, 1558–1625* (Oxford, Clarendon Press, 1913, 4th ed), at 342–53.

may not only lay impositions but levy a tax within the realm without assent of Parliament' was a 'very dangerous' one,

> for to admit this were by consequence to bring us into bondage. You say that upon occasion of sudden war the king may levy a tax. Who shall be judge between the king and his people of the occasion? Can it be tried by any legal course in our law? It cannot. If then the king himself must be the sole judge in this case, will it not follow that the king may levy a tax at his own pleasure, seeing his pleasure cannot be bounded by law?[39]

Quentin Skinner has suggested that it is in these parliamentary debates on impositions that the first showings of what he has labelled neo-Romanism can be identified, with numerous members of Parliament arguing that it is not only the exercise but the mere existence of the prerogative power to levy impositions that renders Englishman unfree.[40] Skinner cites the contribution of Thomas Wentworth, whom he reports as having suggested that, unless the Commons are 'permitted to question this prerogative, then we might as well be sold for slaves'.[41] In similar vein, Skinner cites also an impassioned intervention from Sir Thomas Hedley who, quoting from Cicero himself, sought to demonstrate, as had Hakewill, that the king's prerogative of impositions reduced the Commons and its members to the status of mere 'bondage'.[42]

The outcome of the debate was an agreement with the king: 'James undertook to remit the most burdensome of the impositions, and the Commons agreed to grant him the remainder on condition that it should be declared illegal by statute to levy impositions in the future without consent of Parliament'.[43] However, before the agreement could be implemented, further disputes arose over other matters, leading James to dissolve Parliament in early 1611. This said, the issue did not go away and even into the 1620s the decision in *Bate's Case* 'was often recalled . . . as a milestone marking the beginnings of the collapse of the Commons' confidence in the judiciary.'[44]

---

[39] GW Prothero, *Select Statutes and other Constitutional Documents, 1558–1625* (Oxford, Clarendon Press, 1913, 4th ed), at 346.

[40] See Q Skinner, 'John Milton and the Politics of Slavery' and 'Classical Liberty, Renaissance Translation and the English Civil War', both in Q Skinner, *Visions of Politics, Volume II: Renaissance Virtues* (Cambridge, Cambridge University Press, 2002), at 290 and 320 respectively. In this chapter these essays are hereafter referred to as 'Politics of Slavery' and 'Classical Liberty', respectively. Skinner's 'neo-Romanism' was discussed in detail in ch 2, above.

[41] Q Skinner, 'Classical Liberty', *ibid*, at 320.

[42] *Ibid.*

[43] See JR Tanner, *English Constitutional Conflicts of the Seventeenth Century 1603–1689* (Cambridge, Cambridge University Press, 1928), at 45.

[44] P Croft, above n 33, at 539. The result in *Bate's Case* was eventually reversed by the Petition of Right in 1628: see further below.

Towards the Petition of Right

James died in March 1625 and his son, Charles I, inherited the throne. Unlike his father, Charles possessed an essentially authoritarian temperament. Whereas James' problem with Parliament had been principally his tactlessness, with Charles the issues were immediately more polarised. When in 1625 the new king met his first Parliament, the Commons refused to make that grant of tonnage and poundage for the king's life which since the days of Henry V had been usual. The Commons would grant it for but one year. The Lords would not pass a bill for so restricted a grant, so Charles dissolved Parliament and meanwhile continued to levy tonnage and other imposts without parliamentary sanction.[45] Indirect taxation, however, no longer sufficed to meet the king's needs, so he had recourse to a forced loan. Five knights who refused to contribute, Sir Thomas Darnel, Sir John Corbet, Sir Walter Erle, Sir John Heveningham, and Sir Edmund Hampden, were imprisoned by order of the privy council for their failure to pay.

In November 1627 the Court of King's Bench granted the five writs of habeas corpus, which required that a cause for their imprisonment be given if they were not to receive bail. Charles' privy council decided that the response to be given was to declare that the five knights had been imprisoned 'by his majesty's special commandment'.[46] The question at issue in the subsequent proceedings in King's Bench was whether this rather vague statement was adequate to satisfy the legal requirement that cause of imprisonment be shown. The council had presumably decided on this response 'to avoid any judicial consideration of the forced loan itself, and it was this evasion of the issue that irritated many'.[47] In other circumstances the Crown's actions might have been uncontroversial 'but the use of argument based on "reason of state" in circumstances where, many felt, the refusal to pay a forced loan was not illegal appeared dangerously like an attempt to use a royal prerogative (in itself possibly legal) to safeguard actions of more dubious legality from investigation.'[48]

The judges refused to bail the prisoners, and sent them back to jail.[49] The court held that it was lawful for men to be detained on the authority of the

---

[45] This summary is derived principally from F Maitland, above n 15, at 307.
[46] See G Burgess, above n 21, at 191.
[47] *Ibid.*
[48] *Ibid.*
[49] The case is reported at (1627) 3 St Tr 1. For commentary, see R Cust, *The Forced Loan and English Politics, 1626–1628* (Oxford, Clarendon Press, 1987) and P Christianson, 'John Selden, the Five Knights' Case, and Discretionary Imprisonment in Early Stuart England' (1985) 6 *Criminal Justice History* 65.

Crown even where the cause of the imprisonment was not declared on the warrant. That is, the very fact that the warrant was issued on the authority of the Crown was itself sufficient. In the words of Lord Hyde, the Chief Justice of the King's Bench, 'we are sworn to maintain all prerogatives of the king . . . if no cause of the [imprisonment] be expressed, it is to be presumed to be for matters of state, which we cannot take notice of.'[50]

We can accept that the king was in a bind: the Tudors had greatly extended the scope and reach of government, but financial machinery remained medieval, and Parliament, as we have seen, was not in a generous mood. Short supply was a constant difficulty for the Stuart kings. David Smith has suggested that 'during the mid and late 1620s, the costs of war were such that the Crown probably needed in the region of £1 million a year. Parliamentary supply amounted to £353,000 in 1624, £140,000 in 1625, and £275,000 in 1628.'[51] In this context it is easy to see why Charles needed to secure binding decisions in the common law courts in favour of special (that is, non-parliamentary) taxes. The problem, however, was that such precedents as there were did not favour the king—the judges were therefore reduced to 'employing oblique and circuitous tactics . . . They so defined the issue as to bring it within the accepted powers of the Crown; they argued very skilfully from analogy; and they discovered general legal principles favourable to their contention. At times they deserted the law for more philosophical and political arguments.'[52]

It was not only the decision of the court in the *Five Knights' Case* which caused alarm. There was also a scandal about the way in which the decision was subsequently recorded.[53] The court's decision was a 'rule of court', not a judgment as such. A rule of court was a decision on a procedural matter—the ruling in this case being that the knights should be refused bail. The knights were then 'to be remanded pending the filing, hearing, and judgment of the substantive charges.'[54] This was the theory. The reality, however, was much more negative for the prisoners, as the king had absolutely no intention of filing substantive charges, because he was desperate to keep the forced loan away from being judicially reviewed. The practical effect of the court's decision was therefore to give the Crown the apparent right to detain the prisoners until such time as the king chose to release them.

Parliament met again in March 1628. John Selden, a member of the Commons, had been counsel for one of the five knights. He checked the

---

[50] See 3 St Tr 51. See also J Kenyon, above n 25, at 97.

[51] D Smith, *The Stuart Parliaments, 1603–1689* (London, Arnold, 1999), at 5.

[52] M Judson, above n 28, at 127.

[53] See J Guy, 'The Origins of the Petition of Right Reconsidered' (1982) 25 *Historical Journal* 289.

[54] *Ibid*, at 292.

record in the Crown Office and was shocked to discover that, erroneously, the report of the case had been recorded as having been a judgment (which would offer the Crown a precedent) and not a mere rule of court.[55] Selden was outraged and brought the matter to the attention of the Commons, whose resolve was hardened by Selden's discovery.[56] The Commons insisted that the king had no right to discretionary imprisonment 'in any circumstances'—a tough line indeed.[57] Charles sought to smooth the Commons' ruffled feathers by reassuring the House that they should—and could—trust him to abide by the rule of law. But it was Selden's discovery, more than any other single factor, which prevented the Commons from accepting the king's assurances. In May 1628 the speaker of the Commons, Finch, informed the king that the Commons did in fact trust him, but that since illegal acts had been committed by his ministers, nothing short of a public remedy would suffice.[58] Ideally, the Commons wanted legislation to this effect, but in the end it had to settle for a petition—the Petition of Right.[59]

The Petition of Right dealt with a series of parliamentary concerns: forced loans, billeting and martial law were all addressed in its text. But the dominant issue was discretionary imprisonment, and of all the concerns addressed in the Petition this was the one which the king most keenly felt, as this was the subject which he knew 'most closely touched his prerogative.'[60] The Commons felt that the judges who had decided the *Five Knights' Case* had lost sight of the fundamentals of English law, enshrined in numerous statutes but most clearly expressed in Magna Carta, which provides: 'no freeman shall be taken or imprisoned . . . but by the lawful judgment of his peers or by the law of the land'.[61] This, perhaps the key provision of Magna Carta, was reproduced in paragraph III of the Petition along with Parliament's insistence that the recent imprisonment of diverse of the king's subjects without cause shown should cease immediately.

Paragraph I of the Petition was concerned with impositions and the forced loan. It provided that 'no tallage or aid should be laid or levied by the king . . . without the good will and assent . . . and by authority of Parliament'. It further provided that 'from henceforth no person should be compelled to make any

---

[55] *Ibid*, at 311.

[56] Selden's outrage concerned the Crown's attempt to *pervert* the record. There was nothing exceptional in the government having a role in settling the record: what was exercising Selden was its abuse of that role: see M Kishlansky, 'Tyranny Denied: Charles I, Attorney General Heath, and the Five Knights' Case' (1999) 42 *Historical Journal* 53, at 67.

[57] J Guy, above n 53, at 299–305.

[58] *Ibid*, at 307.

[59] See generally, E Foster, 'Petitions and the Petition of Right' (1974) 14 *Journal of British Studies* 21 and J Reeve, 'The Legal Status of the Petition of Right' (1986) 29 *Historical Journal* 257.

[60] J Guy, above n 53, at 291.

[61] Magna Carta 1297, cap 29.

loans to the king against his will' and that 'none should be charged by any charge or imposition'. It concluded that no-one should be 'compelled to contribute to any tax, tallage, aid or other like charge not set by common consent in Parliament'.[62] This reversed the result not only of the *Five Knights' Case*, but also of course of *Bate's Case*.

The Petition of Right was the inspiration principally of the House of Commons, and particularly of a number of radical leaders, including John Pym, John Eliot and John Selden. We saw above that what Skinner has referred to as the 'neo-Roman' argument about freedom featured in the parliamentary debates in 1610 on impositions. These arguments were repeated and amplified in the debates of 1628. Skinner cites interventions from numerous members of the Commons, including Eliot, in which it was urged that the very existence—let alone the exercise—of prerogative powers such as the forced loan and discretionary imprisonment reduced the Commons and its members to a state of slavery.[63] As in 1610 so too in 1628, however, this neo-Roman argument was not the only one voiced in the Commons. While (as we shall see) it was to become ever more dominant in the parliaments of the early 1640s, in 1628 the neo-Roman argument had yet to achieve the influence it was later to wield.

Another of the Commons' leaders in the 1628 parliament was the common lawyer Sir Edward Coke. Coke, it will be recalled, had been an active member of the privy council in the early 1620s. James I eventually lost patience with him in 1621, and Coke was even imprisoned for a few months in 1622. By 1628 he had become a leading parliamentarian. It is from his contributions as a parliamentarian in the debates of 1628 that much of Coke's subsequent reputation has been derived. Coke's position in the debates of 1628 and in his contributions to the drafting of the Petition of Right was not to show, along neo-Roman lines, that the existence of the prerogative rendered the Commons unfree, but that the common law judges in cases such as the *Five Knights' Case* had got the law wrong. For him and for the bulk of the Commons the Petition of Right was not a statement of neo-Roman freedom, but a restatement of what the common law truly was. We should always be careful to distinguish Coke's contribution as a member of the Commons from his contribution as a judge. This was a point which was brilliantly made in the Commons in 1628 by the then Solicitor-General, Shelton. Coke had made a long speech to the effect that there was neither precedent, law nor reason to allow the king to detain without showing cause. The Solicitor-General

---

[62] Other passages of special note in the Petition include paragraph VI which concerned billeting, and paragraph VII which concerned martial law.

[63] See Q Skinner, 'Politics of Slavery', above n 40, at 290–91 and 'Classical Liberty', above n 40, at 321–22.

then spoke in reply to Coke. This was, as Mark Kishlansky has described it, Shelton's 'finest moment'. Shelton explained that he had uncovered just such a precedent to uphold the royal prerogative. As Kishlansky tells the story:

> it was clear, unambiguous, and came with impeccable pedigree having been given in King's Bench in the thirteenth year of the reign of James I. The report of the case not only specified that the prisoners had been denied bail on review of a writ by special command but also quoted one of the judges as saying: 'if the privy council commit one, he is not bailable by any court of justice'. That judge was Sir Edward Coke.[64]

When the Petition was presented to the king his first answer was evasive. He did not accept the Petition as such but merely stated that: 'The king willeth that right be done according to the laws and customs of the realm; and that the statutes be put in due execution, that his subjects may have no cause to complain of any wrong or oppressions, contrary to their just rights and liberties, to the preservation whereof he holds himself as well obliged as of his prerogative.'[65] The Commons was not satisfied with this and refused to confirm its grant of supply until, five days later, Charles gave a second answer using the conventional formula for consent to a petition: '*soit droit fait comme est désiré*.' However, Charles' subsequent behaviour undid much of the good that his acceptance of the Petition might otherwise have achieved. The Petition was entered as a statute on the Parliament Roll, but Charles ordered his unsatisfactory first answer to be printed alongside his formal assent. This was a 'deliberate bid to cause uncertainty'[66] about whether the Petition had the force of law and resulted in the majority of common law judges disregarding the Petition in future years, most notoriously (as we shall see) in the *Ship-money Case*. Even after the Petition of Right the common law courts remained unprepared to 'forsake their traditional role as servants of the Crown, comfortable and honourable, for the hazardous demagogic role of arbiters between Crown and Parliament.'[67]

Parliamentary Privilege and *Eliot's Case*

On 2 March 1629 there was what Maitland rather euphemistically described as a 'disorderly scene' in the House of Commons.[68] The speaker had the king's command to adjourn the House. Eliot wished to read a remonstrance

---

[64] M Kishlansky, above n 56, at 73.
[65] See D Smith, above n 51, at 117.
[66] *Ibid.*
[67] J Kenyon, above n 25, at 89.
[68] F Maitland, above n 15, at 314.

against the taking of tonnage and poundage without parliamentary sanction. The speaker was forcibly held down in his chair to prevent him from adjourning, so as to enable Eliot to speak. Later that day the king proclaimed that he would dissolve Parliament forthwith. On the following day the king incarcerated seven members: Sir John Eliot, Sir Miles Hobart, Denzil Holles, Walter Long, John Selden, William Strode, and Benjamin Valentine. This was a 'remarkable resort to physical restraint by Charles in attempting to coerce his critics into submission'.[69]

The seven brought a writ for habeas corpus. The king's response cited the cause for arrest, as was now required by the Petition of Right. The members, it was stated, had been arrested for 'notable contempts and for stirring sedition'. The judges of the King's Bench reported to Charles that they were legally obliged to bail the prisoners. Upon hearing this the king moved the seven to the Tower—the royal prison—placing them by his own warrant in the custody of the lieutenant. Counsel for the prisoners requested the opinion of the court on the lawfulness of the detention, but the judges refused to hear the case as, they said, it would have been to no purpose: 'the prisoners could not be bailed, delivered, or remanded'.[70] The seven remained in the Tower during the summer of 1629, without legal redress. After the long vacation, the king offered the prisoners 'bail by letters patent, requiring also a bond of good behaviour, as an act of the royal prerogative.'[71] The prisoners refused this offer. The following year, the Attorney-General brought criminal charges against Eliot (for words spoken in the House)[72] and against Holles and Valentine (for tumult in the House).[73] The defendants argued that as the alleged offences had taken place in the House of Commons, they ought not to answer for them in another court. The judges disagreed, holding in the words of Lord Chief Justice Hyde that 'an offence committed in Parliament, criminally or contemptuously, the Parliament being ended, rests punishable in another court.'[74] The defendants were found guilty of sedition. They were heavily fined and 'imprisoned until they submitted and acknowledged their offences.'[75] When the Long Parliament met eleven years later the Commons

---

[69] J Reeve, 'The Arguments in King's Bench in 1629 Concerning the Imprisonment of John Selden and other Members of the House of Commons' (1986) 25 *Journal of British Studies* 264, at 265.

[70] J Reeve, *ibid*, at 284. See 3 St Tr 286.

[71] J Reeve, *ibid*.

[72] The charge against Eliot was that he had 'publicly and maliciously in the House of Commons, to raise sedition between the king, his nobles, and people, uttered these words: "that the Council and judges had all conspired to trample under foot the liberties of the subjects"'. See 3 St Tr 293.

[73] (1630) 3 St Tr 293.

[74] 3 St Tr 294. Justices Doderidge, Jones and Whitlock agreed with Lord Hyde.

[75] J Reeve, above n 69, at 285.

condemned the proceedings against these men as illegal and against the privilege of Parliament and awarded compensation.[76] By then Holles had escaped and Eliot had died (in the Tower in 1632). Valentine was released in 1640.[77]

Ship-money: *R v Hampden*

After the dissolution of March 1629 Charles was not to call another Parliament until 1640, and even then he did so only with the utmost reluctance. During the 1630s the king's need for money was as great as ever, although—obviously—any sums he was to raise by way of taxation would have to be without parliamentary consent. In 1634 the king resolved that he needed a navy in order, ostensibly, to protect trade. He issued a writ requiring ports to provide ships which were fully equipped. The king consulted his judges on the legality of the writ, and the judges unsurprisingly obliged by confirming its legality. The following year a further writ was issued but this one, significantly bolder, extended not only to the seaports and to the maritime counties but also to the inland counties. This was a novelty: while ship-money had frequently been levied on seaports, it had never previously been levied on inland counties—except once, and that unsuccessfully, in 1628.[78]

The king's increasing demands met with considerable resistance, and with good reason: ship-money was traditionally regarded as a tax on the profits of the maritime trade. As the gentry of inland counties did not tend to share in these profits, why should they be required to pay the tax? Charles turned once again to his judges, who reconfirmed the legality of the king's policy, even in its extended form. The judges stated that, as Craig summarises it, 'the king was the guardian of the country's safety, that this empowered him to raise money for the defence of the kingdom, and that the king was the sole judge as to the best manner of providing for such defence.'[79] Finally in 1636 a third ship-money writ was issued, but with one essential difference: no longer was it possible to pretend that the writs were being issued to meet a war-emergency. As Tanner put it, 'it now became obvious, even to the most

---

[76] *Ibid.* See 3 St Tr 310–15.

[77] Of the other four, Selden and Hobart were freed in 1631, Strode remained in prison until 1640, and it is unclear what happened to Long—he was still in prison in 1632, but when he was released is uncertain—he was a member of the Long Parliament in 1640: see J Reeve, *ibid*, at 285.

[78] See DL Keir, 'The Case of Ship-Money' (1936) 52 *Law Quarterly Review* 546, at 555. For the history of ship-money prior to the seventeenth century, see W Holdsworth, 'The Power of the Crown to Requisition British Ships in a National Emergency' (1919) 35 *Law Quarterly Review* 12.

[79] P Craig, above n 7, at 70.

charitable critics of the king's policy, that ship-money was fast becoming a permanent tax.'[80]

John Hampden refused to pay the amount which had been levied on him by the sheriff of Buckinghamshire (a landlocked county), and he was prosecuted. His case was heard by all twelve common law judges, the majority of whom held for the Crown.[81] On one analysis, the question in the *Ship-money Case* was in essence the same as that in *Bate's Case* and in the *Five Knights' Case*: namely, what was the extent of the king's discretionary power to act for the public good? In *Hampden's Case*, 'the majority of the judges held that statutes protecting the subject's property must be read and interpreted with reference to this power, rather than allowed to override it.'[82] Moreover (and here lay the great weakness in the majority's position) the judges 'failed to find any limit to the use of this power except the belief that the king would use it *bona fide*.'[83] Just in case there had been any lingering doubt about the effectiveness of the common law as a bulwark against the arbitrary powers of the Crown, 'the case of ship-money finally wrecked the reputation of the bench'.[84] As even Clarendon expressed it, the judges declared ship-money to be lawful 'upon such grounds and reasons as every stander-by was able to swear was not law.'[85]

Of the twelve judges, seven supported the king. However, any account of the case which assumed that this was a narrow victory, or that five dissenters supported Hampden, would be sorely mistaken. As Keir correctly argued,

> the familiar statement that the Court of Exchequer Chamber had been almost evenly divided, seven being for the king and five for Hampden, obscures the important fact that nine of the twelve had no doubt that ship-money was a legitimate charge on the subject, a tenth expressed no opinion on this issue and decided only on a technical point for Hampden, and [only] two . . . found for him on the main question.[86]

---

[80] JR Tanner, above n 43, at 77.

[81] The case is extensively reported at (1637) 3 St Tr 825–1316. For commentary, see generally DL Keir, above n 78 and W Jones, *Politics and the Bench: The Judges and the Origins of the English Civil War* (London, Allen and Unwin, 1971), at 123–30.

[82] DL Keir, *ibid*, at 548.

[83] *Ibid*, at 550.

[84] J Kenyon, above n 25, at 90.

[85] Edward Hyde, Earl of Clarendon, *History of the Rebellion*, cited by JR Tanner, above n 43, at 78. This was the verdict of an ardent royalist, it should not be forgotten: Clarendon was the future Charles II's 'most trusted adviser' (*Dictionary of National Biography*) during the interregnum, and following the restoration became Lord Chancellor. His *History of the Rebellion*, composed in part between 1646 and 1648, but mainly after 1667, was the first major history of the period, and was first published in Oxford in 1702–04.

[86] DL Keir, above n 78, at 546.

These two, Hutton and Croke, were the only judges in the case to speak 'decidedly against the king.'[87] Yet Hampden's argument in the case could hardly be described as having been extreme: indeed, his lawyers had conceded a great deal to the royalists. They admitted, for example, that 'the king possessed as part of his general-welfare power the power of defence, that he alone could judge when his kingdom was in danger, and that "means of defence" were in his hands.'[88] Thus, Hampden's argument was not that the king did not possess discretionary powers, but rather that in exercising them he must do so lawfully. Even this relatively moderate argument, however, was too much for the overwhelmingly royalist judges.

Sir Robert Berkeley, a judge of the King's Bench, delivered one of the most outspoken judgments in the case. Hampden's counsel, in Berkeley's words, had argued that it was a 'fundamental policy in the creation of the frame of this kingdom, that in case the monarch of England should be inclined to exact from his subjects at his pleasure he should be restrained, for that he could have nothing from them, but upon a common consent of Parliament.' Berkeley's response was blunt. He described Hampden's argument as being 'utterly mistaken'. This 'fancied policy,' he exclaimed, 'I utterly deny. The law knows no such king-yoking policy. The law is of itself an old and trusty servant of the king's.'[89] For Berkeley, the king and the law were one and the same: 'I never read nor heard that Lex was Rex; but it is common and most true, that Rex is Lex, for he is a "lex loquens"; a living, a speaking, an acting law.'[90] Sir John Finch, the Chief Justice of the Court of Common Pleas (and formerly the speaker of the House of Commons in the 1628 parliament) delivered a judgment which was truly shocking to parliamentarians and which flatly contradicted the Petition of Right. Finch declared that 'acts of Parliament to take away his royal power in the defence of the kingdom are void; they are void acts of Parliament to bind the king not to command the subjects, their persons and goods, and I say their money too; for no acts of Parliament make any difference'.[91]

What did the royalist judges think Parliament was for? Berkeley ruled that its proper function was for peers and commons to 'shew the estate of every part of the kingdom; . . . make known their grievances (if there be any) to their sovereign, and humbly petition him for redress'.[92] In his view, granting supply was 'not merely a benevolence of the people, but . . . an act of justice

[87]   F Maitland, above n 15, at 308.
[88]   M Judson, above n 28, at 270.
[89]   See 3 St Tr 1098.
[90]   *Ibid.*
[91]   See 3 St Tr 1235.
[92]   See 3 St Tr 1098.

and duty to the king.'[93] As Judson put it, 'to the royalists, Parliament was the king's council, meeting when the king called it, dispersing when he dissolved it, and, when it was in session, granting the taxes and passing the laws which the monarch in his great wisdom deemed necessary.'[94] Needless to say, when Parliament was allowed to meet again it took a completely different view. By an Act of the Long Parliament passed in August 1641 the judgment in *R v Hampden* was pronounced void, the writs for the collection of ship-money were declared unlawful, and Berkeley and Finch were impeached.

Before we leave ship-money, let us briefly return to the argument we considered at the beginning of this chapter: namely, the suggestion as put by Paul Craig that, far from demonstrating the failure of the common law constitution, the early seventeenth century should be seen as a moment of common law triumph, as the moment at which the common law courts showed that in disputes between the Crown and Parliament, they would 'consistently back Parliament'. How does this interpretation account for a case such as *Hampden's Case*? In discussing the case Craig concedes, as he must, that the Crown 'emerged victorious in these legal disputes' but insists that this 'should not serve to mask the fact that . . . the victory was premised on the ground that the exercise of the power in question could properly be regarded as within the bounds of the prerogative.'[95] This may be true, but it is hard to see how it meets the point. The judges held that the law grants to the king the discretionary power which he had exercised. This is a very long way indeed from the court showing support for or backing Parliament's claims. The reality is that by 1637 'the discord between legislature and judiciary could hardly have been more complete.'[96] In the eyes of the common law, not only had ship-money become a regular tax but, moreover, 'the power of legislation had been usurped from king and Parliament by the king and the judges.'[97]

Craig goes on to state that, in any case, 'Parliament ultimately won'. We know that this is true, of course, as the result of the *Ship-money Case* was indeed reversed by statute, but the point is that this was a battle which Parliament won *despite* the courts, not *because of* them. As Maitland put it, 'the contest was . . . between the sovereignty of a king, and the sovereignty of a king in Parliament. We know how the contest was decided—by Civil War and revolution.'[98] Indeed, by parliamentary and military might: not through judicial review. Contrary to Craig's view, by the 1640s the parliamentary leaders knew

[93]   See 3 St Tr 1099.
[94]   M Judson, above n 28, at 149.
[95]   P Craig, above n 7, at 71.
[96]   DL Keir, above n 78, at 546.
[97]   W Jones, above n 81, at 129.
[98]   F Maitland, above n 15, at 300.

that the common law courts would be always against them. Indeed, when Parliament was finally recalled in 1640 'almost its first order of business was to impeach and imprison those members of the common law bench whom they felt had been complicitous in the king's unconstitutional policies'.[99] Far from the courts consistently backing Parliament, the reality of the common law constitution—and the reason for its failure—was that, as Coke himself explained it in the House of Commons in 1628, 'in a doubtful thing, interpretation goes always for the king.'[100]

II THE RISE OF THE REPUBLICAN CONSTITUTION

The Development of the Neo-Roman Case

Whereas in the 1628 parliament the majority view had been that it was the judicial interpretation of the common law rather than the law itself that needed correction, by 1640 a remarkable transformation began to occur. The 'neo-Roman' argument that had been voiced by a handful of parliamentarians in 1610 and 1628 started to come centre-stage as the Commons realised that what was required was not a re-interpretation of old law but new, parliamentary law to replace the old and manifestly inadequate law of the common law courts. Those courts had shown, over and again, that for whatever reason they were either unable or unwilling to do the job of checking the unconstitutional actions and decisions of the king's government. Parliament had tried to help, with the Petition of Right setting out an authoritative statement that could have been used by the courts to assist them in their task. But *Hampden's Case* showed that such a strategy was doomed.

Parliament quickly got to work on seeking to right the constitutional wrongs of the near past. It possessed two main weapons, and both were pressed into service with some urgency. The first was impeachment. All the leading architects of the 'personal rule', those who had shaped and directed government policy in years since 1629, came within Parliament's sights. The first target was the biggest: Thomas Wentworth, the Earl of Strafford, the leading politician of the personal rule and symbol of Caroline government. He was charged with treason and was sent to the Tower to await trial. While the king at first tried to save him, it proved an impossible task and Strafford was executed in 1641. Parliament moved also against Laud, the Archbishop

---

[99] J Hart, above n 13, at 72.
[100] Sir Edward Coke, House of Commons, 6 July 1628. Cited by M Judson, above n 28, at 264.

of Canterbury, against numerous bishops, against the king's political advisers and against several of the common law judges who had decided *Hampden's Case*.[101]

Parliament's second weapon was legislation. If impeachment was designed to remove the architects of the personal rule, the legislation of the Long Parliament was designed to destroy its very foundations. A Triennial Act was passed in February 1641, requiring the king to call a Parliament at least once every three years. The Court of Star-chamber was abolished by an Act of July 1641, as was the Court of High Commission. Ship-money was abolished and its future collection declared illegal by an Act passed in August 1641.[102] The effect of this legislation should not be under-estimated. It transformed the face of English government. The Triennial Act curtailed one of the monarch's oldest and most important prerogative powers—the power to decide when, indeed whether, to call a Parliament. It provided that no Parliament could be dissolved or prorogued within fifty days of its first meeting without the consent of both Houses and it provided for machinery whereby a Parliament could be assembled even if the Crown neglected to summon it after the three-year period had elapsed. The Act was repealed after the restoration in 1660 and there was one four-year period at the end of Charles II's reign in which no Parliament was called. But a new Triennial Act was passed in 1694, since which time there has been a Parliament every year. The other 1641 constitutional legislation has remained in force ever since it was passed. Neither Star-chamber, nor the Court of High Commission, nor ship-money have ever been revived, even temporarily.[103]

As Parliament was no longer trying to mend the common law but was instead seeking to make what amounted to a new legal order, its legislation required a source of legitimacy. From 1640 on, that source came increasingly from the neo-Roman, or republican, argument about freedom. The references to and growing reliance upon that argument in the period between the recall of Parliament in April 1640 and the outbreak of the Civil War in August 1642 have been traced in two important essays by Quentin Skinner.[104] Skinner considers the use of the neo-Roman argument both within the Commons and beyond it, particularly in the large number of political tracts and pamphlets that were published and circulated at this time. Among the

---

[101] For an overview, see J Hart, above n 13, at 176–82. For more extensive treatment, esp of the impeachments of Strafford and Laud, see DA Orr, *Treason and the State: Law, Politics and Ideology in the English Civil War* (Cambridge, Cambridge University Press, 2002), chs 2–4.

[102] For the full texts of these statutes, see SR Gardiner, *Constitutional Documents of the Puritan Revolution, 1625–1660* (Oxford, Clarendon Press, 3rd ed, 1906), at 144, 179, 184 and 189 respectively. For an overview, see J Hart, *ibid*, at 182–88.

[103] On the revolutionary nature of this legislation, see D Cressy, above n 3, esp at 40–42.

[104] See above n 40.

most significant and influential of these was *The Case of Ship-money Briefly Discoursed*, written by Henry Parker and published to coincide with the meeting of the Long Parliament in November 1640.[105] Parker, described as 'the leading pamphleteer in favour of Parliament'[106] at this time, defended not the claim that the prerogative should be brought within the ambit of the common law, but the more ambitious argument that 'the very existence of the prerogative leaves everyone enslaved'.[107] Parker's tract denounced the king's prerogative powers to collect ship-money as being 'incompatible with popular liberty' and as having the effect of turning Englishmen into 'the most despicable slaves in the whole world'.[108]

A strong theme of Parker's tract is the link between property and liberty. Impositions, the forced loan and ship-money each constituted what we would now recognise as various forms of taxation. Prerogative taxation, in Parker's neo-Roman argument, made men not only poorer—a relatively uncontroversial argument—but rendered them also unfree. It was a theme taken up by the Long Parliament, which produced a 'general statement to the effect that we forfeit our freedom whenever our properties are made dependent on the will of the king'.[109] If prerogative powers of taxation could render men unfree, it was but a short step to view further prerogatives of the Crown in the same light. In 1641–42 it was first the prerogative to control the militia and secondly the prerogative of the 'negative voice' (as it was then called—what we now know as the 'royal assent' to legislation) that became most controversial.

The great early-modern theorist of sovereignty, Jean Bodin, listed the control of the militia as one of the indisputable 'marks' of sovereignty.[110] For Parliament to insist, as it did in its Militia Ordinance of March 1642, that the control of the militia should be vested exclusively in persons approved by the two Houses was a direct assault on the king's prerogative authority. When Parliament continued immediately thereafter to suggest that the king had no right to withhold his assent to legislation, it re-doubled its assault. In both instances Parliament sought to justify itself entirely in neo-Roman terms.[111]

---

[105] Reprinted in J Malcolm (ed), *The Struggle for Sovereignty: Seventeenth-Century English Political Tracts* (Indianapolis, Liberty Fund, 1999), at 93–125. On Parker generally, see M Mendle, *Henry Parker and the English Civil War* (Cambridge, Cambridge University Press, 1995).

[106] Q Skinner, 'Politics of Slavery', above n 40, at 293.

[107] *Ibid.*

[108] H Parker, above n 105, at 96 and 108.

[109] Q Skinner, 'Classical Liberty', above n 40, at 324.

[110] See Q Skinner, *ibid*, at 325, citing J Bodin, *Six Livres de la République* [1576]. For a modern English edition, see J Bodin, *On Sovereignty* (ed J Franklin, Cambridge, Cambridge University Press, 1992).

[111] Q Skinner, 'Classical Liberty', above n 40, at 326.

Parliament took its stand squarely on Cicero's fundamental maxim, that *salus populi suprema lex est* (the safety of the people is the supreme law).[112]

Parliament accepted that, in normal political circumstances, England was a mixed monarchy—that the highest legislative authority could be exercised only when king, Lords and Commons act together as the three Estates of the Realm—but insisted that these were not normal circumstances. King Charles, in the view of the majority in Parliament, had been seduced by a 'malignant party', whose advice to him amounted to an attempt to destroy the English constitution by subverting its fundamental laws, and whose leading members, as we have seen, Parliament now impeached. He had ruled for eleven years without calling Parliament, he had issued the forced loan and the writs for ship-money, he had raised an army in Ireland that Parliament feared could be used to destroy English liberty, he had sought peace rather than war with Catholic Spain and in his domestic religious policy he had licensed Arminian books, persecuted puritans, extended the jurisdiction of the ecclesiastical courts and forced an Anglican liturgy on Scotland.[113] All of these the majority in Parliament vehemently opposed. In short, this was an emergency, such that the mixed monarchy could no longer be sustained. The king had become 'incapable of recognising the gravity of the situation', so completely had he become 'hoodwinked by the malignant party':

> Given this predicament, with one of the three Estates effectively disabled from pursuing the public good, it [became] the positive duty of the other two Estates to act together in the name of *salus populi*, even if this involve[d] defying the sadly misguided king.[114]

Thus did Parliament arrive in early 1642 at its revolutionary conclusion that, at least in an emergency, the highest legislative authority was vested not in the King-in-Parliament but in Parliament alone.

The Emergence of Republican Accountability

In June 1642 Parliament ordered to be printed one of the most important constitutional documents of the period immediately preceding the outbreak of the Civil War, its *Nineteen Propositions*.[115] In this document Parliament set out its vision of how to rescue the constitution from the evils of the malignant party. It opened by insisting that all members of the privy council

---

[112] Q Skinner, 'Classical Liberty', above n 40, at 326.

[113] See C Roberts, above n 2, at 79–80.

[114] Q Skinner, 'Classical Liberty', above n 40, at 329.

[115] Reprinted in SR Gardiner, above n 102, at 249–54 and in J Malcolm, above n 105, at 145–78. Malcolm's edition includes also the king's *Answer to the Nineteen Propositions*.

should be expelled from it save for those expressly approved of by Parliament. Replacements for those expelled should be similarly subject to parliamentary approval. The second proposition sought to end the possibility of a return to government without Parliament, by insisting that 'the great affairs of the kingdom . . . may be debated, resolved and transacted only in Parliament, and not elsewhere'. It continued that anyone seeking to govern without Parliament shall be subject to Parliament's 'censure and judgment'. The third proposition concerned judicial and ministerial appointments, requiring that ministers and senior judges be appointed only with the 'approbation of both Houses of Parliament'. Proposition 11 required all privy councillors and judges to take an oath 'for the maintaining of the Petition of Right'. Further propositions concerned the education of the king's children, royal marriages and exclusion of Catholics from government office, all designed to secure Protestant government, free from Catholic influence. A final incursion into the prerogative was made by proposition 17, which concerned foreign policy. It directed the king to enter into 'a more strict alliance' with the (Protestant) United Provinces 'for the defence and maintenance' of the Protestant religion 'against all designs and attempts of the Pope and his adherents to subvert and suppress it'.

The importance of the *Nineteen Propositions* for our purposes is twofold. Its first importance lies in its striking articulation of the principles and requirements of what we now call ministerial responsibility. The *Nineteen Propositions* contain the first clear parliamentary statement of the core idea of republican constitutional design: namely, the doctrine of responsible government. All of the doctrine's ingredients are there: the appointment of government personnel is subject to parliamentary approval; once in office government personnel are removable at the instigation of Parliament; and the course and conduct of government policy—both domestic and foreign—are matters that are ultimately to be determined by, and may at any point be changed by, Parliament.

King Charles famously answered the *Nineteen Propositions*. His *Answer*, drafted on his behalf by Viscount Falkland and Sir John Colepeper and issued on 18 June, is an extraordinary document. In it, the king set out a constitutional vision quite at odds with the conventional royalist line. The usual royalist position in the early seventeenth century had been that kings ruled by divine right. This was the view that Charles' father had set out in his *Trew Law of Free Monarchies* of 1598. According to the *Trew Law* 'the king is above the law, as both the author and giver of strength thereto'. Although 'a good king will frame all his actions to be according to the law, yet is he not bound thereto but of his good will'.[116] The king is accountable only to God and to

---

[116] James VI and I, 'The Trew Law of Free Monarchies' [1598], in James VI and I, *Political Writings* (ed J Sommerville, Cambridge, Cambridge University Press, 1995), at 75.

his conscience. Under no circumstances is he accountable to any earthly authority.

In stark contrast to the *Trew Law*, Charles' *Answer to the Nineteen Propositions* presented the monarchy as one of three apparently equal estates, alongside Lords and Commons in the constitutional hierarchy. The *Answer* was based not on the divine right of kings, but on an altogether different constitutional theory, derived from the second-century BCE Greek historian of ancient Rome, Polybius. According to Polybius,

> Kingship, the earliest government, inevitably becomes corrupt and passes into tyranny. The best men in the community then unseat the tyrant and institute an aristocracy. But their descendants are corrupted by the opportunity to gratify their desires and so become oligarchs. Thereupon the community overthrows the oligarchy and institutes a democracy. Next, the people are debauched by evil leaders, and the collapse of the society brings in a monarch once more.[117]

For Polybius, the only way out of this vicious circle was to mix monarchy with elements of aristocracy and democracy. Whereas each of the three forms alone tends to corrupt, in combination they may achieve stability—indeed, in Polybian theory to combine the three is the only way to achieve stable government. The king's *Answer to the Nineteen Propositions* sought to apply Polybian theory to the English constitution. It argued that:

> The ill of absolute monarchy is tyranny, the ill of aristocracy is faction and division, the ills of democracy are tumults, violence and licentiousness. The good of monarchy is the uniting of a nation under one head, to resist invasion from abroad and insurrection at home. The good of aristocracy is the conjunction of counsel in the ablest persons of a state for the public benefit. The good of democracy is liberty and the courage and industry which liberty begets. In this kingdom the laws are jointly made by a king, by a House of Peers, and by a House of Commons chosen by the people, all having free votes and particular privileges.[118]

The *Answer* sought to defend the king's role in the legislative process, rebutting the attack on the prerogative of the negative voice that had followed the controversy over the Militia Ordinance. In doing so, however, it made extraordinary concessions to the parliamentarian argument. Indeed, Pocock has argued that by reducing the king to a mere estate of the realm, the *Answer* can be seen in 'the most paradoxical of lights, as the introduction by Charles I's

---

[117] FD Wormuth, *The Origins of Modern Constitutionalism* (New York, Harper Bros, 1949), at 22. On Polybius, see FW Walbank, *Polybius* (Berkeley, University of California Press, 1972).

[118] J Malcolm, above n 105, at 168. For discussion, see CC Weston, *English Constitutional Theory and the House of Lords, 1556–1832* (London, Routledge, 1965) and A Fukuda, *Sovereignty and the Sword: Harrington, Hobbes, and Mixed Government in the English Civil War* (Oxford, Clarendon Press, 1997).

counsellors of a republican component' into ostensibly royalist constitutional thinking.[119]

Pocock's suggestion is arresting but we do not have to accept it to see that the 'republican component' was pushed much further by the parliamentarians than it was by the likes of Falkland and Colepeper. The *Answer's* use of the Polybian language of mixed monarchy is concerned primarily with balance. That is, it is concerned with a sense of the representation of each of the three estates within society (monarchy, aristocracy and commoners). Its aims were stability, internal peace and unity and the prevention of collapse into anarchy. As such it was a survival mechanism. It was not designed to make government fairer, more open or more responsive, but simply to make it last a while longer. It sought to address not the quality or the accountability of government, but its durability. The parliamentarians, on the other hand, *were* concerned with the quality and accountability of government—hence the emergence, indeed the prominence, of republican notions of ministerial responsibility and responsible government in the *Nineteen Propositions*.

The second importance of the *Nineteen Propositions* and of the king's *Answer* brings us back to Henry Parker. We encountered above Parker's first great political intervention, his tract on the case of ship-money, published in 1640. His second was the publication of his *Observations upon some of His Majesty's late Answers*, which first appeared in July 1642 and can be regarded as 'a semi-official statement of Parliament's case'.[120] The *Observations* return to the second great republican theme at work in the summer of 1642 and remind us that, alongside the republican concern for responsible government lay the neo-Roman argument about freedom. Parker's *Observations* constituted the most sophisticated demolition of Charles I's defence of his legislative role (that is, his prerogative of the negative voice). Parker's argument was that:

> If this prerogative . . . is indeed pivotal to the operation of the mixed constitution, then we cannot speak of the English as a free nation at all. The effect of the negative voice is to take away the liberty not merely of individual subjects but of the people as a whole. It converts the English from a free people into a nation of slaves.[121]

After the publication of Parker's *Observations* the neo-Roman argument about freedom was more and more confidently taken up in the parliamentary cause against the king. It can be seen in parliamentary Declarations

---

[119] See JGA Pocock, *The Ancient Constitution and the Feudal Law: A Study of English Historical Thought in the Seventeenth Century: A Reissue with a Retrospect* (Cambridge, Cambridge University Press, 1987), at 309.

[120] See A Cromartie, above n 4, at 81.

[121] See Q Skinner, 'Classical Liberty', above n 40, at 335.

issued throughout July and August 1642 as well as in a series of political tracts and pamphlets published at the same time.[122]

Civil War, Commonwealth and Protectorate

By the end of August England was at Civil War, with the king having raised his standard at Nottingham on 22 August to symbolise the formal commencement of hostilities. After several years of fighting the war was won by Parliament's New Model Army, led by Oliver Cromwell, Thomas Fairfax and Henry Ireton. The king was executed in January 1649, the House of Lords was abolished two months later and the Commons, purged since the end of 1648 of those members who had opposed the army's line, ruled alone, albeit that the army was never far from its thoughts. England was, for the first and thus far the only time in its history, a formal republic, known by the seventeenth-century English translation of the word, 'Commonwealth'.[123] It was not to last. The Commonwealth survived only until 1653 when it was replaced under Cromwell's leadership with what amounted to a religious and military dictatorship, known as the Protectorate.[124] The Protectorate governed Britain[125] for the remainder of Cromwell's life. He died in September 1658. Less than two years later Charles II, son of Charles I, was restored to the throne and the nation has remained a monarchy ever since.[126]

The period between the execution of Charles I in 1649 and the restoration of Charles II in 1660 witnessed both an explosion of republican writing and a series of constitutional experiments. There was little connection between the two, however. Certainly Cromwell's *Instrument of Government*—the constitution of the Protectorate—contained little of which a republican could approve, elevating as it did the authority (including the law-making authority) of one man over that of the representative.[127] The fact that the one man styled himself Protector rather than King made little difference to those who had sought—and indeed fought for—'national liberation from servitude'.[128]

---

[122] See Q Skinner, 'Classical Liberty', above n 40, at 338–42.

[123] The leading study is B Worden, *The Rump Parliament, 1648–1653* (Cambridge, Cambridge University Press, 1974).

[124] See A Woolrych, *Commonwealth to Protectorate* (Oxford, Clarendon Press, 1982).

[125] Britain was formed through a Union of England and Scotland in 1654. Upon the restoration of Charles II the Union was dissolved and until 1707 the two nations reverted to their pre-war status as separate states, albeit sharing the same monarch, as they had between 1603 and 1649. Scotland is considered in more detail below.

[126] For a detailed study, see R Hutton, *The Restoration: A Political and Religious History of England and Wales, 1658–1667* (Oxford, Oxford University Press, 1985).

[127] For the text, see SR Gardiner, above n 102, at 405–17.

[128] Q Skinner, 'Classical Liberty', above n 40, at 343: see ch 2 above at 56.

The republican writing of the 1650s came in two varieties. First there were the tracts and polemics that sought to justify the regicide and to clothe the new regime with some form of legitimacy. This was the task undertaken by Milton in his *Tenure of Kings and Magistrates* of 1648 and by Marchamont Nedham in his newspaper editorials.[129] The more substantial republican writing of the time, however, was designed not to support the new regime but to criticise it. The collapse of the Commonwealth and its replacement by the Protectorate was roundly condemned by republicans such as Harrington. For them, as we saw in the previous chapter, the all-important distinction was that between a government whose authority was imposed from above and a system of self-government. Cromwell's Protectorate was unambiguously an example of the former and not of the latter.

Little time will be spent here on the details of either Cromwellian government or the republican critique of it. Our principal concern is with the influence of republican thought and action on the making of the British constitution as it is, not as it would have been had Cromwell lived longer or had his *Instrument of Government* developed into a lasting settlement. For better or for worse, few of the institutional innovations of the 1650s were able to make an impression on subsequent constitutional practice. When Charles II was restored to the throne in 1660 all the constitutional arrangements that had been put in place since 1642 were simply swept aside. This is not to say, however, that all of the constitutional *thinking* of the period was immediately lost. While the *institutions* of the Commonwealth and Protectorate did not survive into the restoration period, some of the ideas developed in the political writing of the time exerted considerable influence on the shaping of the constitution after 1660. Indeed, notions of the separation of powers and of executive accountability to Parliament were among the 'most enduring legacies of the Commonwealth period. Englishmen never again placed the executive power immediately in Parliament. Yet they never ceased criticising in Parliament those to whom the king entrusted it.'[130]

The Restoration of the Republican Constitution

What was restored in 1660 was more than the Stuart line. What was restored was the constitution as the Long Parliament had amended it in 1641. This is an extremely important point: what was restored in 1660 was not the constitution that James I had come to when he inherited the English Crown in

---

[129] See above, at 53.
[130] C Roberts, above n 2, at 153.

1603. Nor was it the constitution that Charles I and his advisers had sought
to create during the personal rule of the 1630s. What was restored was the
constitution that the Long Parliament had shaped in its ground-breaking legislation of 1640–41. All the reforming legislation that the Long Parliament
had passed in those years remained on the statute book. The victory in the
battle against arbitrary taxation was confirmed as ship-money and the like
remained illegal. Neither the Court of Star-chamber nor the High
Commission were revived. Those of the Crown's feudal rights that had been
abolished by the Long Parliament (such as wardship and certain knighthood
fines) remained abolished.[131] Even the Triennial Act remained, at least to
start with.[132]

Much of what Parliament had gained after 1641, however, was lost, at least
for the time being. Two Militia Acts of 1661 and 1662 restored sole control of
the militia to the Crown, contrary to the Militia Ordinance of 1642.[133] The
king remained able to choose his own ministers, contrary to the *Nineteen
Propositions*. Similarly, he was 'free to determine both foreign and domestic
policy, to appoint all officers of state, and although obliged to consult with
Parliament, he had the power of vetoing legislation and of dispensing individuals from the provisions of parliamentary statutes.'[134] It must be remem-
bered, though, that the king was restored in a blaze of reaction against the later
years of Cromwell's dictatorship. In such a climate it is hardly surprising that
some of the political gains made after 1641 were reversed and that some of the
parliamentary initiative was lost. Such gains 'were not forgotten for long, and
they were not lost permanently.'[135] Some, as we shall see, were not recovered
until 1688 but others were quicker to return. In 1673 Parliament passed a Test
Act, which required all holders of civil and military office to take the Anglican
sacrament and to make a declaration against the Catholic doctrine of transub-
stantiation. As well as providing a considerable restraint on the king's freedom
to choose his own ministers, this Act also had the consequence of exposing
the heir presumptive, the Duke of York, as a Catholic.[136]

[131] See A Woolrych, *Britain in Revolution, 1625–1660* (Oxford, Oxford University Press, 2002), at 66.

[132] This Act was repealed in 1664; there was one four-year period (1681–85) in which no Parliament was called; and it was not until 1694 that an effective mechanism to secure regular Parliaments was again put in place.

[133] However, this may have had more to do with indemnifying officers for actions commit-ted by them on the authority of royal directions after 1660 than it was a reflection of constitu-tional principle that control of the militia belonged properly to the Crown rather than to Parliament: see R Hutton, above n 126, at 155–56.

[134] T Harris, *Politics under the later Stuarts: Party Conflict in a Divided Society, 1660–1715* (Harlow, Longman, 1993), at 34.

[135] A Woolrych, above n 131, at 795.

[136] See T Harris, above n 134, at 56–57. For an edited text of the Act, see J Kenyon, above n 25, at 385. On the Catholicism of the Duke of York (the future King James II), see further below.

Moreover, despite the king's apparent freedom in terms of the direction of policy, he was subject to significant constraint in another dimension: money. As his father's had been, the government of Charles II was desperately short of money. But unlike his father he could not resort to extra-parliamentary forms of taxation. If, after the restoration, Parliament continued to depend more on the king than its predecessors in the 1640s would have considered ideal, so too did the king depend heavily on Parliament. This may have been less the result of a deliberate attempt to shackle the Crown than it was the accident of financial miscalculation[137] but, whatever the cause of it, the fact was that, from the point of restoration on, for the Crown to govern effectively it needed money, for money it depended ever more heavily on grants made by Parliament, and for access to such grants the price to be paid was full co-operation.

Even though the parliamentary cause had lost some ground, the one thing the restoration settlement clearly did not amount to was a clear victory for the royalists. As Hutton has suggested, even by 1662 Charles II would not have felt 'much like a victor', as his religious policy, his desire for a standing army in the provinces, as well as various of his other domestic policies had been defeated by Parliament, on top of which he had become 'the first English monarch since the Middle Ages to be successfully defied by his leading churchmen.' Further, his 'direct power over the community was truncated by the permanent abolition of the prerogative courts' and even his ability to wage war depended on the goodwill of Parliament.[138]

The restoration settlement, then, was a rather uneasy compromise.[139] For a while it worked well enough, with both sides fuelled by a strong desire not to revisit the destruction of the 1640s. But the relatively smooth politics of the 1660s could not last, as various tensions came inevitably to the fore. During the 1670s serious arguments broke out between the Commons and Charles' court over finance, foreign policy, religion and the law. Overshadowing everything were the extensive popular and parliamentary fears of Catholicism and its influence at court.[140] That such fears could sometimes be irrational did not lessen the intensity with which they were felt. Neither did it reduce their extraordinary impact on the polity. When the Great Fire of 1666 wreaked its havoc in London, Catholics were blamed for starting it even though the official line was always that it was an accident. When rumours were fabricated about a 'popish plot' to kill the king and to

---

[137] See T Harris, *ibid*, at 34.

[138] R Hutton, above n 126, at 181.

[139] Roberts has described it as lying in a 'state of unresolved equilibrium': see C Roberts, above n 2, at 139.

[140] See T Harris, above n 134, at 54–57.

massacre thousands of English Protestants, 'such was the paranoia about Catholicism that few English Protestants doubted [their] veracity'.[141]

Charles had no heir, so upon his death the Crown would pass to his brother James, the Duke of York, whose own Catholicism had become public knowledge as a result of the Test Act and whose second wife (whom he married in 1673) was devoutly Catholic. James had two daughters by his first marriage—Mary and Anne—both of whom were Protestants. If, however, he were to have a son by his new wife, the son would leapfrog Mary and Anne in the order of succession. With two Catholic parents he would presumably be raised and educated as a Catholic, introducing the prospect of a never-ending succession of Catholic monarchs. Such was the fear and loathing of popery that significant factions in Parliament grew desperate to exclude the Duke of York from the succession. Those in favour of his exclusion became known as Whigs; those against as Tories. The argument between them, known as the 'exclusion crisis', dominated domestic politics in the final years of Charles II's reign.[142]

The Republican Constitution Threatened

Charles died in 1685 and the Crown duly passed to his brother, who became King James II. James' reign was to last less than four years but despite (or perhaps because of) its brevity, it was to be both memorable and hugely significant in the making of the republican constitution. Its significance lies in the reasons why and in the manner in which his reign came to an abrupt end.

James' views of kingship developed directly from those of his namesake grandfather. For him as for James I the monarchy was a sacred institution: 'its powers and the principle of hereditary succession were, he believed, divinely ordained'.[143] While kings had responsibilities as well as rights over their peoples, for James II such duties were to do God's work—God's work meaning 'the advancement of Catholicism'.[144] Such a theory of kingship ran directly counter to the theory on which the restoration settlement had been based. That theory, closer to the view espoused by Falkland and Colepeper in the *Answer to the Nineteen Propositions*, was that the constitution was a mixed monarchy in which the king, the Lords and the Commons each had an equal role to play. This is an approach to kingship with which James' notions of

---

[141]   *Ibid*, at 80.

[142]   For a good account, see *ibid*, ch 4.

[143]   J Miller, *James II* (New Haven, Yale University Press, 2000), at 124.

[144]   *Ibid*, at 125.

divine right were utterly incompatible, as both he and his political opponents knew well.

During the exclusion crisis, James and his Tory allies had defended his right to succeed to the throne in part on the basis of a tract written many years earlier but not published until 1680. The tract was Sir Robert Filmer's *Patriarcha*, which, along with James I's *Trew Law of Free Monarchies*, became one of the most important and influential defences of divine right theory in the seventeenth century.[145] *Patriarcha* was adopted by James and the Tories as their official manifesto. The significance of its publication cannot be exaggerated, not only because of its re-introduction into English politics of the dreaded theory of divine right, but also (in the longer term) because of the works that were written to oppose its arguments, most notably Algernon Sidney's great republican work, *Discourses concerning Government* and John Locke's *Two Treatises of Government*.[146]

By the time of James' accession, then, the political atmosphere was already heated with fears both religious and constitutional. Not only was there a Catholic on the throne, but his approach to kingship and to government was positively hostile to the delicate compromise of mix and balance on which the restoration settlement had been based. The opening months of his reign confirmed the worst fears of those who had sought to exclude him from the succession, that a Catholic king would mean 'popery and arbitrary government'.[147] From the first, James was determined to promote the interests of Catholics. Among the many instruments he used for this purpose were the always controversial—indeed, the overtly contested—prerogative powers of dispensing with and suspending statute law. And among the statutes in respect of which he was most eager to use such powers, of course, was the Test Act. The Whigs were horrified: so much was only to be expected. But by such tactics the new king managed with alarming rapidity not only to appal his political opponents but also (and much more damagingly) to alienate the Tory Anglicans who had formerly supported him by opposing his exclusion.

As parliamentary support ebbed away from him, James followed in his father's footsteps by turning to the common law courts. What he sought was

---

[145] See R Filmer, *Patriarcha and other Writings* (ed J Sommerville, Cambridge, Cambridge University Press, 1991). For the 'Trew Law' see above, n 116.

[146] Both were written in the early 1680s. Sidney's *Discourses* were first published in 1698, fifteen years after his (wrongful) conviction of and execution for treason. Locke's *Treatises* were first published in 1690. For modern editions, see A Sidney, *Discourses concerning Government* (ed T West, Indianapolis, Liberty Fund, 1996) and J Locke, *Two Treatises of Government* (ed P Laslett, Cambridge, Cambridge University Press, 1960).

[147] A slogan widely used in the 1670s and 80s: see, eg, Andrew Marvell's tract, *An Account of the Growth of Popery and Arbitrary Government in England* [1678]. The Bill of Rights 1689 speaks of William III 'delivering [the] kingdom from popery and arbitrary power'. See further on the Bill of Rights below.

a judicial endorsement of the legality of his use of the dispensing power. By packing the court with judges sympathetic to his cause and by contriving a suitable test case, *Godden v Hales* in 1686,[148] he got the result he wanted, Lord Chief Justice Herbert delivering a judgment that echoed the rampant royalism of Berkeley and his colleagues half a century earlier in *Hampden's Case*. Herbert ruled in sweeping terms, summing up his argument with the following propositions:

> 1. That the kings of England are sovereign princes. 2. That the laws of England are the king's laws. 3. That therefore 'tis an inseparable prerogative in the kings of England to dispense with penal laws in particular cases and upon particular necessary reasons. 4. That of those reasons and those necessities the king himself is sole judge . . . 5. That this is not a trust invested in or granted to the king by the people, but the ancient remains of the sovereign power and prerogative of the kings of England, which never yet was taken away from them, nor can be.[149]

If ever there needed to be a reminder that parliamentarians could not safely rely on the common law courts, here it was. Even though the king was able to secure results such as that in *Godden v Hales* only through dismissing judges who were unsympathetic to his position and by packing the court with his allies, it remained the case in the 1680s as it had been in the 1630s that the common law was largely an instrument of the king's, not of Parliament's.

The controversy of the court's decision in *Godden v Hales* lay less in its holding that there existed a prerogative power of dispensing statute law than in its ruling that James had not abused the power by applying it so liberally. The purpose of the dispensing power was to allow the monarch, as the fountain of justice, to excuse an individual from having to suffer an iniquitous or unjust application of statute, such as in circumstances beyond those that Parliament had had in mind when passing it. It was not designed to allow the monarch unilaterally to bypass significant chunks of statute law simply in order to promote his own religious sensibilities. Yet that is precisely what James had done, and here were his judges upholding the legality of his actions.

While the courts could not be relied on to secure opinions favourable to Parliament, however, neither by the 1680s could they always be safely relied on by the king. That there were limits to the extent that the courts would comply with the constitutionally dubious actions of the Crown was demonstrated by the *Case of the Seven Bishops*.[150] In April 1688 James issued a Declaration of Indulgence, which he ordered to be read in all Anglican

---

[148] *Godden v Hales* (1686) 11 St Tr 1165. For discussion, see AF Havighurst, 'James II and the Twelve Men in Scarlet' (1953) 69 *Law Quarterly Review* 522.

[149] *Ibid*, at 1199.

[150] (1688) 12 St Tr 183.

churches on two successive Sundays. The Declaration expressed James' wish that all his subjects would convert to Catholicism and his 'will and pleasure' that the oaths required by the Test Act 'shall not at any time hereafter be required to be taken'.[151] This amounted to a wholesale suspension of statute law. While there were precedents in favour of (a limited use of) the prerogative of dispensing with statutes in particular cases, the altogether broader prerogative of suspending the laws had never been widely accepted. Indeed, Parliament had several times declared that in its view it was illegal, most notably in 1663 and again in 1673.[152] Nonetheless, James persisted.

The Archbishop of Canterbury and six bishops presented a petition to the king in which they asked him to withdraw the order that his Declaration be read in every Anglican church. The bishops were charged with seditious libel and were tried. Four judges presided at the trial, headed by the Lord Chief Justice, Lord Wright. After Lord Wright had summed up, two of the more junior judges (Powell and Holloway) spoke in the bishops' favour, arguing that English law recognised no prerogative power to suspend the law. Notwithstanding the strong rebuke they received from the Lord Chief Justice for doing so, the interventions of Powell and Holloway appear to have had an impact, as the following day the jury returned verdicts of not guilty.

In June 1688, while the bishops awaited their trial, probably the single most important factor in the downfall of James' reign occurred: his queen gave birth to a son. The prospect of a never-ending Catholic succession had finally materialised. This was the event that all Protestant England now dreaded: not only James' Whig opponents but also the Tory Anglicans, who had been thoroughly alienated by the king's aggressively pro-Catholic policies. The immediate consequence was the despatch of an extraordinary invitation to William of Orange. Seven leading statesmen, representing both Whigs and Tories, invited William to invade England, no less, in order, as they put it, to safeguard her 'liberties and properties'.[153] William, as well as being avowedly Protestant, was married to James' daughter Mary. Politicians suspicious of James had been communicating with William since the late 1670s about the possibility of him forcibly replacing James in order to secure a Protestant succession and Mary's inheritance. The birth of a new Catholic prince may have been the development James' opponents most feared but it was also a contingency in respect of which they had long been planning.

At the end of September William issued a Declaration, effectively accepting the invitation, in which he outlined both the grievances afflicting the

---

[151] For the text, see J Kenyon, above n 25, at 389–91.

[152] See J Miller, above n 143, at 185.

[153] For the text of the invitation, see EN Williams, *The Eighteenth-Century Constitution: Documents and Commentary* (Cambridge, Cambridge University Press, 1960), at 8–10.

nation and what he saw as the appropriate remedy. Several grievances were cited: James' use (that is, his abuse) of the dispensing power; the failure of the common law judges to put a stop to such abuse; the advancement of and James' 'open profession of the Popish religion' and the attempted suspension of the Test Act—all were listed in William's Declaration as amounting to the overturning of 'the religion, laws and liberties' of England.[154] The Declaration singled out the decision in *Godden v Hales* for particular opprobrium: 'as if it were in the power of the twelve judges to offer up the laws, rights and liberties of the whole nation to the king, to be disposed of by him arbitrarily and at his pleasure, and expressly contrary to laws enacted for the security of the subjects. . .'. William's proposed remedy, of course, was 'the calling of a Parliament for securing the nation against the evil practices of [these] wicked counsellors.'

William's invasion forces landed at Torbay on 5 November 1688. Hampered by inadequate preparation, indifferent health and bad intelligence, James advanced as far west as Salisbury before deciding, in the face of significant desertions to William and an outbreak of violent anti-Catholic rioting in London, to retreat to the capital. Back in London he was left with only two options: to fight or to flee. He chose the latter, finally arriving in France at the end of December. In the so-called 'Glorious Revolution' that saw the Crown pass from James to his son-in-law, barely a shot was fired in anger between the two men's armies.[155]

The Confirmation of the Republican Constitution

William immediately summoned an ad hoc 'Assembly of Commoners', composed of those who had sat in Parliament during the reign of Charles II along with leading representatives from the City of London. The Assembly invited William to assume administrative office for the time being and advised him to call elections for a 'Convention Parliament' to meet at the end of January. This advice William accepted. It was to the Convention Parliament that the task fell of conferring formal constitutional legitimacy onto William's military coup.

The starting point was William's Declaration of the previous September. The Convention Parliament developed William's statement into what it termed a Declaration of Rights. This document listed twelve grievances

---

[154] For the text, see *ibid*, at 10–16.

[155] Contrary to popular mythology the events of 1688 were not entirely 'bloodless'. As well as the anti-Catholic rioting in London there were minor skirmishes between the two armies at Wincanton and at Reading: see J Scott, above n 5, at 217.

against 'the late king James II', as he was described, that is to say, twelve respects in which the former king, 'by the assistance of diverse evil counsellors, judges and ministers . . . did endeavour to subvert and extirpate the Protestant religion and the laws and liberties' of the kingdom. It then declared a series of thirteen rights or statements of law.

The Declaration of Rights was formally read out to William and Mary at their coronation in February 1689. It constituted the terms and conditions set out by Parliament according to which their reign—and indeed all subsequent reigns—must be governed. Its terms were incorporated into statute later in the year. This statute, the Bill of Rights 1689, which remains in force to this day, can be seen as constituting the formal resolution of the troubles of the seventeenth century. As such, it cements the republican constitutional order that the Long Parliament had started to lay down in the early 1640s.[156] The Bill of Rights is in three parts: the first concerns grievances, the second rights and the third the succession to the Crown.

The grievances it lists are relatively familiar. James, his advisers, his ministers and his judges are accused of having attempted to subvert the law in the following ways: by assuming and exercising a power of dispensing with and suspending laws and the execution of the laws without the consent of Parliament; by imprisoning and prosecuting the seven bishops for petitioning to be excused from complicity in such illegality; by 'levying money for and to the use of the Crown by pretence of prerogative for other time and in other manner than the same was granted by Parliament'; by raising and keeping a standing army in peacetime without the consent of Parliament; by violating the freedom of election of members to serve in Parliament; by prosecutions in the common law courts for 'matters and causes cognisable only in Parliament'; by imposing excessive bail and excessive fines; and by inflicting 'illegal and cruel' punishments; 'all of which,' it was declared, 'are utterly and directly contrary to the known laws and statutes and freedom of this realm'.

More important than the grievances as to the past that the Bill of Rights recites, however, are the rights and the legal statements that it goes on to proclaim. These include the following:

I. The pretended power of suspending the laws or the execution of laws by regal authority without consent of Parliament is illegal.

II. The pretended power of dispensing with laws or the execution of laws by regal authority, as it hath been assumed and exercised of late, is illegal . . .

IV. Levying money for or to the use of the Crown by pretence of prerogative, without grant of Parliament, for longer time or in other manner than the same is or shall be granted, is illegal.

[156] For the full text of the Bill of Rights, including the terms of the Declaration of Rights, see EN Williams, above n 153, at 26–33.

V. It is the right of the subjects to petition the king, and all commitments [ie, imprisonments] and prosecutions for such petitioning are illegal.

VI. Raising or keeping a standing army within the kingdom in time of peace, unless it be with consent of Parliament, is against law . . .

VIII. Election of members of Parliament ought to be free.

IX. The freedom of speech and debates or proceedings in Parliament ought not to be impeached or questioned in any court or place out of Parliament.

X. Excessive bail ought not to be required, nor excessive fines imposed, nor cruel and unusual punishments inflicted . . .

XIII. For redress of all grievances and for the amending, strengthening and preserving of the laws, Parliaments ought to be held frequently.

These rights and statements cover all of the major political and constitutional issues that divided Parliament and the Crown from the early 1640s on. And on every one of them, we should note, the parliamentary position prevails over that of the Crown. We saw above that in 1660 what Parliament had gained from the Crown in 1640–41 was kept in place: there was no return to the non-parliamentary taxes of ship-money and the like, and there was no revival of the prerogative courts. What happened in 1689, however, was not merely that these gains were reconfirmed but that, unlike in 1660, they were now enshrined in positive law. This is true not only for the prohibition against non-parliamentary taxation in article IV but also for the safeguarding of parliamentary privilege in article IX, so that no more could the king march into the Commons to arrest members who spoke against him and no longer could he take legal action against them in the common law courts.

Moreover, much of what Parliament had won after 1642 but had then lost after 1660 was now restored to it. Control of the militia is perhaps the most notable example. Parliament, it will be recalled, had sought to establish control of the militia in its Ordinance of 1642, only for the Crown to regain this power in the early 1660s. Article VI of the Bill of Rights re-establishes full parliamentary control, at least in peacetime, and this power has remained with Parliament ever since. Of the political issues that had divided Parliament and the Crown it is only the question of the frequency of Parliament that was not unambiguously resolved in Parliament's favour by the Bill of Rights. Article XIII provides that 'Parliaments ought to be held frequently' but in comparison with the Bill's other articles, and indeed in comparison with earlier legislation on this issue—the Triennial Act of 1641, for example—this provision is surprisingly lame. As we shall see, however, it was quickly supplemented and strengthened in further legislation.

On the third issue addressed by the Bill of Rights, that of succession to the Crown, the aim of the legislation was to secure a firmly Protestant succession. To this end, the Bill of Rights provides that 'whereas it hath been found by experience that it is inconsistent with the safety and welfare of this Protestant kingdom to be governed by a Popish prince or by any king or queen marrying a Papist' it is enacted that 'all and every person and persons that is, are or shall be reconciled to or shall hold communion with the see or church of Rome, or shall profess the Popish religion, or shall marry a Papist, shall be excluded and be forever incapable to inherit, possess, or enjoy the Crown and government of this realm'.

The Bill of Rights was supplemented by two further pieces of constitutional legislation: the Triennial Act 1694, which strengthened article XIII, and the Act of Settlement 1701. The Triennial Act (also referred to as the Meeting of Parliament Act) put back into place a mechanism for ensuring that Parliament would meet at least every three years. The Act of Settlement (whose long title was 'an Act for the further limitation of the Crown, and better securing the rights and liberties of the subject') added to the provisions of the Bill of Rights concerning the Protestant succession. Inspired by Louis XIV's announcement that upon the death of James II France would recognise as the rightful king of England James' young son, the Act of Settlement made detailed provisions specifying the line of succession should William and Mary and Mary's sister Anne die without children. In such circumstances (as of course occurred when Anne died in 1714)[157] the Act provided that the Crown should pass to the house of Hanover, effectively by-passing no fewer than fifty-seven individuals, all of whom had better claims to the Crown than the Hanoverians but all of whom, unlike the Hanoverians, were Catholics.

As well as making specific provision for the line of succession the Act of Settlement imposed four further sets of restrictions on the Crown. The first two arose out of the likelihood that future monarchs would come from overseas. To combat any perceived negative consequences of this development, Parliament legislated on the one hand that 'this nation be not obliged to engage in any war for the defence of any dominions or territories which do not belong to the Crown . . . without the consent of Parliament' and on the other that certain office-holders, including members of Parliament and members of the privy council, had to have British nationality, thus excluding many friends of and close advisers to what would turn out to be the future Hanoverian monarchs.

The second set of further restrictions on the prerogative related to aspects of what we would now call the separation of powers. The Act of Settlement sought to secure greater separation (or independence) from the Crown for two institutions: the common law courts and the House of Commons. With regard to the judiciary the Act provided that judicial tenure should be *quamdiu*

---

[157] Mary died in 1694; William in 1702. Anne was queen from 1702–14.

se bene gesserint (on good behaviour) rather than at the pleasure of the Crown; that judicial salaries should be 'ascertained and established' rather than alterable by the Crown; and that judges should be removable only upon an address of both Houses of Parliament. This provision of the Act of Settlement brought into force a concession Parliament had drawn from Charles I in 1641. Charles, as his sons were later to do, had interfered insensitively with judicial appointments, removing judges not to his liking and inserting his favourites in their place. In 1641 the House of Lords petitioned him to stop doing so and, remarkably, he acquiesced and all judges appointed during the remainder of his reign were appointed *quamdiu se bene gesserint*.[158] For a few years after the restoration, this remained the practice. But it was one that neither Charles II nor James II could maintain.[159] The provision in the Act of Settlement is the single most important provision in English law concerning the independence of individual judges, once appointed, from interference by the Crown.[160]

With regard to the House of Commons the Act provided that 'no person who has an office or place of profit under the king, or receives a pension from the Crown, shall be capable of serving as a member of the House of Commons'. This provision would have secured a complete separation of personnel between Commons and Crown but it was never brought into effect. Instead, the Succession to the Crown Acts of 1705 and 1707 provided that members of the Commons who were appointed to certain Crown offices were required to resign their parliamentary seats, albeit that they could then stand for re-election. This practice continued until well into the twentieth century and marked an important compromise between, on the one hand, securing the separation of the Commons from the power and influence of the Crown while, on the other, enabling the Commons to hold those in governmental office to regular account. We shall return to this theme in chapter four, below.

It is sometimes remarked that, for what I am calling a republican settlement, the Bill of Rights and its successor legislation left a considerable amount of Crown prerogative intact. The historian Tim Harris, for example, has gone as far as to suggest that

> most of the Crown's powers were left intact in 1689. The monarch remained the chief executive in the state: he alone continued to determine all matters of policy

---

[158] See CH McIlwain, 'The Tenure of English Judges' (1913) 7 *American Political Science Review* 217, at 222.

[159] On the former, see AF Havighurst, 'The Judiciary and Politics in the Reign of Charles II' (1950) 66 *Law Quarterly Review* 62 (part 1) and 229 (part 2). On the latter, see AF Havighurst, above n 148.

[160] See further on this issue, ch 4 below.

(foreign and domestic); he had the right to choose his own ministers; he retained the right to veto legislation; and he was left with the power to determine the summoning, proroguing and dissolution of Parliament.[161]

Yet to see the settlement of 1689–1701 as leaving the Crown with substantial power over Parliament is gravely mistaken. Harris is unwise to freeze the moment of settlement in 1689 and not to read the Bill of Rights alongside the additional reforms that strengthened it, further augmenting Parliament's position over the Crown as William's reign progressed. As we have seen, the monarch's ability solely to determine policy—particularly foreign policy— was significantly curtailed by the Act of Settlement. Contrary to Harris' view, the monarch's ability to choose his own ministers had been curtailed even before the Bill of Rights, through legislation such as the Test Act, and remained restricted after it. Similarly, the monarch's powers to summon and dissolve Parliament were also limited by statute.

But the most significant curtailment of the monarchy's powers, of its independence and of its room for manoeuvre came not as much through the formal enactments of legislation as from its permanent shortage of money. That there has been a Parliament in England every year since the 1690s is principally due not to any statutory provision but to the fact that government is prohibitively expensive. The government is in permanent need of finance and, as we have seen, it was perhaps Parliament's greatest single victory in the constitutional struggles of the seventeenth century to place itself as the major source of supply. Without parliamentary supply there can be no government: it is as simple as that. In order to secure parliamentary supply the Crown is effectively required to elicit and maintain the support of Parliament. Appointing ministers of whom Parliament disapproves or dissolving Parliament without its consent are measures simply beyond the reach of a Crown whose government is reliant on Parliament for revenue.

It is essential not to overlook this point. It is true that there is no statutory equivalent in the Bill of Rights or the Act of Settlement of the parliamentary claim made in the *Nineteen Propositions* of 1642 that ministers of the Crown be subject to prior parliamentary approval before taking office. To insist on this power was not at the front of Parliament's mind in 1688 (as it had been in 1642) partly because under James II (unlike under Charles I) it was not the king's *ministers* of whose policies Parliament disapproved: it was the policies of the king himself.[162] However, to compare only the *texts* of the *Nineteen Propositions* with the Bill of Rights and Act of Settlement, to see the inclusion of extensive requirements as to parliamentary approval of ministers in the

---

[161] T Harris, above n 134, at 134.
[162] See C Roberts, above n 2, at 245.

one but not in the other, and to conclude that Parliament had by the end of the century either surrendered or somehow lost the claims it had made in 1642 is wholly to miss the point that by 1689 Parliament no longer needed to make such claims. The financial *context* of government meant that, irrespective of the text of statute law, no government could survive without parliamentary support. In 1689 Parliament 'deliberately voted William an inadequate revenue. They intended to make it impossible for him to protect his ministers by governing without Parliament. As a result William was unable to retain any minister against whom the House of Commons voted an address.'[163] Such remains the position today: no government collectively nor any minister individually can survive in office for long once the support of the House of Commons has been lost.

Thus, of the four instances of 'intact' Crown prerogatives cited by Harris, only the veto—the royal assent or the negative voice—remains. Even here it is important not to exaggerate. While the negative voice was of significant concern in the 1640s, after the restoration it was never to return anywhere near to the top of Parliament's priorities. Charles II refused his assent to legislation only twice in his twenty-five year reign. James II never did so. William refused three times, but in each instance Parliament eventually won out: in 1692 he vetoed a Bill that would have established judicial tenure on the basis of good behaviour, as the Act of Settlement achieved nine years later; in 1693 he vetoed a Triennial Bill, but as we have seen a Triennial Act was passed the following year; and in 1694 he vetoed a Place Bill that would have limited the number of members of the Commons who could hold office under the Crown, but again the result of this veto was reversed in subsequent legislation.[164] Queen Anne, as every constitutional law student in the country knows, was the last monarch to refuse her assent, to the Scottish Militia Bill in 1708. This was her only refusal, it 'went unchallenged by the Commons, and is remarkable only because it was the last'.[165]

Conclusion—Our Republican Constitution

The case for constitutional transformation that Parliament in 1640–42 had constructed out of neo-Roman arguments of freedom and republican ideas

---

[163] See C Roberts, above n 2, at 437. During the reign of Queen Anne 'Parliament preferred to censure ministers by condemning the policies which they advocated, rather than by requesting their dismissal, but whatever the form a vote of no confidence took, no minister could long survive the hostility of the Commons' (*ibid*, at 437–38).

[164] See B Kemp, *King and Commons, 1660–1832* (London, Macmillan, 1957), at 27.

[165] *Ibid*.

of governmental accountability emerged victorious from the settlement of 1689–1701. It had taken sixty years, but the result was unambiguous. All of the key reforms craved by Parliament before the Civil War were secured in Parliament's favour by the end of the century. The Crown's powers of discretionary non-parliamentary taxation were gone forever, as were its pre-rogative courts, its control over the tenure of individual common law judges, its control of the militia and its powers to suspend or sweepingly to dispense with Parliament's laws. But the biggest prize that Parliament had secured for itself was the one it had set out at the beginning of the *Nineteen Propositions*: responsible government. The Crown and its government had become fully accountable to Parliament. Through a combination of its statutory powers and its control over the purse, Parliament could now determine the destiny of the monarchy (who shall be king?) as it could govern the direction of the monarchy (what shall be the king's policies?) and control the servants of the monarchy (who shall for the time being be entrusted with office?). It was a remarkable achievement. As John Milton had expressed it in 1660, what Parliament had done was to remove the 'unnecessary, burdensome and dangerous' architecture of kingly rule and to replace it with a constitution that could now blossom into a fully 'free commonwealth'.[166]

III AN ENGLISH OR A BRITISH REPUBLIC?

This book argues that the British constitution is profoundly informed, indeed shaped, by republican ideas and practices. This chapter has demonstrated that the republican dimensions to our constitutional order date principally from the seventeenth century. This was a time, of course, before the legal creation of Britain. That event did not formally occur until the Union of 1707,[167] although the two kingdoms, England and Scotland, shared the same monarch from 1603–49 and again after 1660. The history discussed in this chapter is English rather than British. This raises the delicate question of whether (and if so how) an English political history can have created a British constitutional order. This is a famously knotty problem, which can be addressed only in outline here. The legal, political and constitutional relations between England, Scotland and Britain are both complex and, at least in some quarters, passionately contested. This is as true in the early twenty-first century as it was in the seventeenth.

Confusingly, seventeenth-century Scottish political history has both similarities with and marked differences from its English counterpart.

[166] See above n 1.
[167] Cromwell's union of 1654 was dissolved in 1660.

Scotland's seventeenth-century political story is not simply a northern version of England's, yet neither are the two unrelated to one another. In some respects England followed Scotland; other times the reverse was the case. In other instances the two kingdoms followed quite different paths from one another.[168] Like England, Scotland found Charles I and his government impossible. As in England so too in Scotland Charles I attempted to rule for protracted periods without Parliament. The 1630s saw politically explosive trials in both places: Lord Balmerino's trial for and conviction of treason in 1635 more than once having been described as 'Scotland's ship-money case'.[169] Rebellion and Civil War erupted both north and south of the border, Scotland collapsing into war by 1639, England three years later. Reforming legislation was passed by the Scottish Parliament in 1640–41 as it was at Westminster. There was a Scottish Triennial Act to match the English one[170] and as in London so too in Scotland did Parliament assert its rights to vet nominations to the privy council and to the judiciary. As Michael Lynch has summarised it, this was 'political revolution, for it can hardly be called anything less . . . [Although it] did not have the dramatic impeachments and show trials of the king's servants which the English Parliament went through . . . it was root and branch reform.'[171]

Similarities such as these may be more apparent than real, however. The immediate causes of the war in Scotland, for example, seem to have been more narrowly focused on religious issues than was the case in England. As we have seen, in England the disputes between Parliament and king concerned political and constitutional issues as well as religious matters. In Scotland, by contrast, arms were raised against the king primarily because of his religious policies—not least his imposition of the Anglican prayer book on the Kirk. The Covenanting movement that emerged to oppose Charles' religious policies in Scotland provided the drive to rebellion and on to war. Its key texts, whether the National Covenant itself, or the later writings of Samuel Rutherford (whose 1644 work *Lex, Rex* is perhaps the fullest statement of the Covenanters' ideals) emphasise over and again the religious tensions of the time, saying relatively little about any broader political and constitutional concerns.[172]

[168] For an overview, see W Ferguson, *Scotland's Relations with England: A Survey to 1707* (Edinburgh, John Donald, 1977).

[169] *Balmerino's Case* is reported at (1635) 3 St Tr 591. For the comparison with *Hampden's Case*, see M Lee, *The Road to Revolution: Scotland under Charles I, 1625–1637* (Urbana, University of Illinois Press, 1985), at 160 and M Lynch, *Scotland: A New History* (London, Pimlico, 1992), at 268.

[170] More accurately, the English one matched the Scottish: the Scottish Act was passed eight months earlier than the English one.

[171] See M Lynch, above n 169, at 272.

[172] On Rutherford, see J Coffey, *Politics, Religion and the British Revolutions: The Mind of Samuel Rutherford* (Cambridge, Cambridge University Press, 1997).

On one level this is surprising, as there was at the beginning of the seventeenth century a far richer tradition of political argument critical of royal rule in Scotland than there was in England. George Buchanan had written his extraordinary *De jure regni apud Scotos* in 1567, publishing it twelve years later, in which he justified the killing of Mary Queen of Scots on the ground that a people had the right to resist the rule of a tyrant. This was an argument Buchanan developed directly out of the great Roman republican writer, Cicero. Kings, according to Buchanan, are appointed to office: a king is one 'who gains power by popular consent, who rules by law, and who is subject to law'.[173] Kings are appointed by the 'people' to serve in the interests of the 'people'.[174] If they exercise their powers not in the interests of the people but for their own personal gain, they become tyrants. And tyrants the people have the legitimate right to resist, even depose.[175]

In justifying their armed opposition to Charles I, however, Rutherford and the Covenanters relied less on the largely secular arguments of Buchanan and more on 'explicitly theological arguments' derived from the Old Testament.[176] While there are intermittent echoes in Rutherford's *Lex, Rex* of the political position adopted by Henry Parker and his allies in England, and while there is even occasional reference to Roman law, 'rather than presenting an argument for the secular right to resist, *Lex, Rex* concentrated on the religious duty to resist. The cause of true religion was always pre-eminent in Rutherford's mind, and, in comparison with it, other concepts paled into insignificance. He hinted, for instance, that the grievance over ship-money was not a good enough pretext for resistance to a king'.[177] In all of these respects, then, Scottish and English experiences were quite different from one another. As David Mathew wrote in his survey of *Scotland under Charles I*:

> In the seventeenth century the climate of Scottish opinion and the organisation of Scottish social life bore little resemblance to the habits of thought . . . which characterised the southern kingdom. In considering Scotland and England in the years before the Civil Wars it is difficult to find a common factor.[178]

[173] R Kingdom, 'Calvinism and Resistance Theory, 1550–1580', in JH Burns and M Goldie (eds), *The Cambridge History of Political Thought, 1450–1700* (Cambridge, Cambridge University Press, 1991), at 217. It was just this argument that Buchanan's pupil, James VI and I, sought to rebut in his 'Trew Law': see above n 116.

[174] By 'people' Buchanan meant the aristocracy: the nobles, magnates and clan chiefs. See C Kidd, *Subverting Scotland's Past: Scottish Whig Historians and the Creation of an Anglo-British Identity, 1689–c1830* (Cambridge, Cambridge University Press, 1993), at 20.

[175] For discussion, see JH Burns, *The True Law of Kingship: Concepts of Monarchy in Early Modern Scotland* (Oxford, Clarendon Press, 1996), ch 6 and essays by R Bushnell, RA Mason and JH Burns in RA Mason (ed), *Scots and Britons: Scottish Political Thought and the Union of 1603* (Cambridge, Cambridge University Press, 1994), chs 4–6.

[176] See J Coffey, above n 172, at 80 and 148.

[177] *Ibid*, at 181.

[178] D Mathew, *Scotland under Charles I* (London, Eyre and Spottiswoode, 1955), at 15.

After the Civil Wars the differences between England and Scotland become more marked. The regicide was a uniquely English development. Within a few days of it the Scottish Parliament proclaimed Charles II as king not only of Scotland but of England and Ireland also (meanwhile the English Parliament was abolishing monarchy). Cromwell's forces twice engaged with armies from Scotland, with the Battles of Dunbar in 1650 and of Worcester in 1651 both resulting in overwhelming Cromwellian victories. The restoration settlement, somewhat like the regicide, was an English rather than a British affair, responsibility for resolving the contentious matters having been handed to the English Parliament.[179] Post-restoration politics, too, took different courses in the two kingdoms, with a 'landslide of royalist sentiment' north of the border resulting in a Scottish Parliament and privy council 'a good deal more royalist' than even Charles II had imagined possible.[180] Whereas in England the Long Parliament's reforming legislation of 1640–41 remained in force after the restoration, in Scotland 'nothing was salvaged from the constitution of 1641'.[181] An Act of 1661 'annulled all legislation since 1633 and thus paved the way for the return of . . . tight royal control of church, Parliament, privy council and judiciary . . . The new government seized its opportunity to push the prerogative to unprecedented lengths and at the same time voted Charles a large supply for life, thus dealing a further crippling blow to the Parliament.'[182]

The collapse of the restoration settlement and the crisis of the 1680s were likewise English rather than British phenomena, with their roots wholly in England, it being 'hard to find any trace of the same in Scotland'.[183] Yet while there was no Scottish 'revolutionary caucus' in support of William's claim to the Crown, neither was there any significant rallying to James: even Aberdeen, 'that bastion of loyalty to the Stuarts' accepted the proclamation of William as king 'without opposition'.[184] In the constitutional politics of the late seventeenth and early eighteenth centuries, all the shots, it seems, were called in England.[185] The choice of the Hanoverians to succeed to the throne in the event that William and Mary and Anne died without heirs was taken by the English Parliament, without even consulting the Scots. Even

[179]   See M Lynch, above n 169, at 287.
[180]   *Ibid*, at 288–89.
[181]   W Ferguson, above n 168, at 150.
[182]   *Ibid*.
[183]   M Lynch, above n 169, at 297.
[184]   *Ibid*, at 300. Jacobitism was to rise as a force only later, most notably of course in 1715 and 1745: see J Shaw, *The Political History of Eighteenth-Century Scotland* (London, Macmillan, 1999).
[185]   The first formal Scottish political discussion of William's coup did not take place until the middle of March 1689, some three months after James' flight to France: see C Jackson, *Restoration Scotland, 1660–1690: Royalist Politics, Religion and Ideas* (Woodbridge, Boydell Press, 2003), at 191.

before the Union of 1707 the future of Scottish politics was being shaped in London, just as it was in London where the Anglo-British republican constitution was forged. Thus it is not Anglo-centric to view the development of the British constitution from an Anglo-oriented perspective. As Colin Kidd has described it, 'Scottish economic and institutional retardation' in the seventeenth century had created a 'simulacrum of mixed constitutionalism' but the reality was that 'Scotland's was only a half-baked medieval mixed constitution which, consisting only of aristocratic and monarchic elements, was, unlike England's, incapable of generating or protecting the liberty and property of the commons.'[186]

Two factors explain why Scotland's contributions to the making of the republican constitution were not greater. The first is institutional and the second intellectual. The institutional reason concerns the powers of the Scottish Parliament. England was able to secure a republican dimension to its constitution only through the efforts of generations of parliamentarians. Such parliamentarians were able to be successful only because of the power of the institution (the House of Commons) to which they belonged. If the Commons had had no powers over the Crown it would clearly have been no more able to force the king into making the constitutional concessions of 1640–42 than it would have been able to change the identity of the monarch in 1688–89.

In contrast with the position at Westminster, the Scottish Parliament was considerably less able to assert its independence from and powers over the Crown. On the one hand the Parliament's internal structure inhibited its independence from the Crown and on the other the Scottish Parliament (unlike its English counterpart) never acquired the all-important power of the purse. The central component of the Scottish Parliament's structure was the Committee of the Articles. When the Parliament met, instead of considering legislation for itself, it would appoint a committee—the Committee of the Articles—to consider it. Only later would the Parliament then reassemble to give its approval. The Committee of the Articles, however, was

> little more than an agent of the king or council, who had gone far towards framing legislation before Parliament met. Timetables show that this was so: the Parliament of 1633 met on 20 June to elect the committee, and when it met again on 28 June it passed 168 statutes *en bloc*. The Committee of Articles can have done little more than approve measures already prepared. This procedure gave little, if any, opportunity for debate, and the brevity of sessions of Parliament also meant that there was little time to organise an opposition.[187]

[186] C Kidd, above n 174, at 209.
[187] G Donaldson, *Scotland: The Shaping of a Nation* (Newton Abbot, David and Charles, 1974), at 97.

If the relative impotence of the Scottish Parliament is the institutional factor, the intellectual factor lies in the fact that the seventeenth century was not Scotland's finest moment in terms of the production of radical or critical political thought. While Scottish thinkers have made internationally significant contributions to the development of republicanism, they did so in the sixteenth and eighteenth centuries, rather than in the seventeenth.[188] If the moment of British constitution-making had occurred either before or after the 1600s it would surely have been shaped far more considerably by Scottish writers than it was. In the sixteenth century it was the Calvinist resistance theory of George Buchanan that was ground-breaking: in the eighteenth century it was the political thought of the figures of the Scottish Enlightenment. Republican thought was taken significantly forward in the work of Andrew Fletcher, Francis Hutcheson, Adam Ferguson, Adam Smith, David Hume and John Millar.[189] But the direction in which these writers moved republicanism was away from the classical domain of constitution-making and towards the rather more modern concern of the analysis of political economy. To the extent that they were interested in constitutional design, their ideas were either defeated or never carried out. As Caroline Robbins observed of the less well-known English Commonwealthmen of the eighteenth century, no constitutional achievements of any consequence can be attributed to them.[190]

For good or ill, Britain's republican constitution was made in England. It has been subjected to numerous reforms since the close of the seventeenth century, of course, not least the emergence in the early twentieth century of mass democracy. But no such changes—not even those which may appear to be the most fundamental ones—have altered the seventeenth-century, English foundations on which the constitution was built. How in twenty-first century Britain we can construct a constitutional politics that breathes new life into the old ideal of a free commonwealth is the question addressed in the final chapter.

---

[188] As David Reid has suggested, 'we need only compare it with what English writers of the time achieved or what Scottish writers would achieve in the next century to have the meagreness, the backwardness of the literary culture of the Scottish seventeenth century brought home to us': see D Reid (ed), *The Party-Coloured Mind: Prose Relating to the Conflict of Church and State in Seventeenth-Century Scotland* (Edinburgh, Scottish Academic Press, 1982), at 1.

[189] For an overview, see C Robbins, *The Eighteenth-Century Commonwealthman* (Cambridge, Harvard University Press, 1959), ch 6.

[190] See *ibid*, at 1 and 179.

4

Republican Constitutional Reform

—————⇒•←—————

'Our laws [are] but cobwebs indeed, made only to catch flies,
but not to hold wasps or hornets.'[1]

I A WARNING TO LEGAL CONSTITUTIONALISTS

THE FIRST LESSON we should learn from the constitutional
history of Britain's seventeenth century is a deep scepticism about
seeking to rely on the courts to curb the government. As we saw in
the previous chapter, once upon a time the common law courts were placed
centre-stage. Once upon a time the constitution did rely on the common law
courts to do the job of holding the government to account. And as we repeatedly saw, those courts comprehensively failed. Ours was a common law constitution. But that constitution proved incapable of doing its job and
had—forcibly—to be replaced by a new constitutional order, in which the
Crown and its government become subject, above all, to the will of
Parliament. Before seeking a return to a common law constitution (as the
legal constitutionalists desire) should we not at least ensure that the factors
contributing to the common law's failure in the early seventeenth century
have been sufficiently dealt with?

The Independence of the Judiciary

There is one factor that has changed: judicial tenure. One of the Crown's
main weapons against judges whose judgments were inconvenient to it was
its ability to remove them from office. We saw in the previous chapter how
the Act of Settlement sought to protect judicial tenure from the whim of the

---

[1] William Allen (ie Edward Sexby), 'Killing No Murder' [1657], in D Wootton (ed), *Divine
Right and Democracy* (Harmondsworth, Penguin, 1986), at 372.

Crown, so that judges became appointed *quamdiu se bene gesserint* (on good behaviour), rather than at the pleasure of the Crown, and became removable only upon an address of both Houses of Parliament. It should be noted that the Act was not completely successful. Even after 1701 a number of judges lost their patents upon the death of the monarch: this practice did not come to an end until the accession of George III in 1760.[2] Nonetheless we must accept that, once they are appointed, individual judges enjoy a security of tenure now that was largely unavailable in the seventeenth century. However, this is far from the end of the issue. Two problems remain: the first concerns the *appointment* of individual judges and the second concerns the independence of the judiciary not individually but *collectively*.

The first of these is relatively widely recognised as being unsatisfactory. Senior judges in England and Wales are appointed by the queen on the recommendation of the prime minister, who receives (but is not required to follow) the advice of the lord chancellor. The Department for Constitutional Affairs (formerly the Lord Chancellor's Department) employs a team of civil servants to acquire and sift the information that forms the basis on which appointments are made. The appointments process has three stages: application, consultation and interview. Since 2001 there has been a Commission for Judicial Appointments to which complaints of discrimination, unfairness or maladministration may be made. The Commission publishes an annual report. In its most recent report it has subjected the present appointments process to strong criticism.[3] Although no appointments may now be made without the candidate first applying for the position, the lord chancellor reserves the right to approach those who have not applied, inviting them to do so. The Commission is very critical of the way in which such largely unreviewable discretion limits the extent to which the process is fully transparent and meritocratic.

But it is the consultation stage of the process that is most controversial. According to the Commission, it is very costly and it produces information of only limited quality. In addition, given the fact that all appeal court judges (including all House of Lords judges) are confidentially consulted on all senior appointments, the consultation process cannot but perpetuate the impression that the judiciary is a club, open only to those of whom existing judges, almost all of whom are white, upper-middle class and male, approve. Whether the impression is accurate or not is frankly beside the point. While

---

[2] See CH McIlwain, 'The Tenure of English Judges' (1913) 7 *American Political Science Review* 217, at 224.

[3] The Commission's annual and other reports are available on its website: see <www.cja.gov.uk>. Scotland has its own system of judicial appointments: see <www.judicialappointmentsscotland.gov.uk>.

this form of confidential consultation remains part of the process and while the judges remain in fact so lacking in social diversity, the impression will inevitably remain.

The lack of diversity among the judiciary, especially the senior judiciary, remains one of its most notable and, given the courts' increasing constitutional power, most worrying features. In the Commission's view what is required is to remove the judicial appointments process entirely from the government and to establish a fully independent judicial appointments commission. The government announced in July 2003 its intention to bring about such a reform[4] and in February 2004 it introduced legislation to this effect.[5] The legislation contains provisions on other matters that have proved controversial (the abolition of the office of lord chancellor, for example, and the replacement of the judicial committees of the House of Lords and the privy council with a new United Kingdom supreme court) and its progress though Parliament has been slow.[6]

The question of judicial appointments is undoubtedly important. Recent constitutional reforms such as devolution and the coming into force of the Human Rights Act have, just as undoubtedly, made the issue more pressing and, quite fittingly, it is a matter that now receives considerable attention.[7] Nevertheless, there is a greater problem with regard to judicial independence that lies elsewhere and that is, by contrast, generally overlooked. This is that judges, like government ministers, are ultimately servants of the Crown: it is from the legal authority of the Crown that they derive their power. The more we seek to rely on the courts to hold the government to constitutional account, the more the courts' dependency upon the Crown becomes problematic. In other words, the nearer we get to the model of legal constitutionalism, the more critical the issue becomes. For how can the judiciary be expected to hold the government effectively to account if, ultimately, it lacks constitutional independence? To emphasise, I am not here talking of the independence of individual judges but rather of the judiciary as a whole—of the judges collectively.

---

[4] See its consultation paper, 'Constitutional Reform: A New Way of Appointing Judges', CP 10/03.

[5] See the Constitutional Reform Bill (HL Bill 91, Feb 2004).

[6] At the time of writing the legislation remains bogged down in the House of Lords, the House of Commons not yet having commenced its scrutiny of the measure. For commentary on the government's various proposals, see the essays collected in the special issue of *Legal Studies*: [2004] *Legal Studies* 1–293.

[7] See, eg, K Malleson, *The New Judiciary* (Aldershot, Ashgate, 1999) and 'Safeguarding Judicial Impartiality' (2002) 22 *Legal Studies* 53.

Judicial Authority and the Crown

For all the recent advances in the power of the courts and for all the writing on legal constitutionalism, there has, perhaps surprisingly, been very little legal or broader constitutional analysis of the source of judicial power in our legal system. In other jurisdictions there may be no great mystery about this: Article III of the US Constitution, for example, clearly provides for judicial power to be exercised under the authority of the Constitution, in the same way as is stipulated for legislative power in Article I and for executive power in Article II.[8] Similarly, Article 220 EC confers judicial power on the Courts of Justice and of First Instance. Are there equivalent provisions in the British constitution? If so, where are they? In the previous chapter we saw what seventeenth-century judges such as Berkeley and Herbert had to say on the matter (in the *Case of Ship-money* and in *Godden v Hales*, respectively). For them, both the courts and the law they enforced were instruments entirely of the Crown's. The question for us is the extent to which this remains the position today.

The leading modern case on the relationship between the law and the Crown is *M v Home Office*, decided by the House of Lords in 1994.[9] The question for their lordships was whether the courts have the power to find a minister of the Crown in contempt of court. M was an asylum seeker. His application for asylum was unsuccessful and he sought judicial review of the decision to refuse him leave to remain in the United Kingdom. His application for judicial review was likewise unsuccessful. He then changed his lawyers and was advised to renew his application for judicial review on substantially different (and stronger) grounds. His renewed, emergency application was heard by the duty judge on the very day M was due to be deported to Zaire (as it then was). The duty judge, Garland J, desired to adjourn the proceedings until the following morning and in the meantime sought—and thought he received—an undertaking from Home Office counsel that M would not be deported before his case could be fully heard. M was deported, however, counsel for the Home Office being apparently unaware of the fact that Garland J had understood him to have given an undertaking that M would not be deported.

When, in the middle of the night, Garland J was informed by M's lawyers that M had been deported, the judge immediately granted an injunction

---

[8]   Article III, §1 provides that 'The judicial power of the United States shall be vested in one Supreme Court and in such inferior courts as the Congress may from time to time ordain and establish'.

[9]   [1994] 1 AC 377.

requiring the home secretary 'by himself, his servants or his agents' to return M to the United Kingdom so that his application for judicial review could be properly heard. This the home secretary declined to do. Having taken political advice from his junior minister that the underlying asylum decision had been the correct one and legal advice that Garland J's injunction was made without jurisdiction and was therefore voidable, the home secretary, Kenneth Baker MP, instructed his officials to cancel the return flight from Zaire on which M had been booked. The government's legal team then returned to court to seek the annulment of Garland J's midnight order on the ground that it amounted to an injunction against the Crown, no such remedy being known in English law.[10] The court duly annulled the order, M went into hiding and we do not know what became of him.

M's lawyers then commenced contempt proceedings against the Home Office. While Garland J's order was ultimately annulled by the court, until it was formally annulled it remained in force and, crucially, it was in force at the time when the home secretary instructed that M's return flight should be cancelled. In giving and carrying out these instructions, the home secretary and Home Office had acted against the order of the court, such action being in contempt of court. It is uncontentious that action taken in violation of an order of the court constitutes a contempt. The controversy of the case concerns not whether the offence was made out (it clearly was) but whether the courts have the jurisdiction to find a minister of the Crown, such as the home secretary, in contempt of court.

On the face of it, it may seem absurd that such an apparently simple question should have proved so difficult that it required determination in the highest court in the land. In a modern constitutional system based on the rule of law and some form of separation of powers between the judicial and the executive branches it would be axiomatic that the courts of law would have the power to enforce their judgments as against the executive. But if one thing is evident from the analysis in the preceding chapters it is that the British constitution is neither especially modern nor based on the rule of law. Rather, the British constitution struggles today just as it struggled in the seventeenth century to find ways of bringing the Crown and its ministers within the coercive scope of the law. This is because both courts and ministers share the same ultimate source of authority: namely, the Crown.

It is surely clear that the government is the Crown's government. The prime minister is appointed directly by the queen herself. All ministers are subsequently appointed by the queen on the advice of the prime minister. Ministers are known as 'ministers of the Crown' as the government is known

---

[10] See Crown Proceedings Act 1947, s 21(2).

as 'Her Majesty's government'. While the government is (of course) able to exercise significant power conferred upon it by statute, so too may it exercise a considerable number of prerogative powers: that is, powers which in former times would have been exercised by the monarch personally but which have now passed to ministers. The making of treaties, the deployment of the armed forces, the conduct of diplomacy and the employment and organisation of the civil service are all examples of prerogative powers exercised by government ministers.

So too with the judges. The queen is the fount of justice. 'All jurisdiction is exercised in her name, and all judges derive their authority from her commission.'[11] The High Court and the Court of Appeal transact much of their business in a building called the '*Royal* Courts of Justice'. Senior judges, like cabinet ministers, are all 'Right Honourable' members of the privy council and, again like ministers, are appointed by the queen on the recommendation of the prime minister. The judicial oath is to the Crown (not to the people, not to the law, not to the constitution and certainly not to Parliament).

Given the ubiquity of the Crown's authority we can perhaps begin to see why *M v Home Office* raised such an acute question of law. The question in the case ('do the courts have the jurisdiction to find a minister of the Crown in contempt of court?') was difficult because in British constitutional law it unravels into a nonsense. It amounts to asking whether the Crown's courts have the power to find the Crown's ministers in contempt of the Crown's courts, or whether the Crown may be found to be in contempt of itself and, if so, whether the Crown may, through its courts, say so. As numerous commentators have observed, in Britain we do not have a modern, sophisticated legal concept of the state, divided into difference branches (or separate powers). Instead, we have the Crown.[12] And when two dimensions of the Crown clash, as they did in *M v Home Office*, there is no possibility of the law being able to proceed rationally.

What ought to have happened is straightforward. What the courts should have been able to say is that no-one is above the law and that, if you violate an order of the court you have acted in contempt of court and that this is so regardless of your position. Whether you are a teacher, a nurse, an insurance salesman, a secretary of state or even the head of state should be utterly immaterial. The law should apply equally to all, irrespective of anyone's job.

But of course this is not how the courts ruled. No such approach was available because under the common law status is anything but immaterial.

---

[11]   See M Loughlin, 'The State, the Crown and the Law', in M Sunkin and S Payne (eds), *The Nature of the Crown: A Legal and Political Analysis* (Oxford, Oxford University Press, 1999), at 58.
[12]   See *ibid.*

The leading speech in the House of Lords in *M's* case was given by Lord Woolf.[13] It is not an easy read. Far from proceeding on the basis of the equal application of the laws, his lengthy and convoluted speech was dominated by the theme of status and by the problem of whether the law allowed the courts to conceive of themselves as being sufficiently separate from the Crown as to enable them to coerce ministers of the Crown into obeying the law. After thirty pages of dense and often arcane analysis Lord Woolf came to the conclusion that the courts do have the jurisdiction to *find* ministers of the Crown in contempt of court but that they lack the power to punish them for it. Even this limited ruling Lord Woolf was able to arrive at only after he had severed the Crown in two. The Crown-as-executive (government ministers and the like) may be found in contempt of court, whereas the Crown-as-monarch (the head of state) may not be. Against the monarch the courts continue to lack even this limited power. In the Divisional Court Simon Brown J had ruled that the relationship between the Crown and judiciary is merely 'one of trust.' Lord Woolf's speech in the House of Lords effectively endorsed this view: 'the Crown's relationship with the courts,' he ruled, 'does not depend on coercion.'[14]

On one level the decision in *M v Home Office* was a minor breakthrough: after all, never before had an English court clearly held that a minister of the Crown may be found to be in contempt of court. It is for this reason that the case has been celebrated by a number of lawyers as a great triumph for the rule of law.[15] But to focus only on this ruling is to see less than half the picture for, in the course of its decision in the case, the House of Lords unanimously upheld the old maxim that 'the Crown can do no wrong' and it unanimously ruled (1) that ministers of the Crown cannot be punished for contempt of court and (2) that the Crown-as-monarch cannot even be found in contempt of court. These are not the opinions of long-gone royalist hardliners from the courts of Charles I or James II. These are the unambiguous rulings handed down by the highest court of the land in 1994.

What they show is that the courts remain as wrapped up in the authority of the Crown now as they were in the seventeenth century. Individual judges may not be dismissible at the unilateral instigation of Crown or government, but the judiciary as a whole lacks now as it lacked in the 1600s a genuinely independent source of authority. For all their supposed radicalism in other respects, it should be noted that the present government's proposed reforms

---

[13] Lord Templeman gave a short concurring speech. The remaining law lords (Lords Keith, Griffiths and Browne-Wilkinson) agreed with Lord Woolf.

[14] *M v Home Office* [1994] 1 AC 377, at 425.

[15] See, eg, HWR Wade, 'The Crown, Ministers and Officials: Legal Status and Liability', in M Sunkin and S Payne, above n 11, ch 2.

on the establishment of a new supreme court for the United Kingdom will make no difference to the issues raised here. Clause 1 of the Constitutional Reform Bill that is currently before Parliament guarantees judicial independence, but such independence is described throughout as 'continuing'. It is concerned with prohibiting ministerial interference in the administration of justice in particular cases, not with placing judicial authority on a new basis, independent of that of the Crown. Even if this legislation is eventually passed, British judges will not become 'lions over the throne' (in Bacon's famous phrase) but will remain tethered firmly beneath it, as they are now. They are 'the queen's lions with an irrational reverence for her Crown'.[16] They allow the enforcement of the rule of law to be diluted by adding to it 'a mystical notion of a Crown that can do no wrong'.[17]

M v Home Office is not the only modern case to illustrate the difficulties which the courts face. The *GCHQ* case,[18] *Rehman*,[19] *Shayler*[20] and the Chagos Islands litigation[21] all serve to illustrate the overwhelming reluctance or inability of today's common law courts to subject the Crown's government to searching scrutiny. In the *GCHQ* case in 1984 the House of Lords unanimously ruled that the exercise of numerous prerogative powers remained beyond judicial review. All of those exercised by the queen herself (the appointment of the prime minister, the dissolution of Parliament, the dismissal of ministers and the royal assent to legislation) as well as several of those exercised by ministers (such as the making of treaties and the deployment of the armed forces) were held to be beyond any judicial oversight. In addition the House of Lords ruled that all questions in relation to government powers concerning national security, whether the powers derived from the prerogative or from statute, were, as Lord Diplock put it, 'par excellence . . . non-justiciable' questions.[22] *Rehman* and *Shayler* we encountered in chapter one where we saw that even after the Human Rights Act the courts continue to show extraordinary deference to the Crown, the state and the government where it is asserted that matters of national security are at issue.

But that it is not only in the sensitive arena of national security where the courts continue to defer to the Crown is illustrated by the final case I wish to consider here: the recent claim of the exiled and displaced Chagos Islanders for compensation for their illegal treatment at the hands of the Crown in the

---

[16] See JWF Allison, *A Continental Distinction in the Common Law: A Historical and Comparative Perspective on English Public Law* (Oxford, Oxford University Press, 2000, rev ed), at 107.

[17] *Ibid.*

[18] *Council of Civil Service Unions v Minister for the Civil Service* [1985] AC 374.

[19] *Secretary of State for the Home Department v Rehman* [2003] 1 AC 153.

[20] *R v Shayler* [2003] 1 AC 247.

[21] *Chagos Islanders v Attorney General* [2004] EWCA (Civ) 997, judgment of 22 July 2004.

[22] See above n 18, at 412. See also Lord Fraser at 402.

1960s and 1970s. The Chagos Islands, of which the largest is Diego Garcia, were from 1814–1965 part of the British colony of Mauritius. In 1965 they were severed from Mauritius and became the British Indian Ocean Territory. In the 1960s the United States decided that it required a military base in the Indian Ocean. It asked Britain whether it could have the Chagos Islands. After Britain agreed to the proposal it became clear that the Americans desired to have the islands unpopulated, so Britain started forcibly to remove the islands' inhabitants, some to Mauritius (over 1000 miles away) and others to the Seychelles, where large numbers of them starved to death, literally rotting in the slums. Estimates of the numbers involved vary, but it is possible that as many as two thousand people were moved, including in the region of 430 Ilois, a people indigenous to the Chagos with no connection either to Mauritius or the Seychelles.

In 2000, in an important judgment, the Divisional Court in London held in a case called *Bancoult* that the Crown had acted unlawfully in exiling the Ilois from their homes.[23] On the basis of the judgment in *Bancoult* the Chagos Islanders commenced legal action in the English courts seeking compensation for the loss they had suffered as a result of the Crown's illegal actions. Their action was struck out and their appeal against the order to strike out was unsuccessful, Sedley LJ giving the judgment of the Court of Appeal.[24] A number of reasons were given in Sedley LJ's judgment, including the reason that, as a matter of law, it is simply impossible to sue the state. Indeed, as Sedley LJ expressed it, 'the English common law has no knowledge of the state'. Public law recognises instead the Crown and, as we have seen, the starting point even now in the law's relationship with the Crown is the notion that the Crown can do no wrong. We know from *Bancoult* that the exile of the Ilois was illegal—indeed it was contrary to Magna Carta, no less. But to turn what Sedley LJ described as a 'public law wrong' into an actionable tort in respect of which damages may be awarded would require, as he put it, 'a legal system in which the Crown, in private law, can do wrong; and this . . . we do not have.'

English public law is a small world. The Sedley LJ who decided the Chagos Islands case is the same Stephen Sedley who was M's counsel in *M v Home Office* in the High Court and the Court of Appeal (by the time *M's* case went to the House of Lords, Sedley had been elevated to the bench). Writing after the House of Lords had dispensed with *M's* case but before the Chagos Islands litigation, Sedley wrote extra-judicially in praise of *M v Home Office*. He suggested that the decision showed that we had

---

[23] See *R (Bancoult) v Secretary of State for the Foreign and Commonwealth Office* [2001] QB 1067; for commentary, see A Tomkins, 'Magna Carta, Crown and Colonies' [2001] *Public Law* 571.

[24] See above n 21.

reached a point at which, in the undemonstrative way of the common law, the state in the shape of the executive and in the name and right of the Crown can be recognised as an entity capable of being impleaded and subjected to the legal processes *which alone can make the rule of law a reality*.[25]

His own judgment in *Chagos Islanders v Attorney General* shows that this is not so, for the Crown cannot be impleaded. It cannot be sued. As far as the law is concerned, it can do no wrong. And, as Sedley himself wrote, it is *only* by changing this that the rule of law can become a reality.

This is the first lesson, then, of the story told in this book. Our laws are indeed but 'cobwebs', made to catch the 'flies' of government officials but not to hold the 'wasps or hornets' of the Crown itself.[26] Unless and until this is reformed, the model of legal constitutionalism can never be successfully applied in Britain. It is incumbent on those who favour adopting the model to address this point. While the Crown remains immune to the rule of law we should be extremely wary of seeking to rely on the courts as our principal means of securing accountable government for, at the heart of the law's conception of government lies the Crown and at the heart of the law's relationship with the Crown is its continuing insistence, even into the twenty-first century, that it can do no wrong.

II PARLIAMENTARY GOVERNMENT TODAY

The republicanism of our constitution is to be found neither in the courts nor in the common law but in Parliament. In the previous chapter we saw how the neo-Roman idea of freedom as non-domination and the republican conception of political accountability combined in the seventeenth century to produce a constitutional order deeply informed by, indeed based on, republican values. It is a constitution that was described above as one that could allow Britain to 'blossom into a fully free commonwealth'.[27] The values of such a commonwealth were outlined at the end of chapter two: popular sovereignty, non-domination, open government, civic virtue, equality and, of course, the political accountability that is required to secure responsible government. The final questions to be considered here are: how far do these values feature in contemporary British constitutional practice and, to the extent that they do so inadequately, how may they be encouraged to come further to the fore?

---

[25] S Sedley, 'The Crown in its own Courts', in C Forsyth and I Hare (eds), *The Golden Metwand and the Crooked Cord* (Oxford, Clarendon Press, 1998), at 257, emphasis added.

[26] See above n 1.

[27] See above at 109.

The Worst-Case Diagnosis

It might be said that, from the standpoint of our republican values, the present position is poor, perhaps even dire. The worst-case diagnosis might run something like this. The British government, re-elected to power in 2001 on little more than forty per cent of the votes cast in an election in which less than two-thirds of the registered electorate voted at all, enjoys an enormous majority of seats in the House of Commons—410 Labour MPs in a House of 659 seats, or 62 per cent. Such a majority hands to the government effective control not only of the proceedings in the chamber of the House of Commons but also in the various select and standing committees of the House that are designed to examine the detail of the government's policies, decisions and legislative proposals. A Commons that is so dominated by backbench MPs who come from the same political party as forms the government is, it might be thought, a rather unlikely place in which to find effective scrutiny or political accountability.

Meanwhile the House of Lords, while not dominated by the governing party, remains utterly lacking in democratic legitimacy and in the authority that comes with it. Its membership is entirely appointed, save for the small group of 92 hereditary peers who have been allowed to remain in the House pending further reform of its composition. Moreover, the powers of patronage and appointment to the House reside in those same political parties that dominate proceedings in the Commons.

While Parliament is so weak the government, by contrast, is stronger than ever, or so the worst-case diagnosis would suggest. The government is apparently all-powerful. It may introduce any legislation into either House in any session for any reason. Equally, it may refuse to introduce any legislation, no matter how earnestly desired by the public and no matter how much its enactment may be shown to be for the public good. Such legislation as it does introduce is almost invariably passed, no matter how controversial, illiberal or ill thought through. Moreover, most of the levers controlling the extent to which Parliament will be permitted to deliberate upon the government's proposals lie in the hands of the governing party.

The passage of the Bill which became the Anti-terrorism, Crime and Security Act 2001 provides a useful example. This is the legislation that marked the British government's formal response to the terrorist attacks in the United States of America on 11 September 2001. Despite the fact that it took the government more than two months to prepare the Bill, its 129 sections and eight schedules were rushed through Parliament in a mere three weeks. The Commons debated the measure for sixteen hours, the Lords for nine days. This, despite the fact that the Act constituted the most draconian single piece of legislation passed in peacetime in Britain in over a century, requiring a derogation from core international human rights treaty obligations.[28] Among other matters the most notorious part of the Act—part IV— provides for the indefinite detention without trial of those certified by the home secretary as being or having links with suspected international terrorists.[29]

In 2003 the Blair government controversially took the country into a war with Iraq despite unprecedented opposition internationally, popularly and in Parliament. Could any other act so clearly justify the worst-case diagnosis? Internationally, the government failed to persuade many of its key European allies that the war was needed. Nor could the United Nations security council be cajoled into providing clear authorisation for the use of force. At the same time, literally millions of Britons took to the streets in a series of mass protests against the war and, in Parliament, two Commons votes were staged in which unprecedented numbers of Labour MPs voted against the government. These were the biggest backbench rebellions since the passing of the corn laws in the middle of the nineteenth century.[30] Yet despite all of this, the government pressed ahead—military action in Iraq commenced a mere 28 hours after the second Commons vote.

Re-assessing the Parliamentary Record

With the government's vast Commons majority, with the continued impotence of the House of Lords, with legislation such as the Anti-terrorism, Crime and Security Act being rushed through Parliament and with the government's decision to go to war in Iraq, the picture of modern British parliamentary government can seem bleak indeed from the standpoint of our republican values. It is no part of my argument to suggest that the government has not become too powerful or that Parliament has not on occasion been painfully disappointing. But, contrary to the legal constitutionalists

---

[28] For detailed commentary, see A Tomkins, 'Legislating against Terror' [2002] *Public Law* 205 and H Fenwick, 'A Proportionate Response to 11 September?' (2002) 65 *Modern Law Review* 724.

[29] The legality of the derogation and of the measures in part IV of the Act have been challenged in the courts. The Court of Appeal ruled that they were not unlawful: see *A v Secretary of State for the Home Department* [2003] 2 WLR 564. At the time of writing an appeal to the House of Lords has been heard but the Lords' judgment has not yet been handed down.

[30] In the first vote (on 26 February 2003) 121 Labour MPs voted against the government on the issue; in the second (on 18 March 2003) 139 Labour MPs did so: for details, see P Cowley and M Stuart, 'Parliament: More Bleak House than Great Expectations' (2004) 57 *Parliamentary Affairs* 301, at 304–8.

whose views were considered in chapter one, I do want to insist that the remedy lies within the republican values of parliamentary accountability and not in the courts. The worst-case diagnosis makes for grim reading, for sure. But does it give a complete view of what has been happening? It seems to me that the position is not actually as bad as the worst-case diagnosis makes out. Let us take another look at the two events considered above: the passage of the Anti-terrorism legislation in 2001 and the decision to go to war in 2003.

The Anti-terrorism, Crime and Security Act is a straightforwardly nasty, indeed brutal, measure designed, or so the home secretary would have us believe, to counter what is perhaps an even more straightforwardly brutal threat. Notwithstanding the government's repeated warnings about the enormity and the novelty of the threat now faced by the United Kingdom from international terrorism, we should do well to remember that the context in which the 2001 Act was passed was that, as the home secretary himself explained in Parliament, 'there is no immediate intelligence pointing to a specific threat to the United Kingdom'.[31] Never is it more difficult for Parliament to set limits to new executive powers than in times when the executive is asserting that national security requires it to possess such powers.

Yet despite the fact that it was given only a matter of hours to debate the Bill and despite the fact that the government tried to treat its passage as that of an emergency measure, Parliament actually did remarkably well in seeking to curb some of the worst excesses desired by David Blunkett's Home Office. Controversial provisions that would have created new offences of inciting religious hatred were included in the Bill when it was published but removed as a result of pressure during its passage through Parliament. Several safeguards against abuse of new executive powers regarding the collection and retention of personal data were added at Parliament's insistence. The home secretary's powers to detain without trial were watered down, so that he would have to show that he 'reasonably' suspected an individual of being an international terrorist.[32] And both the Act as a whole and part IV in particular were made subject to a variety of reviews as well as to an eventual sunset clause (so that the powers will lapse after a certain point).[33]

Despite the acute shortage of time that was made available to Parliament to debate the measure, no fewer than five select committee reports were

---

[31] See HC Deb, col 925, 15 October 2001.

[32] On the critical importance of this amendment, see *Secretary of State for the Home Department v M* [2004] 2 All ER 863. Compare *Liversidge v Anderson* [1942] AC 206.

[33] When the committee of privy counsellors appointed to review the Act reported in December 2003 its review was scathing, especially with regard to part IV. The all-party committee unanimously recommended that the power indefinitely to detain without trial should be repealed and replaced with provisions that did not require derogating from international human rights law: see HC (2003–04) 100.

published on the Bill as it passed through the legislature. The Joint Committee on Human Rights published two reports and the Delegated Powers and Regulatory Reform Committee, the Home Affairs Committee and the Defence Committee each published one.[34] In the drawing up of their reports these committees called on a variety of witnesses to provide them with oral and written evidence. The reports on the Bill served three useful purposes. They significantly augmented the range of expert information on which Parliament was able to draw in its deliberations on the Bill, reducing the extent to which parliamentarians were reliant on the government as a source of information.[35] They brought into the legislative process a degree (albeit, considering the time available, a necessarily limited degree) of popular participation, with a variety of interest and pressure groups as well as a number of individuals being called to give evidence. And they highlighted in detail a number of the most controversial aspects of the legislation, allowing Parliament quickly to focus and to force concessions from the government.

This was a considerable achievement and we should not under-estimate it. Parliament was legislating in the most difficult of circumstances. The government, let us not forget, despite the absence of 'immediate intelligence pointing to a specific threat to the United Kingdom', was insistent that the emergency now faced by the country was so grave as to require a derogation from international human rights law—such derogations being lawful only in time of war or 'other public emergency threatening the life of the nation'.[36] The Anti-terrorism, Crime and Security Act was passed in the context of the government saying to Parliament that the United Kingdom faced a public emergency which threatened the very life of the nation. Yet despite this, despite the emergency context, despite the enormity of the Labour party's majority in the Commons and despite the acute shortage of time, Parliament managed to deliberate upon the measure in a way which enabled it to secure its own independent sources of information, allowing it to come to a judgment of its own on the merits (or otherwise) of the government's proposals.[37] Of course, the Act was passed, part IV included. And the government got much, perhaps most, of what it wanted. But the full story of the enactment of the Anti-terrorism, Crime and Security Act shows that, for all the faults and flaws in the system and in the people who currently operate it, the

---

[34] For details, see A Tomkins, above n 28.

[35] This was particularly the case with regard to the reports of the Joint Committee on Human Rights, which were extensively cited and relied upon in the debates on the Bill in the House of Lords.

[36] See European Convention on Human Rights, Art 15(1).

[37] See further D Feldman, 'The Impact of Human Rights on the UK Legislative Process' (2004) 25 *Statute Law Review* 91, at 101–2.

position—even in the always difficult context of emergency legislation—is not quite as bad as the worst-case diagnosis makes out.

A closer look at the decision in 2003 to go to war in Iraq reveals much the same. Two things are noteworthy about the decision-making process here. The first is that votes were taken in the House of Commons on the issue at all and the second is the size of the backbench rebellions. The waging of war is governed in British constitutional law not by statute but by the royal prerogative. When the government declares war or commits Britain's armed forces in combat it is exercising prerogative, not statutory, authority. Parliament's role on such occasions is normally extremely limited. But in 2003, as we have seen, there were two votes in the Commons on the government's proposed use of force in Iraq. Had the Commons voted against the government's policy, the prime minister would have resigned from office, or so the media were briefed.[38]

Thus, the government's decision to go to war was not one which, ultimately, it was able to make alone or for itself. Parliament forced its way into the decision-making process and moreover, it did so not as a bit-part player but as a body whose decision could effectively *determine* whether British troops were sent into combat.[39] Whether we like or approve of the outcome is not the point. The point is that the prime minister's decision to wage war in Iraq was one in respect of which Parliament ensured that he would be fully constitutionally responsible.

It has not been only over the matter of the Iraq war that the House of Commons has witnessed significant backbench rebellions since the 2001 election. The government Bill to introduce so-called 'foundation hospitals' in the NHS was the subject of the largest rebellion at the second reading stage since the mid 1980s and at one point in the legislative process the government's nominal Commons majority of over 160 was reduced to one of a mere seventeen votes.[40] As a result of intense parliamentary pressure the government was forced to make a series of concessions on its proposed scheme. In

[38] Despite the large numbers of Labour backbenchers prepared to vote against the government on the issue, there was in reality little danger of the prime minister resigning while the opposition Conservative party supported his plans for military action. It is to be noted that, like the government, the Conservatives also experienced significant parliamentary rebellion over the Iraq war: a total of 21 Conservative MPs defied their party whips over the issue and four front bench spokesmen resigned over it: see P Cowley and M Stuart, above n 30, at 306.

[39] On the basis that had Parliament voted against the use of force the prime minister would have resigned. It is possible, of course, that an incoming prime minister would have overridden Parliament's objection, but unless and until Parliament changed its position such a course of action must surely be considered highly unlikely.

[40] The last government Bill to be defeated at the second reading stage was the Shops Bill in 1986. On the votes over foundation hospitals, see P Cowley and M Stuart, above n 30, at 309–10.

the following session of Parliament this story repeated itself over the issue of university tuition fees.

The Blair government is not the only recent administration to have found itself subject to rebellious backbenchers. The small size of the Conservatives' majority between 1992 and 1997 meant that John Major's government was constantly having to make deals with and concessions to parliamentarians of all sorts of political persuasions, most famously (but certainly not only) over issues of European integration. What is notable about events since 2001 is that the House of Commons has demonstrated that the same fate awaits governments with far larger majorities. A long-standing concern among constitutional and political commentators in Britain has been that the big Commons majorities which the first-past-the-post electoral system used in general elections can sometimes throw up is bad for our democracy, as it makes for a government that is too easily able to control Parliament. Experience since 2001 suggests that this fear should not be exaggerated. Even with a majority of more than 160, the Labour government has been forced to fight for its policies and, on a wide range of issues, to make numerous changes to them. Even with a three-figure majority, the House of Commons has shown that it is the government that is accountable to Parliament, and not the other way around.

Conclusion

The preceding re-assessment of the recent parliamentary record shows that the worst-case diagnosis is not justified. Despite everything, Parliament continues to have both the means and the will to check the government of the day. It would have been easy for Parliament to atrophy. The Commons could easily have been overwhelmed by the unprecedented weight of Labour's majorities since 1997. The Lords could equally easily have been silenced by virtue of their abject lack of democratic authority. The government could have played up, even more than it did, the terrorist threat and forced even more coercive legislation through Parliament. We now know that there were indeed pressures inside the Home Office and/or the intelligence services to do just that—in 2001 the home secretary was strongly urged by some of his officials that in order to prevent a future terrorist attack on the United Kingdom Parliament needed to authorise a vastly more extensive detention of all asylum-seekers seeking entry into the UK. That the government rejected such advice must have at least something to do with its assessment that it would have been unable to secure majority support in Parliament for such a measure.[41]

[41]   See D Feldman, above n 37, at 101–2.

Parliament generally and the House of Commons in particular have grown stronger under the Blair government. The detailed rules of ministerial responsibility to Parliament were clarified in a pair of important parliamentary resolutions passed in 1997, a step designed to prevent future governments from being able to repeat the constitutional abuses that occurred under John Major's premiership.[42] Since 1997 a growing number of government Bills have been published in draft, enabling markedly greater parliamentary scrutiny over a wide range of measures.[43] The powers and influence of select committees have considerably increased in recent years.[44] Tony Blair is the first prime minister in history regularly and frequently to be called to give account to a select committee.[45] When in 2001 the Labour whips tried to remove certain MPs from the chairs of a number of committees which in the previous Parliament had been critical of government policy, the Commons revolted and the MPs were immediately re-instated, much to the government's embarrassment. It was a powerful reminder that these are *parliamentary* committees and are not the playthings of government. In October 2003 the Commons voted to pay the senior and experienced backbench MPs who chair select committees an enhanced salary so that there is now, for the first time, the beginnings of a career structure within the House of Commons that is independent of the pursuit of ministerial office.

III A REPUBLICAN FUTURE?

This is all well and good—these are all small steps in the right direction, that will enhance the ability of Parliament and especially of the House of Commons to hold the government to account. But there is so much more that we could be doing to bring the republican values on which our political constitution was founded more openly to the fore. What follows in this final section is an outline of a republican reform agenda designed to achieve that end.

There are four items on the agenda, each of which relates to at least one of the values of republican constitutionalism identified in chapter two. Some of

---

[42] For details, see A Tomkins, *Public Law* (Oxford, Oxford University Press, 2003), at 148–59.

[43] For a valuable appraisal, see A Kennon, 'Pre-legislative Scrutiny of Draft Bills' [2004] *Public Law* 477.

[44] For an overview, see A Tomkins, 'What is Parliament for?', in N Bamforth and P Leyland (eds), *Public Law in a Multi-Layered Constitution* (Oxford, Hart Publishing, 2003), ch 3.

[45] The prime minister gives evidence once every six months to a public meeting of the House of Commons Liaison Committee, which is composed of the chairs of all Commons select committees.

these items may at first sight appear quite radical, even wild, but I hope that the preceding analysis has shown that even far-reaching republican reforms may be seen as pushing with the grain of the British constitution, not against it. The four sets of proposals are as follows: (1) all prerogative powers, privileges and immunities should be abolished and, where necessary, replaced with statutory powers; (2) current freedom of information laws should be repealed and replaced with legislation that would secure genuinely open government; (3) Parliament should be reformed so that both Houses are democratically elected and so that both are able to operate freely, without the constraints imposed by party loyalty; and (4) the Crown and the queen should be removed from the constitutional order, with the monarch's powers being transferred to the House of Commons. Let us now consider each of these in a little more detail.

Prerogative Powers

The starting principle for executive power should be the same for central government as it already is for local government: namely, that the government may exercise only those powers which are expressly (or by necessary implication) conferred upon it by statute. If this is sufficient for local government there is no reason why it should not also be sufficient for central government. To achieve this it is necessary for Parliament to pass legislation revoking all prerogative powers. Both those exercised by the queen herself and those exercised on her behalf by ministers of the Crown should be revoked. There is no justification compatible with republican constitutionalism for distinguishing between the two sorts.

In Britain's parliamentary democracy we do not elect our government. Rather, we elect our Parliament (or at least, one half of it). The *personnel* of the government is already drawn from Parliament and once in office the government is of course accountable to Parliament for its *policies*. Given this, there is no reason not to extend the control by Parliament over the government also to its *powers*. Government should possess only those powers which the people, through their elected representatives in Parliament, have expressly or by necessary implication conferred upon it by statute. This is a principle of the highest importance to republican constitutionalism. It is a reflection of the first theme of republicanism identified in chapter two above: namely, popular sovereignty.

But it is not only a matter of principle. The reform suggested here would have significant practical consequences. Prerogative powers are not marginal. They concern governmental activities that are critical and may often be both politically and legally controversial. Consider, for example, Mrs Thatcher's reliance on the prerogative to ban civil servants at GCHQ from joining trade unions, or the Major government's use and abuse of the prerogative to issue public interest immunity (or PII) certificates in the Matrix Churchill trial and other, related prosecutions. Yet when exercising prerogative powers ministers have, as a Commons committee recently expressed it, 'very wide scope to act without parliamentary approval'.[46] And as we saw above, in no area of public law are the courts as reluctant to review government actions and decisions as when they touch upon the prerogative. This lack of parliamentary oversight and judicial review applies to a wide range of governmental powers. It applies to the making and ratification of treaties, to the conduct of diplomacy, to the governance of British overseas territories, to the deployment of the armed forces both overseas and within the UK, to the appointment and removal of ministers, to the appointment of peers, to the grant of honours, to the organisation of the civil service, to the granting and revoking of passports and to the granting of pardons.[47]

Even this list, compiled by the House of Commons Select Committee on Public Administration, is incomplete. It does not include, for example, powers to claim Crown privileges or immunities, such as the power to issue PII certificates. Indeed, there is no authoritative list of all the prerogative powers possessed by ministers. Parliament has repeatedly asked to be provided with one but successive governments have steadfastly refused. As the Public Administration Committee recently expressed it, 'Parliament does not even have the right to know what these powers are.'[48] This matters: as we saw in chapter two, ministers do from time to time claim new prerogative powers for themselves and when they do the courts have not demonstrated great eagerness to stop them.[49]

The way forward is simple. Parliament should pass a Prerogative (Abolition) Act. The Act should contain two sections. Section 1 should provide that 'all prerogative powers shall be abolished' and section 2 should provide (with a nice touch of irony) that 'section 1 shall come into force one year after this Act receives the royal assent'. This would give the government one year in which to introduce legislation that, when passed, would confer on the government such powers as Parliament considers it needs in place of its former prerogative powers. There would be a Treaties Act, a Deployment of

[46] House of Commons Select Committee on Public Administration, fourth report of session 2003–04, *Taming the Prerogative: Strengthening Ministerial Accountability to Parliament*, HC 422, March 2004, para 12.

[47] See *ibid*, para 10.

[48] See *ibid*, para 12.

[49] See *R v Secretary of State for the Home Department, ex parte Northumbria Police Authority* [1989] QB 26 and *Ruddock v Vadarlis (The MV Tampa Case)* (2001) 183 ALR 1, considered above, ch 2.

the Armed Forces Act, a Civil Service Act and so forth, in each of which Parliament would lay down the terms according to which the government may exercise its powers. There would also have to be legislation dealing with powers that were formerly exercised by the queen—this issue is considered below.

Unfortunately, when the House of Commons Public Administration Committee recently considered the issue of how to 'tame the prerogative' (as it put it) and how to strengthen ministerial responsibility to Parliament in respect of the exercise of prerogative powers, it was not so forthright. The recommendations contained in the committee's report were, for what has on the whole been one of Parliament's most ambitious and forward-thinking committees, uncharacteristically limp. For one thing the committee considered only the prerogative powers exercised by ministers, leaving the position of the queen entirely untouched. For another it recommended only that the government should 'initiate a public consultation exercise' on the future of ministerial uses of prerogative powers.[50]

This is self-evidently not going to happen. The principal *beneficiary* of prerogative power is the government of the day. No government can realistically be expected to volunteer to surrender such powers: this is not the way politics works. The Stuart kings in the seventeenth century did not volunteer to surrender power. They were forced into it, first by Parliament and subsequently as a result of military action. The Public Administration Committee would be better advised, instead of calling on the government to act, to seek to persuade Parliament to act. If the prerogative is going to be wrested away from the government it is going to be as a result of parliamentary insistence, not government self-sacrifice. Parliament showed as long ago as the 1640s that it has the power to achieve this. In the seventeenth century Parliament significantly curbed the Crown's prerogative. What Parliament should do now is to finish the job and remove the prerogative entirely from the British constitutional order.

Open Government

In order for effective scrutiny of government to be possible information about what the government is doing and is proposing to do must be freely available. No system of accountability, whether parliamentary, judicial or of any other kind, can hope to be successful without an informed understanding of what the government is doing and is proposing to do. The ideal of a

---

[50] *Taming the Prerogative*, above n 46, para 60.

contestatory, deliberative and inclusive democracy that follows from the republican principle of freedom as non-domination and that was outlined in chapter two will remain but that—an ideal—without genuinely open government. Mechanisms of tracking the interests of citizens and of seeking to ensure that government acts for the public good rather than in the interests of a particular group or faction likewise require systematically open government.

While it was in opposition the Labour party appeared to appreciate the importance of freedom of information, aided no doubt by the various unscrupulous, indeed unconstitutional, ways in which Conservative ministers behaved in seeking to withhold information from Parliament over what had been their covert policy of encouraging British trade, including trade in arms, with Saddam Hussein's Iraq. This policy became both embarrassing and public at a time when British troops were at war with Iraq in what has now become known as the first Gulf War, of 1990–91. When it emerged that the government had been seeking to withhold such information not only from Parliament but also from the criminal courts, it found itself embroiled in a scandal from which it could not escape without a detailed and lengthy public inquiry—the famous Scott inquiry of 1992–96.[51]

The Scott inquiry had several consequences in the area of freedom of information. The government drew up guidance regulating ministerial answers to parliamentary questions (PQs). Parliament's ability to ask questions of ministers is one of its key means of obtaining government information and the guidance significantly tightened previous practice in a number of respects.[52] The government also drew up a *Code of Practice on Access to Government Information*. The Code, enforced though the House of Commons by the parliamentary ombudsman, was, like the guidance on answering PQs, a modest but nonetheless important step in the direction of greater freedom of information.[53]

When the Labour government came to power in 1997 it seemed at first that it was eager to take these developments considerably further and that it would introduce a sweeping Freedom of Information Act. The Cabinet Office published a hugely encouraging white paper to this effect in December 1997[54] but six months later the government seemed to suffer a severe change of mind, as responsibility for freedom of information was shifted from the Cabinet Office to the notoriously more guarded, some

---

[51] For a detailed account, see A Tomkins, *The Constitution after Scott: Government Unwrapped* (Oxford, Clarendon Press, 1998), esp chs 1–5.

[52] See *ibid*, at 96–103 and B Hough, 'Ministerial Responses to Parliamentary Questions: Some Recent Concerns' [2003] *Public Law* 211.

[53] See A Tomkins, *ibid*, at 112–24.

[54] See *Your Right to Know*, Cm 3818, 1997.

would say secretive, Home Office, which in 1999 announced its decision to ditch the proposals contained in the white paper and to introduce instead draft legislation that was far less ambitious.[55]

Despite persistent pressure from the vigilant Public Administration Committee of the House of Commons, in a long and drawn-out legislative process Parliament never managed to secure in the Act that was eventually passed anything like the same radical edge that had informed the 1997 white paper. Indeed, in many respects the regime under the Act allows for less openness than had been the case under the non-statutory scheme of the Code of Practice. In the words of one of Britain's most experienced academic commentators on matters of freedom of information, what the 2000 Act amounts to is the legislative enshrining of 'a discretionary power to choose what information to disclose' that returns us 'to an all-pervasive culture of secrecy and of seeking to find a reason for not disclosing'. As this commentator bluntly but correctly concludes, the Freedom of Information Act 2000 is no less than 'a fraud on democratic accountability'.[56]

Given the critical importance of open government and freedom of information to the republican insistence upon political accountability, the starting point for republican reform in this context should be that all government information is presumed to be open and freely available both to Parliament and to the public unless it can be objectively shown (and independently verified) that its disclosure would cause substantial harm to a specified public good. Such a prima facie obligation of openness should apply right across government, exceptions to disclosure should be narrowly drawn, the burden of proof resting always on the government and never on the party seeking disclosure, and the exceptions to disclosure should be strictly interpreted by an information commissioner appointed by and accountable to Parliament.

Parliament and Party

If lack of adequate information is the greatest practical obstacle to securing political accountability and the deliberative, contestatory style of democracy craved by republicans, the most significant political impediment lies in the

---

[55] See now the Freedom of Information Act 2000, which is due to come fully into force in 2005. Compare the (slightly) more impressive Scottish legislation: the Freedom of Information (Scotland) Act 2002, on which see J Munro, *Public Law in Scotland* (Edinburgh, Green, 2003), ch 9.

[56] R Austin, 'The Freedom of Information Act 2000—A Sheep in Wolf's Clothing?', in J Jowell and D Oliver (eds), *The Changing Constitution* (Oxford, Oxford University Press, 2004, 5th ed), at 415.

problem of party. Both political accountability and contestatory democracy rely for their success on a separation of interests as between government ministers on the one hand and parliamentarians on the other. Party eats away at this separation. Instead of backbench MPs being constitutionally loyal to the public good or to the interests of Parliament as an institution responsible for holding the government to account, they become loyal to their political parties. If their political party is the one which happens to be in government, the logic of party loyalty dictates that they support the government regardless of the greater public good. Conversely, if their political party is in opposition, MPs can seek to obstruct government policy for the sake of party political point-scoring, even where the government is acting in the public good.

It has been customary to see the principal dynamic in Parliament, and particularly in the House of Commons, as being that between the two front benches, that is to say, as being that between government and opposition.[57] But important as it undoubtedly is, there is a deeper dynamic at work in the constitutional understanding of Parliament than the relationship of government to opposition. This is the dynamic between Crown and Parliament, between front bench and back, or between minister and parliamentarian. As we saw in the previous chapter this is something that pre-dates by some margin the emergence in Britain of both political party and democracy. Parliament began to win for itself the right to hold the Crown's government to account as long ago as the early 1640s. The question in the modern era is how to re-energise this dynamic in the age of mass democracy and party politics.

In the previous section of this chapter we saw that since 2001 the House of Commons has witnessed a series of considerable backbench rebellions against, in particular, the Labour party line over a range of foreign and domestic policy issues. More generally the ever growing prominence and importance of the all-party and uniquely backbench select committees of the House of Commons has established over the past twenty years or so a healthy working pattern of cross-party (and usually not overly partisan) backbench scrutiny of government policy. In these ways it can be seen that there are already in the House of Commons a number of senses in which parliamentarians find themselves not being governed only, or even mainly, by party loyalty.

Welcome and valuable as these developments assuredly are, however, in the present scheme of things there is no way of securing or guaranteeing that parliamentarians will not allow loyalty to party to obscure or even to obstruct loyalty to Parliament's constitutional function of holding the government to

---

[57] An excellent example is offered in WI Jennings' pioneering study, *Parliament* (Cambridge, Cambridge University Press, 1939).

account. What is needed, therefore, is just such a security—some method of preventing or prohibiting party from replacing the public good as the interest for which our representatives in Parliament work.

The constitution has attempted to tackle this problem before. In the previous chapter we saw how the Act of Settlement 1701 had sought to remove the Crown's placemen—including all ministers—from the Commons. This solution is not altogether attractive, however, as it is the location of ministers in Parliament that enables Parliament readily to call them to account. It is not the existence of ministers in Parliament that causes the crucial separation of Crown from Parliament to become blurred: it is party. What is required is the removal not of ministers from the institution of Parliament, but the removal of party and of party loyalty from the working of Parliament. Thus, whips should be prohibited. There should be no whipped votes. There should be no whips' offices through which parliamentary office-holding (such as the chairing of select committee) can be fixed. There should be no institutional means—save for seeking to justify the merits of their policies in open parliamentary debate—by which the government is able to secure parliamentary support.

At first sight this may appear an implausible suggestion. I readily admit—indeed I hope—that if implemented it would bring about radical changes in the ways in which Parliament works, particularly on the floor of the House of Commons. But as the last twenty years' experience of select committees shows, it is not a suggestion that flies in the face of everything the British parliament currently stands for. As with all the reforms advocated here, this is one that can be read as being compatible, not in conflict, with the republicanism that this book argues is already inherent within our constitutional order.

As for the composition of Parliament, it is obvious that the republican principle of popular sovereignty requires both Houses to derive their authority either directly or indirectly from the people. The House of Commons needs a second, revising chamber that can take an additional look at the government's proposals. The upper House currently supports the Commons rather well, in that its powers and functions complement those of the lower House. This is particularly the case with regard to Parliament's committee structure. Whereas the committees of the Commons are generally organised along departmental lines, those of the Lords are more cross-cutting, looking at issues of policy that span government departments—science and technology and European Union matters being notable examples.

It is not with regard to the powers and functions of the upper House that reform is needed: it is with regard to its composition. Two solutions are attractive from the republican point of view. The upper House could either be directly elected, but using a different electoral system from that used for elections to the Commons (some form of proportional representation rather than first-past-the-post, perhaps). Alternatively, it could be indirectly elected, so that directly elected local councillors and members of devolved assemblies could send representatives to form the upper House. Either method would generate a newly invigorated and democratically legitimate upper House that could continue to complement the work of the House of Commons and that would vastly enhance Parliament's ability to provide the forum in which the republican values of deliberative and contestatory democracy could be practised.

The Crown

The fourth item on the republican constitutional reform agenda returns to the monarchy itself. There are all sorts of reasons, some stronger than others, as to why the British monarchy should be abolished. The degrading rituals of pomp and circumstance that surround the queen and her entourage. The way in which generation after generation of the royal family have sought to find ways of limiting their contributions to the exchequer.[58] The unhelpful political interventions of various princes and others on matters as wide-ranging as architecture, town planning, agriculture and blood sports. And the rumours of all sorts of unsavoury activities taking place behind closed doors in various of the royal palaces. All of these and more have contributed in recent years to a growing sense of popular restlessness that the royals have outlived their usefulness.

But even if the first family were composed of the brightest and most virtuous of Britons, there would still be two compelling reasons for abolishing the Crown. The first is that, as we saw in chapter two, the existence of the Crown is straightforwardly incompatible with the core republican requirement of freedom as non-domination. As the seventeenth-century parliamentarians argued, being subjects of the Crown rather than citizens of a free commonwealth effectively reduces us to the status of slaves. The second reason is that, as we have seen over and again, the Crown simply gets in the way of the constitutional project of trying to find ways of holding the government to account.

Neither Parliament nor the courts are in a position to review or scrutinise any power exercised by the queen herself. And both political and legal

---

[58] See P Hall, *Royal Fortune: Tax, Money and the Monarchy* (London, Bloomsbury, 1992) and A Tomkins, 'Crown Privileges', in M Sunkin and S Payne, above n 11, ch 7.

institutions have struggled, not particularly successfully, to bring the ministerial exercise of prerogative power within the scope of their oversight. The abolition of the Crown would bring about the strengthening of both parliamentary and judicial review of government action. It is difficult to conceive of a good constitutional objection to such a move. It is impossible to conceive of a republican objection.

One question that naturally follows from advocating that the Crown be abolished is what it should be replaced with. My answer is that there is no need to create any new office as a replacement. The constitutional powers of the queen should simply be transferred to the House of Commons. Either Parliament could legislate to place the queen's powers on a statutory basis, to be exercised on Parliament's behalf by the speaker of the House of Commons—that is, by the member of the House freely elected by the House as a whole to represent its interests. Or Parliament could legislate so as in effect to remove the need for the powers. Instead of it being in the queen's, the prime minister's, the speaker's or anyone else's discretion as to when to dissolve Parliament and to call a general election, we could move to fixed-term sessions, as we already have for local and devolved authorities. Similarly, instead of it being in the queen's or in the speaker's discretion as to whom should be appointed as prime minister, Parliament could pass an Act providing that the Member of Parliament able to command majority support in the House of Commons shall assume the office of prime minister for as long as such support remains. Statutes could become law upon their passage through both Houses of Parliament, with no need for any third-party assent.

Constitutionally we do not need the queen. Nor do we need any presidential head of state to replace her. All the monarch's constitutional powers could—and should—be vested in the House of Commons. In a republican constitutional order what we do need is a strong parliament, able fully and properly to represent the sovereign authority of the polity: namely, the people who are its citizens. To this end, *all* the government's powers should be derived from Parliament and the government should be responsible to Parliament for the exercise of *all* of its powers, irrespective of subject-matter.

IV AFTERWORD

The republican reform agenda sketched in the previous section constitutes only an outline and only a beginning. There is much more work that can and, I hope, will be done to suggest ways in which the values of republican constitutionalism can come to shape the future direction of our government, in Britain, in the European Union and beyond. How do we ensure that government really does track the interests of its citizens? Beyond freedom of information and parliamentary reform, how do we best promote practices of informed deliberation and contestatory democracy? And how do we encourage citizens to rediscover the value of civic virtue? All of these and more are issues of political theory, political science and constitutional law on which considerably more work is required.

What I hope has been offered here is a series of four first steps that we in Britain could relatively easily and quickly take, steps which would revive the republicanism that was injected into the constitutional order in the seventeenth century and that would, as John Milton envisaged, allow Britain at last to blossom and to realise its long-promised but as yet still dormant status of a fully free commonwealth.

Bibliography

K ABRAMS, 'Law's Republicanism' (1988) 97 *Yale Law Journal* 1591

B ACKERMAN, 'The Rise of World Constitutionalism' (1997) 83 *Virginia Law Review* 771

—— 'The New Separation of Powers' (2000) 113 *Harvard Law Review* 633

TRS ALLAN, *Law, Liberty and Justice: The Legal Foundations of British Constitutionalism* (Oxford, Clarendon Press, 1993)

—— 'Common Law Constitutionalism and Freedom of Speech', in J Beatson and Y Cripps (eds), *Freedom of Expression and Freedom of Information* (Oxford, Oxford University Press, 2000), ch 1

—— *Constitutional Justice: A Liberal Theory of the Rule of Law* (Oxford, Oxford University Press, 2001)

JWF ALLISON, *A Continental Distinction in the Common Law: A Historical and Comparative Perspective on English Public Law* (Oxford, Oxford University Press, 2000, rev ed)

H ARENDT, *The Human Condition* (Chicago, University of Chicago Press, 1958)

—— 'What is Freedom?', in H Arendt, *Between Past and Future: Eight Exercises in Political Thought* (London, Penguin, 1977)

ARISTOTLE, *Politics* (ed and trans CDC Reeve, Indianapolis, Hackett, 1998)

D ARMITAGE, A HIMY and Q SKINNER (eds), *Milton and Republicanism* (Cambridge, Cambridge University Press, 1995)

R AUSTIN, 'The Freedom of Information Act 2000 – A Sheep in Wolf's Clothing?', in J Jowell and D Oliver (eds), *The Changing Constitution* (Oxford, Oxford University Press, 2004, 5th ed), ch 16

W BAGEHOT, *The English Constitution* (ed P Smith, Cambridge, Cambridge University Press, 2001)

B BAILYN, *The Ideological Origins of the American Revolution* (Cambridge, Harvard University Press, 1967)

S BARBER, *Regicide and Republicanism: Politics and Ethics in the English Revolution, 1646–1659* (Edinburgh, Edinburgh University Press, 1998)

—— *A Revolutionary Rogue: Henry Marten and the English Republic* (Stroud, Sutton, 2000)

A BARNETT, *This Time: Our Constitutional Revolution* (London, Vintage, 1997)

—— C ELLIS and P HIRST (eds), *Debating the Constitution: New Perspectives on Constitutional Reform* (Cambridge, Polity Press, 1993)

J BELL, *French Constitutional Law* (Oxford, Clarendon Press, 1992)

S BENHABIB (ed), *Democracy and Difference: Contesting the Boundaries of the Political* (Princeton, Princeton University Press, 1996)

I BERLIN, 'Two Concepts of Liberty', in I Berlin, *Liberty* (ed H Hardy, Oxford, Oxford University Press, 2002)

T BINGHAM, 'The European Convention on Human Rights: Time to Incorporate' (1993) 109 *Law Quarterly Review* 390

B BIX, *Jurisprudence: Theory and Context* (London, Sweet and Maxwell, 2003, 3rd ed)

G BOCK, Q SKINNER and M VIROLI (eds), *Machiavelli and Republicanism* (Cambridge, Cambridge University Press, 1990)

J BODIN, *On Sovereignty* (ed J Franklin, Cambridge, Cambridge University Press, 1992)

V BOGDANOR (ed), *The British Constitution in the Twentieth Century* (Oxford, Oxford University Press, 2003)

J BRAITHWAITE, 'On Speaking Softly and Carrying Big Sticks: Neglected Dimensions of a Republican Separation of Powers' (1997) 27 *University of Toronto Law Journal* 305

—— and P PETTIT, *Not Just Deserts: A Republican Theory of Criminal Justice* (Oxford, Clarendon Press, 1990)

R BRAZIER, 'The Downfall of Margaret Thatcher' (1991) 54 *Modern Law Review* 471

—— 'A British Republic' (2002) 61 *Cambridge Law Journal* 351

P BREST, 'Further Beyond the Republican Revival: Toward Radical Republicanism' (1988) 97 *Yale Law Journal* 1623

L BROWNE-WILKINSON, 'The Infiltration of a Bill of Rights' [1992] *Public Law* 397

G BURGESS, *The Politics of the Ancient Constitution: An Introduction to English Political Thought, 1603–1642* (Pennsylvania, Pennsylvania State University Press, 1993)

JH BURNS, *The True Law of Kingship: Concepts of Monarchy in Early Modern Scotland* (Oxford, Clarendon Press, 1996)

—— and M GOLDIE (eds), *The Cambridge History of Political Thought, 1450–1700* (Cambridge, Cambridge University Press, 1991)

N BURROWS, *Devolution* (London, Sweet and Maxwell, 2000)

N BUTTLE, 'Republican Constitutionalism: A Roman Ideal' (2001) 9 *Journal of Political Philosophy* 331

P CHRISTIANSON, 'John Selden, the Five Knights' Case, and Discretionary Imprisonment in Early Stuart England' (1985) 6 *Criminal Justice History* 65

CICERO, *The Republic and the Laws* (ed and trans N Rudd, Oxford, Oxford University Press, 1998)

—— *On Obligations* (ed and trans PG Walsh, Oxford, Oxford University Press, 2000)

J COFFEY, *Politics, Religion and the British Revolutions: The Mind of Samuel Rutherford* (Cambridge, Cambridge University Press, 1997)

B CONSTANT, *Political Writings* (ed and trans B Fontana, Cambridge, Cambridge University Press, 1988)

P COWLEY and M STUART, 'Parliament: More Bleak House than Great Expectations' (2004) 57 *Parliamentary Affairs* 301

P CRAIG, *Public Law and Democracy in the UK and the USA* (Oxford, Clarendon Press, 1990)

—— 'Prerogative, Precedent and Power', in C Forsyth and I Hare (eds), *The Golden Metwand and the Crooked Cord* (Oxford, Clarendon Press, 1998)

—— 'Competing Models of Judicial Review' [1999] *Public Law* 428

—— 'Constitutional Foundations, the Rule of Law and Supremacy' [2003] *Public Law* 92

D CRESSY, 'Revolutionary England, 1640–1642' (2003) 181 *Past and Present* 35

P CROFT, 'Fresh Light on *Bate's Case*' (1987) 30 *Historical Journal* 523

A CROMARTIE, 'The Constitutionalist Revolution: The Transformation of Political Culture in Early Stuart England' (1999) 163 *Past and Present* 76

R CUST, *The Forced Loan and English Politics, 1626–1628* (Oxford, Clarendon Press, 1987)

G DONALDSON, *Scotland: The Shaping of a Nation* (Newton Abbot, David and Charles, 1974)

G DREWRY (ed), *The New Select Committees* (Oxford, Clarendon Press, 1989, 2nd ed)

R DWORKIN, *Taking Rights Seriously* (London, Duckworth, 1977)

KD EWING, 'The Bill of Rights Debate: Democracy or Juristocracy in Britain?', in KD Ewing, C Gearty and BA Hepple (eds), *Human Rights and Labour Law: Essays for Paul O'Higgins* (London, Mansell, 1994), ch 7

—— 'Social Rights and Constitutional Law' [1999] *Public Law* 104

—— 'The Futility of the Human Rights Act' [2004] *Public Law*, forthcoming

—— and C GEARTY, *Freedom under Thatcher: Civil Liberties in Modern Britain* (Oxford, Oxford University Press, 1990)

—— and C GEARTY, *The Struggle for Civil Liberties: Political Freedom and the Rule of Law in Britain, 1914–1945* (Oxford, Oxford University Press, 2000)

R FALLON, 'What is Republicanism and is it Worth Reviving?' (1989) 102 *Harvard Law Review* 1695

D FELDMAN, 'Human Dignity as a Legal Value' [1999] *Public Law* 682 (Part I) and [2000] *Public Law* 61 (Part II)

—— 'The Impact of Human Rights on the UK Legislative Process' (2004) 25 *Statute Law Review* 91

H FENWICK, 'A Proportionate Response to 11 September?' (2002) 65 *Modern Law Review* 724

W FERGUSON, *Scotland's Relations with England: A Survey to 1707* (Edinburgh, John Donald, 1977)

R FILMER, *Patriarcha and other Writings* (ed J Sommerville, Cambridge, Cambridge University Press, 1991)

Z FINK, *The Classical Republicans: An Essay in the Recovery of a Pattern of Thought in Seventeenth-Century England* (Evanston, Northwestern University Press, 1962, 2nd ed)

E FOSTER, 'Petitions and the Petition of Right' (1974) 14 *Journal of British Studies* 21

D FOXTON, '*R v Halliday, ex parte Zadig* in Retrospect' (2003) 119 *Law Quarterly Review* 455

A FRASER, 'In Defence of Republicanism: A Reply to Williams' (1995) 23 *Federal Law Review* 362

A FUKUDA, *Sovereignty and the Sword: Harrington, Hobbes, and Mixed Government in the English Civil War* (Oxford, Clarendon Press, 1997)

SR GARDINER, *Constitutional Documents of the Puritan Revolution, 1625–1660* (Oxford, Clarendon Press, 1906, 3rd ed)

C GEARTY, 'The Cost of Human Rights: English Judges and the Northern Irish Troubles' (1994) 47 *Current Legal Problems* 19

—— *Principles of Human Rights Adjudication* (Oxford, Oxford University Press, 2004)

S GEY, 'The Unfortunate Revival of Civic Republicanism' (1993) 141 *University of Pennsylvania Law Review* 801

J GOLDSWORTHY, *The Sovereignty of Parliament: History and Philosophy* (Oxford, Oxford University Press, 1999)

—— 'Homogenising Constitutions' (2003) 23 *Oxford Journal of Legal Studies* 483

J GRAY, *Liberalism* (Buckingham, Open University Press, 1986)

—— 'After the New Liberalism', in J Gray, *Enlightenment's Wake* (London, Routledge, 1995)

JAG GRIFFITH, 'The Political Constitution' (1979) 42 *Modern Law Review* 1

—— *The Politics of the Judiciary* (London, Fontana, 1997, 5th ed)

—— 'The Brave New World of Sir John Laws' (2000) 63 *Modern Law Review* 159

J GUY, 'The Origins of the Petition of Right Reconsidered' (1982) 25 *Historical Journal* 289

L HAILSHAM, *The Dilemma of Democracy: Diagnosis and Prescription* (London, Collins, 1978)

C HALL, 'Impositions and the Courts, 1554–1606' (1953) 69 *Law Quarterly Review* 200

P HALL, *Royal Fortune: Tax, Money and the Monarchy* (London, Bloomsbury, 1992)

S HANNETT, 'Third Party Intervention: In the Public Interest?' [2003] *Public Law* 128

I HARDEN and N LEWIS, *The Noble Lie: The British Constitution and the Rule of Law* (London, Hutchinson, 1986)

C HARLOW, 'Export, Import. The Ebb and Flow of English Public Law' [2000] *Public Law* 240

—— *Accountability in the European Union* (Oxford, Oxford University Press, 2002)

—— and R RAWLINGS, *Law and Administration* (London, Butterworths, 1997, 2nd ed)

J HARRINGTON, *The Commonwealth of Oceana* (ed JGA Pocock, Cambridge, Cambridge University Press, 1992)

T HARRIS, *Politics under the later Stuarts: Party Conflict in a Divided Society, 1660–1715* (Harlow, Longman, 1993)

J HART, *The Rule of Law, 1603–1660: Crowns, Courts and Judges* (Harlow, Longman, 2003)

L HARTZ, *The Liberal Tradition in America: An Interpretation of American Political Thought since the Revolution* (New York, Harcourt Brace, 1955)

AF HAVIGHURST, 'The Judiciary and Politics in the Reign of Charles II' (1950) 66 *Law Quarterly Review* 62 (Part I) and 229 (Part II)

—— 'James II and the Twelve Men in Scarlet' (1953) 69 *Law Quarterly Review* 522

L HEWART, *The New Despotism* (London, Benn, 1929)

C HILL, *Intellectual Origins of the English Revolution Revisited* (Oxford, Clarendon Press, 1997)

R HIRSCHL, *Towards Juristocracy: The Origins and Consequences of the New Constitutionalism* (Cambridge, Harvard University Press, 2004)

W HOLDSWORTH, 'The Power of the Crown to Requisition British Ships in a National Emergency' (1919) 35 *Law Quarterly Review* 12

I HONOHAN, *Civic Republicanism* (London, Routledge, 2002)

H HORWITZ, *Parliament, Policy and Politics in the Reign of William III* (Manchester, Manchester University Press, 1977)

M HORWITZ, 'Republicanism and Liberalism in American Constitutional Thought' (1987) 29 *William and Mary Law Review* 57

B HOUGH, 'Ministerial Responses to Parliamentary Questions: Some Recent Concerns' [2003] *Public Law* 211

R HUTTON, *The Restoration: A Political and Religious History of England and Wales, 1658–1667* (Oxford, Oxford University Press, 1985)

C JACKSON, *Restoration Scotland, 1660–1690: Royalist Politics, Religion and Ideas* (Woodbridge, Boydell Press, 2003)

J JACOB, *The Republican Crown: Lawyers and the Making of the State in Twentieth-Century Britain* (Aldershot, Dartmouth, 1996)

JAMES VI and I, *Political Writings* (ed J Sommerville, Cambridge, Cambridge University Press, 1995)

WI JENNINGS, *Parliamentary Reform* (London, Gollancz, 1934)

—— *Cabinet Government* (Cambridge, Cambridge University Press, 1936)

—— 'Public Order' (1937) 8 *Political Quarterly* 7

—— *Parliament* (Cambridge, Cambridge University Press, 1939)

W JONES, *Politics and the Bench: The Judges and the Origins of the English Civil War* (London, Allen and Unwin, 1971)

J JOWELL, 'Of Vires and Vacuums: The Constitutional Context of Judicial Review' [1999] *Public Law* 448

—— 'Beyond the Rule of Law: Towards Constitutional Judicial Review' [2000] *Public Law* 671

—— 'Administrative Law', in V Bogdanor (ed), *The British Constitution in the Twentieth Century* (Oxford, Oxford University Press, 2003), ch 10

M JUDSON, *The Crisis of the Constitution: An Essay in Constitutional and Political Thought in England, 1603–1645* (New Brunswick, Rutgers University Press, 1949)

DL KEIR, 'The Case of Ship-Money' (1936) 52 *Law Quarterly Review* 546

B KEMP, *King and Commons, 1660–1832* (London, Macmillan, 1957)

A KENNON, 'Pre-legislative Scrutiny of Draft Bills' [2004] *Public Law* 477

J KENYON, *The Stuart Constitution, 1603–1688: Documents and Commentary* (Cambridge, Cambridge University Press, 1986, 2nd ed)

C KIDD, *Subverting Scotland's Past: Scottish Whig Historians and the Creation of an Anglo-British Identity, 1689–c1830* (Cambridge, Cambridge University Press, 1993)

R KINGDOM, 'Calvinism and Resistance Theory, 1550–1580', in JH Burns and M Goldie (eds), *The Cambridge History of Political Thought, 1450–1700* (Cambridge, Cambridge University Press, 1991), ch 7

M KISHLANSKY, 'Tyranny Denied: Charles I, Attorney General Heath, and the Five Knights' Case' (1999) 42 *Historical Journal* 53

I KRAMNICK, 'Republican Revisionism Revisited' (1982) 87 *American Historical Review* 629

J LAWS, 'Law and Democracy' [1995] *Public Law* 72

—— 'The Constitution: Morals and Rights' [1996] *Public Law* 622

—— 'The Limitations of Human Rights' [1998] *Public Law* 254

M LEE, *The Road to Revolution: Scotland under Charles I, 1625–1637* (Urbana, University of Illinois Press, 1985)

J Locke, *Two Treatises of Government* (ed P Laslett, Cambridge, Cambridge University Press, 1960)

M Loughlin, *Public Law and Political Theory* (Oxford, Clarendon Press, 1992)

—— 'The State, the Crown and the Law', in M Sunkin and S Payne (eds), *The Nature of the Crown: A Legal and Political Analysis* (Oxford, Oxford University Press, 1999), ch 3

—— *Sword and Scales: An Examination of the Relationship between Law and Politics* (Oxford, Hart Publishing, 2000)

M Lynch, *Scotland: A New History* (London, Pimlico, 1992)

N Machiavelli, *The Discourses* (ed B Crick and trans LJ Walker, London, Penguin, 1998)

R MacKay, 'Coke – Parliamentary Sovereignty or the Supremacy of the Law' (1924) 22 *Michigan Law Review* 215

F Maitland, *The Constitutional History of England* (Cambridge, Cambridge University Press, 1908)

J Malcolm (ed), *The Struggle for Sovereignty: Seventeenth-Century English Political Tracts* (Indianapolis, Liberty Fund, 1999)

K Malleson, *The New Judiciary* (Aldershot, Ashgate, 1999)

—— 'Safeguarding Judicial Impartiality' (2002) 22 *Legal Studies* 53

D Marr and M Wilkinson, *Dark Victory* (Sydney, Allen and Unwin, 2003)

G Marshall, 'The End of Prime Ministerial Government?' [1991] *Public Law* 1

RA Mason (ed), *Scots and Britons: Scottish Political Thought and the Union of 1603* (Cambridge, Cambridge University Press, 1994)

D Mathew, *Scotland under Charles I* (London, Eyre and Spottiswoode, 1955)

C McCrudden, 'A Common Law of Human Rights? Transnational Judicial Conversations on Constitutional Rights' (2000) 20 *Oxford Journal of Legal Studies* 499

CH McIlwain, 'The Tenure of English Judges' (1913) 7 *American Political Science Review* 217

M Mendle, *Henry Parker and the English Civil War* (Cambridge, Cambridge University Press, 1995)

E Mensch and A Freeman, 'A Republican Agenda for Hobbesian America' (1989) 41 *Florida Law Review* 581

F Michelman, 'Foreword: Traces of Self-Government' (1986) 100 *Harvard Law Review* 4

—— 'Law's Republic' (1988) 97 *Yale Law Journal* 1493

—— 'Conceptions of Democracy in American Constitutional Argument: Voting Rights' (1989) 41 *Florida Law Review* 443

J Miller, *James II* (New Haven, Yale University Press, 2000)

J Milton, *Areopagitica and other Political Writings* (ed J Alvis, Indianapolis, Liberty Fund, 1999)

Montesquieu, *The Spirit of the Laws* (ed and trans A Cohler, B Miller and H Stone, Cambridge, Cambridge University Press, 1989)

F Mount, *The British Constitution Now: Recovery or Decline?* (London, Heinemann, 1992)

R Mulgan, ' "Accountability": An Ever-Expanding Concept?' (2000) 78 *Public Administration* 555

J MUNRO, *Public Law in Scotland* (Edinburgh, Green, 2003)

D NORBROOK, *Writing the English Republic: Poetry, Rhetoric and Politics, 1627–1660* (Cambridge, Cambridge University Press, 1999)

D OLIVER, 'Underlying Values of Public and Private Law', in M Taggart (ed), *The Province of Administrative Law* (Oxford, Hart Publishing, 1997), ch 11

—— *Constitutional Reform in the UK* (Oxford, Oxford University Press, 2003)

DA ORR, *Treason and the State: Law, Politics and Ideology in the English Civil War* (Cambridge, Cambridge University Press, 2002)

P PETTIT, *Republicanism: A Theory of Freedom and Government* (Oxford, Clarendon Press, 1997)

—— 'Keeping Republican Freedom Simple: On a Difference with Quentin Skinner' (2002) 30 *Political Theory* 339

—— 'Discourse Theory and Republican Freedom', in D Weinstock and C Nadeau (eds), *Republicanism: History, Theory and Practice* (London, Frank Cass, 2004)

T PLUCKNETT, 'Bonham's Case and Judicial Review' (1926) 40 *Harvard Law Review* 30

JGA POCOCK, *The Ancient Constitution and the Feudal Law* (Cambridge, Cambridge University Press, 1957)

—— *The Machiavellian Moment: Florentine Political Thought and the Atlantic Republican Tradition* (Princeton, Princeton University Press, 1975)

T POOLE, 'Dogmatic Liberalism? TRS Allan and the Common Law Constitution' (2002) 65 *Modern Law Review* 463

—— 'Back to the Future? Unearthing the Theory of Common Law Constitutionalism' (2003) 23 *Oxford Journal of Legal Studies* 435

GW PROTHERO, *Select Statutes and other Constitutional Documents, 1558–1625* (Oxford, Clarendon Press, 1913, 4th ed)

F RAAB, *The English Face of Machiavelli: A Changing Interpretation, 1500–1700* (London, Routledge, 1964)

P RAHE, *Republics Ancient and Modern* (Chapel Hill, University of North Carolina Press, 1992)

J REEVE, 'The Legal Status of the Petition of Right' (1986) 29 *Historical Journal* 257

—— 'The Arguments in King's Bench in 1629 Concerning the Imprisonment of John Selden and other Members of the House of Commons' (1986) 25 *Journal of British Studies* 264

D REID (ed), *The Party-Coloured Mind: Prose Relating to the Conflict of Church and State in Seventeenth-Century Scotland* (Edinburgh, Scottish Academic Press, 1982)

H RICHARDSON, *Democratic Autonomy: Public Reasoning about the Ends of Policy* (Oxford, Oxford University Press, 2002)

C ROBBINS, *The Eighteenth-Century Commonwealthman* (Cambridge, Harvard University Press, 1959)

—— (ed), *Two English Republican Tracts* (Cambridge, Cambridge University Press, 1969)

C ROBERTS, *The Growth of Responsible Government in Stuart England* (Cambridge, Cambridge University Press, 1966)

WA ROBSON, *Justice and Administrative Law: A Study of the British Constitution* (London, Macmillan, 1928)

D RODGERS, 'Republicanism: The Career of a Concept' (1992) 79 *Journal of American History* 11

L SCARMAN, *English Law – The New Dimension* (London, Stevens, 1974)

J SCOTT, *England's Troubles: Seventeenth-Century English Political Instability in European Context* (Cambridge, Cambridge University Press, 2000)

S SEDLEY, 'Human Rights: a Twenty-First Century Agenda' [1995] *Public Law* 386

—— 'The Crown in its own Courts', in C Forsyth and I Hare (eds), *The Golden Metwand and the Crooked Cord* (Oxford, Clarendon Press, 1998)

R SHALHOPE, 'Toward a Republican Synthesis: The Emergence of an Understanding of Republicanism in American Historiography' (1972) 29 *William and Mary Quarterly* 49

J SHAW, *The Political History of Eighteenth-Century Scotland* (London, Macmillan, 1999)

J SHKLAR, *Legalism* (Cambridge, Harvard University Press, 1964)

A SIDNEY, *Discourses Concerning Government* (ed T West, Indianapolis, Liberty Fund, 1996)

Q SKINNER, *Liberty before Liberalism* (Cambridge, Cambridge University Press, 1998)

—— 'John Milton and the Politics of Slavery', in Q Skinner, *Visions of Politics, Volume II: Renaissance Virtues* (Cambridge, Cambridge University Press, 2002), ch 11

—— 'Classical Liberty, Renaissance Translation and the English Civil War', in Q Skinner, *Visions of Politics, Volume II: Renaissance Virtues* (Cambridge, Cambridge University Press, 2002), ch 12

D SMITH, *The Stuart Parliaments, 1603–1689* (London, Arnold, 1999)

J-F SPITZ, 'The Twilight of the Republic?', in D Weinstock and C Nadeau (eds), *Republicanism: History, Theory and Practice* (London, Frank Cass, 2004)

R STEVENS, *The English Judges: Their Role in the Changing Constitution* (Oxford, Hart Publishing, 2002)

A STONE, 'The Australian Free Speech Experiment', in T Campbell, K Ewing and A Tomkins (eds), *Sceptical Essays on Human Rights* (Oxford, Oxford University Press, 2001), ch 21

M SUNKIN and S PAYNE (eds), *The Nature of the Crown: A Legal and Political Analysis* (Oxford, Clarendon Press, 1999)

C SUNSTEIN, 'Beyond the Republican Revival' (1988) 97 *Yale Law Journal* 1539

'Symposium: The Civic Republican Tradition' (1988) 97 *Yale Law Journal* 1493

'Symposium on Republicanism and Voting Rights' (1989) 41 *Florida Law Review* 409

JR TANNER, *English Constitutional Conflicts of the Seventeenth Century, 1603–1689* (Cambridge, Cambridge University Press, 1928)

S THORNE, 'Dr Bonham's Case' (1938) 54 *Law Quarterly Review* 543

A TOMKINS, *The Constitution after Scott: Government Unwrapped* (Oxford, Clarendon Press, 1998)

—— 'Crown Privileges', in M Sunkin and S Payne (eds), *The Nature of the Crown: A Legal and Political Analysis* (Oxford, Oxford University Press, 1999), ch 7

—— 'Responsibility and Resignation in the European Commission' (1999) 62 *Modern Law Review* 744

—— 'Magna Carta, Crown and Colonies' [2001] *Public Law* 571

—— 'In Defence of the Political Constitution' (2002) 22 *Oxford Journal of Legal Studies* 157

—— 'Legislating against Terror' [2002] *Public Law* 205

—— 'The Republican Monarchy Revisited' (2002) 19 *Constitutional Commentary* 737

—— 'What is Parliament for?', in N Bamforth and P Leyland (eds), *Public Law in a Multi-Layered Constitution* (Oxford, Hart Publishing, 2003), ch 3

—— 'The Draft Constitution of the European Union' [2003] *Public Law* 571

—— *Public Law* (Oxford, Oxford University Press, 2003)

—— ' "Talking in Fictions": Jennings on Parliament' (2004) 67 *Modern Law Review* 772

—— (ed), *Devolution and the British Constitution* (London, Key Haven, 1998)

A TRENCH (ed), *Has Devolution made a Difference?* (Exeter, Imprint Academic, 2004)

M TUSHNET, *Red, White, and Blue: A Critical Analysis of Constitutional Law* (Cambridge, Harvard University Press, 1988)

—— *Taking the Constitution away from the Courts* (Princeton, Princeton University Press, 1999)

D UNDERDOWN, *A Freeborn People: Politics and the Nation in Seventeenth-Century England* (Oxford, Clarendon Press, 1996)

M VAN GELDEREN and Q SKINNER (eds), *Republicanism: A Shared European Heritage* (Cambridge, Cambridge University Press, 2002)

M VIROLI, *Republicanism* (trans A Shugaar, New York, Hill and Wang, 2002)

HWR WADE, 'The Crown, Ministers and Officials: Legal Status and Liability', in M Sunkin and S Payne (eds), *The Nature of the Crown: A Legal and Political Analysis* (Oxford, Oxford University Press, 1999), ch 2

HWR WADE and CF FORSYTH, *Administrative Law* (Oxford, Oxford University Press, 2004, 9th ed)

D WAGNER, 'Coke and the Rise of Economic Liberalism' (1935) 6 *Economic History Review* 30

FW WALBANK, *Polybius* (Berkeley, University of California Press, 1972)

J WALDRON, *Law and Disagreement* (Oxford, Clarendon Press, 1999)

—— *The Dignity of Legislation* (Cambridge, Cambridge University Press, 1999)

JHH WEILER, 'To be a European Citizen: Eros and Civilization', in JHH Weiler, *The Constitution of Europe* (Cambridge, Cambridge University Press, 1999)

D WEINSTOCK and C NADEAU (eds), *Republicanism: History, Theory and Practice* (London, Frank Cass, 2004)

JR WESTERN, *Monarchy and Revolution: The English State in the 1680s* (London, Blandford, 1972)

CC WESTON, *English Constitutional Theory and the House of Lords, 1556–1832* (London, Routledge, 1965)

EN WILLIAMS, *The Eighteenth-Century Constitution: Documents and Commentary* (Cambridge, Cambridge University Press, 1960)

G WILLIAMS, 'A Republican Tradition for Australia?' (1995) 23 *Federal Law Review* 133

B WINETROBE, 'The Judge in the Scottish Parliament Chamber' [2005] *Public Law*, forthcoming

G WINTERTON, *Monarchy to Republic: Australian Republican Government* (Melbourne, Oxford University Press, 1994, rev ed)

G WOOD, *The Creation of the American Republic, 1776–1787* (Chapel Hill, University of North Carolina Press, 1969)

—— *The Radicalism of the American Revolution* (New York, Knopf, 1992)

A WOOLRYCH, *Commonwealth to Protectorate* (Oxford, Clarendon Press, 1982)

—— *Britain in Revolution, 1625–1660* (Oxford, Oxford University Press, 2002)

D WOOTTON (ed), *Divine Right and Democracy* (Harmondsworth, Penguin, 1986)

B WORDEN, *The Rump Parliament, 1648–1653* (Cambridge, Cambridge University Press, 1974)

—— 'English Republicanism', in JH Burns and M Goldie (eds), *The Cambridge History of Political Thought, 1450–1700* (Cambridge, Cambridge University Press, 1991), ch 15

FD WORMUTH, *The Origins of Modern Constitutionalism* (New York, Harper Bros, 1949)

IM YOUNG, *Inclusion and Democracy* (Oxford, Oxford University Press, 2000)

Index